Becoming A Mature Christian

Becoming a

MATURE

CHRISTIAN

Emeric Lawrence, O.S.B.

The Liturgical Press
Collegeville, Minnesota

Preface

The title of this book might well have been *Do Catholics Need Conversion?* I did not choose such a title as it might be disturbing and even insulting to some Catholics. "Conversion to what?" they would say. "What's better than Roman Catholicism?" My answer (and conviction) is that nothing is better than Roman Catholicism, but I would want to specify not just any kind of Roman Catholicism. My purpose in this book is to try to show that every Catholic can become a more convinced, more committed Catholic—one whose religious convictions and whose attachment to Christ have been renewed at their roots. This book seeks to lay out the path towards that worthy goal.

I admit that through baptism a person becomes a member of the Catholic Church. In a few pages I shall compare the process of becoming a Catholic in modern times with that of the earliest ages of Christianity. At this point I hardly need to prove that baptism is not identical with conversion, that one can be a life-long Catholic according to all external appearances (Sunday Mass, frequent Communion, participation in parish activities, financial contributions) but not be a convinced Christian whose life is directly involved with the person of Jesus or permeated by the spirit of Christ's Gospel.

It could well be that Catholicism has come too easily to most "cradle Catholics." Few of us have ever had to fight for our faith. In recent decades Catholicism has become "respectable." I am convinced that religion ceases to be a dynamic force when its adherents take it for granted, get too used to it.

In her book *The Man on the Donkey,* H.F.M. Prescott describes a crucifix on the wall of a Reformation-era room as "the image of a tormented man nailed to a tree," and she says that the people in the room live comfortably with it because "they knew it too well to see it for what it was." And John Garvey, who cites this example, comments: "This is the barrier which organized religion presents to the gospel—the very thing it is called upon to preach becomes a convention; it is brought down to the level it was meant to raise us from, so that we can live comfortably with it, which is precisely what we are *not* meant to do" *(Saints for Confused Times* [Chicago: Thomas More Press, 1976], p. 11).

I am convinced that the experience of conversion to Christ, the experience of being "born again" (to quote Jesus himself) is a real necessity for every follower of Christ. This need has been increasingly recognized by the late Pope Paul VI, at the bishops' meetings in Rome, and by the American bishops as well.

It is obvious today that the defection of many Catholics in the last few years points to the one fact that most of them have never really been converted to Christ. It is not merely a matter of instruction in the basic truths of the faith (or lack of it), although the truth is that only a small minority of Catholics today have any more than a bare minimum of theological knowledge to bolster their faith. It is also a matter of encountering Christ, experiencing him in a manner akin to that of the first disciples whom he called and attached to himself.

So . . . whether or not Catholics recognize their need for conversion, the Church herself has no doubts. I have no ambition to propose a secret formula for bringing about sudden conversions after the manner of Saul's conversion to Christ on his way to Damascus. Sudden and dramatic conversions do indeed occur; (how long they last is another question). But for most of us—as I shall spell out later—conversion is a life-long, ever-deepening, experience. And that seems to be the way the Church sees it too. Year after year in her Advent liturgy, the Church confronts us with the stern person of John the Baptist, speaking to us now as he did to the contemporaries of Jesus: "Repent, for the kingdom of heaven is at hand" (Mt. 3:2).

When John the Baptist said to the Jewish multitudes, "Do not begin to say to yourselves, "We have Abraham as our father; for I tell you, God is able from these stones to raise up children to Abraham" (Lk. 3:8), he was insisting that membership in the People of God was not enough to please God. So now in presenting that text to us Catholics during Advent, the Church (using John's words and example) is telling us that mere membership in the Roman Catholic Church hardly suffices.

And few of us would claim that we do not need the message that the Church's liturgy presents to us year in, year out at the beginning of Lent:

"Yet even now," says the Lord,
　"return to me with all your heart,
with fasting, with weeping, and with mourning;
　and rend your hearts and not your garments."
Return to the Lord, your God,
for he is gracious and merciful,
slow to anger, and abounding in steadfast love,
　and repents of evil (Joel 2:12-13).

Ladislaus Boros has written:

> God wants to enter the world in us and through us, he wants to be kind through us. He has taken this extraordinary risk. This is the task that is involved in being a Christian: to be God's goodness, so that men can recognize that goodness and benevolence exist, that, despite everything, being is good. If we are Christians, we must prove to others that tomorrow will be a better day. In this they experience God: total benevolence and infinite love. There are proofs of God that refute unbelief with logical impeccability. But in the grave crises of human existence they mean nothing, or very little. In such times there must be a man whose life is at least a sign that humanity is respected and honoured, that it is taken up into an unconditional friendship, that is, that he really exists who makes all possible: God.
>
> *Meeting God in Man* (New York: Herder and Herder, 1968), p. 16.

So, being a Catholic implies being responsible for conveying Christ's light, truth, and goodness to a seeking, hungry world. It hardly seems possible for any but "converted Christians" to carry out this awesome vocation. This book attempts to outline the way to lasting conversion to Christ. It is only a beginning, but hopefully it will lead readers to further reading, praying, and loving.

February 15, 1979
St. Scholastica Priory
Duluth, Minnesota

Acknowledgments

The credit for the initial idea of this book goes to Mr. John Dwyer, business manager of The Liturgical Press. When he received a copy of the 1974 provisional text of the *Rite of Christian Initiation of Adults,* he wondered if I would be interested in implementing the rite. I was more than willing, but when I studied the rite, I wasn't sure how to fulfill my promise. After more reflection and toying with ideas and rough drafts of the first chapters, the book seemed to want to direct itself more at born Catholics in need of and interested in deepening their faith than towards the instruction and orientation of prospective converts (catechumens).

Actually, I was glad it turned out that way, for this seems to be an even more urgent need than the original plan, and it also seems to be the thrust of much of the work that is increasingly being carried on in more and more dioceses and parishes across the country. So I may hope that this might be the kind of pastoral book that many diocesan leaders and pastors are looking for (besides being—I would hope—of great help to individual Catholics).

I am most grateful to the following friends and colleagues who have helped me prepare the manuscript for publication. First, to John Dwyer for the original idea; to the director of The Liturgical Press, Fr. Daniel Durken, O.S.B., for his excellent critiques of the chapters and his many suggestions for improving them; to Mark Twomey of The Liturgical Press for his gentle editing of the text and his valuable hints for brightening it up; to Chico Anderson of Duluth for having provided a layman's (and prospective lay deacon's) evaluation and for his excellent suggestions; to Sr. Mary Charles McGough, O.S.B., of St. Scholastica's Priory for contributing another of her imaginative and beautiful cover designs, and to Sr. Timothy Kirby, O.S.B., of St. Scholastica's Priory for her constructive critiques of the book.

I am especially grateful to Bishop Paul Anderson of the Duluth Diocese for consenting to write an introduction and to the courageous contributors to the final chapter of personal testimonies of what their faith means to them.

Contents

Introduction

Quite regularly persons in positions of responsibility speak of the tremendous volume of mail that crosses their desks each day. Newspapers, periodicals, advertisements, bills, letters of a personal nature, and memos of one kind or another from a multiplicity of organizations and committees. Bishops of course are no exception to this modern phenomena.

In prioritizing these daily stacks of material, it is interesting to note what falls on the pile marked "most important." Of late, again and again, there surfaces in various ways, shapes, and forms the subject of evangelization. Recently, on top of such a stack of mail, a small brochure entitled *Evangelization of the Modern World*, a summary of the Apostolic Exhortation of Pope Paul VI, caught my eye. It referred to the document written by the late Holy Father following the Fourth Synod of Bishops held in 1974.

The vital importance of both this synod and the document *Evangelii nunciandi* are clearly evident in what has happened during the past four years. In 1976 the bishops of the country reviewed their priorities for the coming years, and specifically the topic of evangelization rose to the top in order of importance. Following that decision, an *ad hoc* committee was set up under the chairmanship of Archbishop Francis Hurley of Anchorage, Alaska. Regional meetings are in the planning stages in various parts of the country. Mini-congresses have already been held in many places searching for an answer to the questions: What has happened to that hidden energy of the Good News which is able to have such a powerful effect on man's conscience? Is the evangelical force of the Gospels capable of transforming lives? What methods should be followed to insure that the Gospel may have its proper impact?

I am not sure that the answers to all these questions are that readily available. But from the pen of both professional theologians and popular writers alike, together with the prayers of a praying Church, at least the beginnings of what it means to evangelize the world in our time will begin to surface.

In the present work of Fr. Emeric Lawrence, I find a special contribution made to the Church's mission of evangelization. In clear and incisive language, he takes the reader from what it means to be a person of mature faith to the very heart of spirituality—the virtue of charity. The way is long, but the reader is guided skillfully through that encounter with Jesus in the Holy Spirit that results in the faith community we call the Church. Like the woman at the well, the discovery and sharing anew of the person, the power and the presence of Jesus the Lord speaks in a powerful way to both those within and without the Church.

It may seem a bit embarrassing for those who have professed faith in the Lord all these years to think and talk in terms of conversion and commitment, but it becomes clear that it was the special grace and genius of Vatican II that brought home the underlying necessity of institutional reform and personal renewal in the Spirit.

A careful reading in a prayerful vein should help both religious and lay persons alike to move from where they are to where they want to be on the Word of someone who loves them. To those who no longer walk that road and to the great body of the unchurched, even a casual reading should give new reason for hope in a hopeless world. To the disciple of the Lord still other delights will be found.

May God bless the efforts of the author and may the Good News continue to bring peace, joy, love, and life to those in deepest need.

+ Paul F. Anderson
Bishop of Duluth

Becoming A Mature Christian

1

Human Maturity:

Basis of Mature Christianity

There are mysterious influences in our lives. You have probably reflected from time to time on your so-called identity and have asked yourself, "Who am I? Who am I as a human being? Who am I as a Christian? How did I get to where I am now? Who are the people who have helped to make me what I am? What would have happened to me if I had not followed along the way that brought me to where I now am? Who brought these people into my life? Why am I looking at these pages, why did I pick up this book? Was it just chance or was there someone who gave me the initial impulse?"

What does life mean to you? What is its purpose, its ultimate goal? What are your values, what is important, what really matters to you? The world is full of men and women whose entire life is directed by some cause or other. The cause may be political, social, educational, financial. In many cases, especially today, the cause that directs the lives of thousands of young people is religious. They have been so won over to a particular religious cause that they willingly give up home, family, a college education, and jobs in order to contribute to this cause. And in it they seem to find satisfaction and meaning for their lives.

Discontent Among Catholics

The May 1977 *The St. Anthony Messenger* has an enlightening (and disturbing) article on the Rev. Sun Myung Moon and his Unification Church. One aspect of this Church that the author touches on is the number of young ex-Catholics who have been won over and what it was

1

that attracted them. One of them said, "I never really considered religion too much. It was a formal, detached thing. I feel I could have been fulfilled spiritually in the Catholic Church if I'd had the desire and been willing to work at it. But the Catholic Church did not come after me. Moon did." Another said, "Most people want a change—they want a radical change. There's a void in young people today." And the author comments, "The asceticism Moon demands is attractive: it adds to the young people's illusion that they're accomplishing a positive change in their lives and working for some positive good."

I have said that the article was disturbing. Any loyal and serious-minded Catholic has to wonder at the large number (some estimate 35 percent) of one-time Catholics who, disappointed in or unchallenged by the Catholic Church, have given it up for the Unification Church. "The Catholic Church did not come after me. Moon did." One of the most pressing hungers of young people today is for the experience of community. They want and they need companionship—the sense of belonging to a caring community. Unable to find satisfaction for this desire in most of our large parishes—many of them simply assemblies of individuals who neither know nor are concerned for one another—they look around until they find parishes (of whatever denomination) or communes where they can really experience an atmosphere of charity, of unity, of mutual concern. The old arguments for the Roman Catholic Church being the one, true Church do not convince them.

Part of the problem may lie in the manner in which most modern Christians receive the faith. The early Christians were converted and won over to Christ when they heard the Gospel, the Good News of Jesus. They were convinced by it and made a personal decision to accept and live by it. They were instructed in the doctrines and practices of Christianity over a period of years (the catechumenate), and only then were they baptized into the Christian community, allowed to take part in the Mass, receive Holy Communion, and contribute to the full life of the community.

Most modern Catholics, on the other hand, are born into Catholic families, they are baptized as infants, they receive their Christianity from their parents, and are instructed in the meaning of the faith by parents and teachers; they observe all the religious practices of the Church. But something seems to be lacking in many of them. Could it be that element of personal conversion experienced by the first Christians? How many of the millions of people who call themselves Catholic would be willing today to make the kind of personal commitment to Christ that is implicit in his demand that they take up their cross and come after him? How many are ready right now to admit that Christ is number one in their lives, the supreme value they place above any other value?

It would seem that many, perhaps the majority, of Catholics have lived as members of their parishes and of the Church without ever having made such a commitment or been challenged to make it. A few years ago a Paris university student decided that he wanted to become a Catholic. He found a priest who agreed to instruct him, and at the end of a long period of instruction during which the young man's desire to become a Catholic became more and more intense, the priest decided that he was ready for baptism. He suggested that the man invite his university friends to the ceremony. When it was over the priest turned to the observers (all of whom had been baptized in their infancy and had also made their First Communion) and asked how many of them at their present stage of life would be willing to make the same kind of commitment to Christ and the Church that their friend had just made. Only a few indicated their willingness. The rest were or had become nominal, apparently unconvinced Catholics.

Need for Evangelization

Judging by a statement of Archbishop Bernardin at the United States bishops' meeting in November 1977 and by the chief topic of discussion at the Synod of Bishops in Rome that same month, the leaders of the Catholic Church are keenly aware of and disturbed about this situation. Archbishop Bernardin asked his fellow bishops how the American Catholic Church could be expected to evangelize eighty million unchurched Americans when so few Catholics had yet to experience conversion themselves.

While aware of a malaise in Christianity caused by secularism and the values of a consumer society, the Roman synod also sensed rising hopes for the future of Catholicism in various parts of the world. In his evaluation of the synod for *The Tablet* (November 5, 1977), Cardinal George Basil Hume of Westminster detected four points of growth—"areas of thought and behaviour which are becoming increasingly important to many people. These are evident at least as seed and promise for the future. They provide a challenge for the united Christian conscience. The four growth-points are prayer, a feeling for universal justice, a respect for human dignity, a longing for community."

Cardinal Hume described each of these growth points and ended with the hope, "Perhaps then the young of today will become the ones to discover the vision and the purpose. That was the aim of the fifth Synod of Bishops." The young may be the ones to whom the bishops look most for renewal, but I am convinced that the desire to enter more thoroughly into the understanding and practice of their faith is gripping Catholics of all ages today. When told of the nature and purpose of this book, their first reaction of some of my former students has been, "Hurry it up! Be sure to see to it that I get a copy. It's just what I have been looking for." It is all too obvious that they are no longer satisfied with the adolescent understanding and practice of the faith that they grew up in. They are eager for a deeper appreciation of religion and a firmer challenge to their maturity. They want to be adult Christians.

What really is mature or adult Christianity? In order to answer that question, we have to know the meaning of the words "mature" and "adult." It is obvious that the human person passes through a variety of psychological and physical changes on the way to becoming an adult. Each state has its peculiar characteristics, beginning with total dependency and progressing to well-controlled and mature independence. A child receives. An adult provides. A child is told what to believe. An adult makes his own decisions. An adult wants to know why he has to believe what he is told to believe. An adult Christian wants to make his own personal response to the question, "What do *you* think of Christ?"

Adult Christianity is undoubtedly more than a knowledge of Catholic doctrine and practice. It is more than the faithful fulfillment of the obligations of parish membership and parish life. It is quite evident that people can know Catholic theology and not be committed Catholics. Knowledge of Catholic teaching is extremely important, and a mature Christian surely requires a knowledge of Catholic teaching that goes far beyond the elementary catechizing received as a child. But unless knowledge descends to the heart, unless it fuels a person's prayer life and forms the basis of his total outlook, it is only a step along the way.

Perhaps, before considering the nature of adult Christianity further, it would be useful to inquire about the nature of mature adulthood itself. What does it mean to be an adult? What follows in this chapter and the next is borrowed heavily from the ideas of a former professor of mine at Lumen Vitae, Brussels, Belgium, Père A. Liégé.

Elements of Human Maturity

According to this theologian, a person has achieved the first quality of human maturity when he has acquired a definite unity of personality. Unlike an adolescent still unsure of himself, the adult has actually found himself, he knows himself. He has discovered his personality resources and is aware of the worth of each of his faculties and talents.

The second quality of the mature adult is that he no longer experiences any need for the kind of boasting that often characterizes adolescent insecurity. He has overcome his inability to become totally involved in a cause. He is capable of sincere reflection and enjoys genuine liberty of spirit. He is able to live up to his convictions. Convictions involve the deepest recesses of the human personality. Convictions concern one's freedom. They endure, they motivate the entire life of the adult person in a critical manner. In a word, one is not only generous and active, but he knows why and for whom he is acting. The adult knows that a person is worth what his heart is worth, the term "heart" being understood in its biblical meaning, namely, the very core of the person's spiritual personality, that "place" where his affirmative and negative decisions determine the very living out of his life.

The third quality of the mature adult is that he knows he is responsible for the totality of his life. He perceives moral existence as a whole and sees himself as being completely involved in every moment and event of life. The adult knows that he has only one life and that everything depends on it. Moreover he sees himself as being totally responsible for the quality of his life as much and even more than for isolated moments of formal morality.

Fourth, the adult is a socialized being. He is well aware of his social roots, his solidarity with others. No longer centered upon himself, he is responsibly and actively open to the beings and things surrounding him.

Finally, the adult is adapted to the whole reality of experience. He prefers daily experience to dreams and imaginary flights of idealism. The adult does not trifle with reality but rather seeks to situate himself in it, accepting its limits and checks. He is capable of dealing honestly and openly with whatever unbalanced elements he has discovered in his personality.

It seems reasonable to suppose that these conditions for human maturity are just as valid and necessary for Christian maturity, that our progress towards Christian maturity will follow the rhythm of human maturity. We are human beings before we are Christians; our Christianity is built on and completes our humanity. The more perfected we become as human beings, the more apt we become for the fullness of Christianity. The saint is the person who is most perfectly and fully human. "The glory of God is man fully alive" is a familiar saying that goes back to St. Irenaeus in the second century.

Accordingly, unity of personality will be established in the Christian's solemn *decision* to undergo a faith-conversion that will freely involve his entire being. Access to gospel *convictions* will again and in a faithful and coherent way motivate the person's entire existence. *Socialization* will be lived out at the level of the Church and all that historically conditions the kingdom of God. Acceptance of reality will introduce a person to the genuine humility of the man who though a sinner has been engraced and is henceforth bolstered by God's own optimism.

Christianity is a religion that makes an appeal directly to human liberty, to consciously chosen motivations. It is a religion that is eminently personal without losing its common property. It makes an appeal to consciences that are truly capable of making decisions, that are literally possessed by their responsibility.

Maturity—A Gradual Evolution

All this does not mean that it is impossible for children and adolescents to live an authentic Christian life. They can indeed live it, though perhaps only partially. However, it seems that the same condition of partially lived Christianity prevails among many modern Catholics who have never totally and responsibly come to terms with their faith. Surely, this is not the ideal presented to us in the Gospel. Jesus demanded a decision from his followers. "He who is not with me is against me," he said. "Who do *you* say that I am?" "Who has first place in your life?"

The history of God's people as depicted in the Old Testament indicates that God brought them along slowly and in a human manner. Man has to be fully awakened and developed before he is ready for the Messiah. So, too, modern men and women; it behooves them to grow into perfect human maturity if they are to enter wholly into the mystery of Christ and his Way.

Valuable and essential conditions can be drawn from the above principles, the first one being that children and adolescents are to be encouraged to grow toward human maturity. Human maturity must be helped along, not feared. To be sure, this involves risk. It involves the possibility of making mistakes, even serious ones, but without freedom and without risk, no one can reasonably develop as a human person. Children and adolescents should be given responsibilities and then allowed to carry them out. They will never develop as human beings (or as Christians) if every moment of their lives is lived under command and threat, if they are never given the opportunity to make a mistake.

There are ways of working towards Christian and human maturity simultaneously. One of the most indispensable elements of reasonable and effective maturity is reflection—reflection on one's own existence and on the exact situation of the world and the humanity in which a person lives his life. Everyone needs to be confronted with the complexity of the real world. And it is obvious that children and adolescents need opportunities to exercise their freedom and to develop the ability to make decisions.

It goes without saying that the above remarks about growth in maturity in no way conflict with our Lord's word, "Unless you turn and become like children, you will never enter the kingdom of heaven" (Mt. 18:3). What Jesus demands here is not childishness. He wants the dependence and openness that characterizes a child over against its parents. It takes real maturity to become a child according to Jesus' ideal. To him, the real Christian is one who, having become satiated with human glory, loaded down with responsibility, wounded perhaps by the experiences of life, knows that he is never anything but a child in the sight of the Father. In the eyes of the world, he is an adult, but in the eyes of the Lord he is eternally only a child. It might well be that the spiritual childhood demanded by the Gospel is the crown of mature Christianity.

2

Elements of a Mature Faith

Before examining what constitutes maturity in faith, it might be well to recall two principles that are almost taken for granted by Catholic theology. First, we must hold that faith is a gift. Both God's call to a person and the power of loving adherence to the God who calls is a gift. It cannot be "merited" or acquired by any human effort. The grace of faith has its own personal history in the life of every believer, and it has its stages. Faith involves the fidelity of God coming together with the fidelity of man.

Second, baptism is the sacrament of faith. Baptism gives the grace of faith. But faith granted in baptism is like a seed that has to grow. The person who is attracted to the faith as an adult naturally aspires to baptism. The catechumen looks forward to baptism as the crown of a faith that has matured. God rarely gives ready-made results or accomplishments. A person must be much more concerned with growing in the faith than with keeping and protecting it.

We are ready now to examine what growing in the faith involves. The adult believer is first a person who has gone through—or is willing to go through—a process of conversion. Consider the story of the young Parisian student and the reaction of his classmates to his solemn baptismal commitment. All had been baptized as infants and brought up "in the faith," but only a couple of them were willing to admit that they would be ready in their current stage of life to take the step their friend had just taken. The faith of the others lacked the solidity of a personal conversion. They had not yet experienced the demands upon them required by the passage from the state of baptized children or adolescent Christians to the situation of baptized adults in full possession of their faith, ready to assume and implement its obligations.

Nature of Conversion

What is conversion? Conversion in the New Testament is called "metanoia," which is probably best translated as "conversion of the heart." The prodigal son underwent a genuine change of heart when he decided to return to his father. In the Gospel the heart is the center of the human personality. It is the "place" of action and of communion of persons with God; it is the source of decisions that involve mind as well as will, liberty as well as fidelity; it is moral conscience responding to the call and judgment of God. In a word, in the presence of God and face to face with himself, the worth of man is the worth of his heart. This is why Christ places personal responsibility at the center of his religion—that responsibility which the adult assumes with his heart when he comes face to face with the Word of God: "For where your treasure is, there will your heart be also" (Mt. 6:21).

Confronted by the call of God, the heart will have to declare its dispositions. If it is true to the terms of the New Testament, the heart will either be open, enlightened, pure, believing, or it will be blinded, hardened, impenitent, dull of mind, wrapped in darkness, hesitant, evil, and faithless.

As mentioned earlier, a conversion that is concerned only with ideas—a purely intellectual change—would not be a conversion in the Gospel sense at all. So too a conversion that involved only religious sentiment, or even one which would only change a person on an ethical plane, with reference only to oneself. It is with one's deepest being, with all that constitutes an adult person—in a word, *with his heart*—that the believer assumes his position in the presence of the Word of God which challenges him. The human heart which has thus welcomed the Word then becomes a heart indwelled by God. St. Paul's prayer for the Ephesians is then fulfilled "that Christ may dwell in your hearts through faith" (Eph. 3:17).

Many modern Christians, both Protestant and Catholic, speak of actually *experiencing* Jesus in a very vivid encounter that changed their lives, as did St. Augustine, Pascal, and many saints years ago. Fr. Ladislaus Boros describes the experience well:

> Suddenly, imperceptibly, and quite unexpectedly, God breaks through to our soul. That is it, but there is something else—God comes to us and is present with us, but he comes with a task. . . . We may not recognize at once what it is that God wants. Or it may be that our task gradually emerges

when we are close to God for a long time. But, if we listen attentively, and listen within, we may hear what God is saying and know what he wants us to do.   *Sign* (July-August 1978), p. 24.

Whether or not such a dramatic experience of Christ is to be expected (or can be "arranged" by human effort) is open to question. I suspect that the more ordinary way to conversion is more like that of a man and woman gradually coming to know one another over a period of time and eventually falling in love.

In any case, being converted means accepting—and totally committing oneself to—the world of Jesus Christ's judgments and values, his concept of happiness, and the demands of life according to Christ. Being converted means welcoming *into one's heart* a new mentality, that of Christ himself.

So, the professing of the Christian faith is much more than simply affirming certain truths about God as being true. Through God's grace and man's decision, the Christian faith is a reshaping of the believer's whole existence; henceforth the believer is obedient only to the call of God. No matter what a person's progress in union with God, conversion in the Gospel sense always appears as a renewal of the heart. It begins with his being enlightened and ends with a total personal adhering to Christ, whom he recognizes behind his signs as Presence and Salvation for every person who opens his heart to the Gospel call. This conversion is simply a clarification and development of the conversion of the heart that constituted the center of the prophetic preaching of the Old Testament.

We must insist that what is at stake is *conversion to Christ*. As Dr. Bernard Cooke says, "The Christian faith is basically neither the acceptance of doctrinal statements, nor conformity to Church law, nor the performance of certain approved religious practices but, rather, a personal acceptance of the risen Jesus as our brother and our savior." He goes on to say that this personal acceptance of Christ as savior does not eliminate or downgrade Church, but rather it lays down priorities. It insists that Jesus is prior in importance to Church; also it forewarns that it is possible (as with the Pharisees) to be a very exact (and exacting) Christian and not be personally involved with Jesus Christ.

The German author Fr. Eugen Weiler adds very useful insights into the variety, the nature and the progress of the encounters of Christians with Christ:

> The Christian's life involves an encounter with Christ, and the manner of the encounter can be different for every individual. The one thing certain is that no matter how it happens it must lead to a decision, for Jesus always summons us to follow him. Every Christian must give his own very personal answer; in fact he must be ever more bent on answering. Perhaps our

journey through life is leading us only slowly and painfully and in a round-about way to a genuine encounter with Jesus? In any event, if we do what he says, if we mull over his words and never think they have no more to say to us, then as the years pass we will begin to realize what he can be and wants to be for us in life and in death.

Jesus, Son of God: Encounter and Confession of Faith
(Chicago: Franciscan Herald Press, 1974), p. 30.

Who Needs Conversion?

The mission of the Church of Jesus Christ can never be anything else than the universal proclaiming of the same message that Jesus himself announced at the beginning of his ministry: "The time is fulfilled, and the kingdom of God is at hand; repent, and believe in the gospel" (Mk. 1:15). The Church has to preach this conversion to *already-converted Christians* whose faith lacks vigor and dynamism, in an attempt to stir up a more complete and permanent decision of their heart. The Church has to preach conversion to *baptized children and adolescents* so that the faith that grabs their hearts will bloom in them at an age when their personality is in the act of being shaped.

The Church will preach conversion to *adults whose religious practice is formalistic,* adults who though baptized are not yet convinced Christians. They have to be delivered from their infantile understanding and practice and brought to the full exercise of their religion which their maturity and age demand. Finally, with all the missionary urgency contained in the Good News of salvation in Christ Jesus, the Church will preach conversion to unbelievers.

Accordingly, every aspect of education in the faith will have Christian conversion as its term and goal, for without it there is no spiritual maturity. Nor does one arrive at conversion in a single day. If it is true that conversion requires the unifying of the personality under the sign of liberty, it is quite evident that the child is not yet capable of it, and even the normal adolescent will manifest only the possibility and promise of conversion.

The faith of a *child* rests its reality on the faith of the milieu in which it lives. The child's faith results mainly from receiving and agreeing with the faith of those around him, even as his freedom is but a participation in the choices and decisions of the adults on whom he depends.

The main task of the *adolescent* will be to work out a reconciliation between the faith of his childhood and the subjective discoveries of the emotive, reflective, and idealistic powers of his body and passions. Will he allow himself to be submerged in the experimental inventory of his interior riches? Will he hesitate to recognize Jesus Christ as the master of his life at the risk of having to renounce coming to satisfying terms with his discoveries? Or rather will he freely agree to submit to Jesus by a conversion in which he turns over to him all the resources of the youthful personality which he has just acquired?

At the threshold of maturity there is a new confrontation which challenges adolescent faith to even further progress. God's call will now come face to face not just with the riches of the adolescent's subjectivity, but with values of adult life: work, love, social personality, and his creative presence in a world which is growing. Will this believing former adolescent, who is still very idealistic and even sentimental, recognize Christ as having absolute dominion over the whole of his life with a conversion firm enough to anticipate the conversion demanded of a mature adult? Will he choose to belong entirely to Christ or will he succumb to the pagan life around him? From now on Christ addresses himself clearly to his liberty, to the whole of his personality. His "heart" is now summoned to declare itself and submit to conversion.

What Kind of God?

If conversion is the first step on the way to maturity in the faith, we have to ask ourselves about the God to whom a person is converted. The moving force of the Christian faith in every age is the God of revelation. For the Christian, believing in God always means believing in the God of Jesus Christ who calls and summons us with his grace-filled Word. But human motives for being interested in God vary, and under the impetus of these motives it sometimes happens that Christians, under the cover of faith, adopt this or that God of philosophies or religions or sociologies who has no resemblance to the God of revelation. As long as the Christian motivation for believing in God does not take first place over any other motivation, as long as the God of the Gospel of Jesus Christ is not recognized in his own personality, there can be no such thing as an adult faith. The conversion we are considering is a conversion to him whom Jesus called "the only true God" (Jn. 17:3).

The unfortunate truth is that conceptions of God exist which correspond to an infantile conception of religion—a kind of demiurge or a "God of the primitives," who acts in the world of nature and arouses a kind of sacred terror. Or it might be the sovereign "God of majesty" who requires slaves and imposes obligations upon them or a "God of the social order" who guarantees the securities of the complacent and is useful in policing human society.

There are also conceptions of God which correspond to an adolescent conception of religion—the "God of the romantics and the esthetes" who gratifies the yearnings of sentiment and often also the needs of folklore. Or there might be the "God of morality" who is concerned simply with being the auxiliary motor of the chivalric or moralizing ideal. Or finally, it could be the "God of idealistic transcendence"—a pure Spirit whose only concern is for individual souls.

It is perhaps inevitable that the faith of an adolescent of a child provisionally takes on one or the other of these notions of God. But genuine growth in faith depends on a person's being able to perceive the inadequacy or even the falsity of a religious dedication motivated solely or principally by religious instinct or by the general sense of the sacred or a moral sense or the search for human security or the need for a psychological calming.

The Christian faith of a mature adult has to be an encounter with the *living and personal* God who, without any kind of paternalism invites us to give free and willing consent to being adopted by the Father; the *loving God* who never forsakes his tenderness even when he demands and judges; the *holy God* who starts us on our way to a superhuman destiny and a new degree of happiness; finally, the *God of the kingdom* who, although already present in history, insists on pursuing the realization of his plan in history, naturally with the collaboration of human persons.

A Definite Choice of Christ

It is important that we be very clear about the distinction between *faith and the religious sense.* Man may be naturally religious, but he is not naturally a believer or a Christian. The religious sense is nourished on the sacred which in different forms proposes a certain transcendence to men, a kind of security and safety in the presence of their limitations, defeats, and the fragility of their experiences. The human need for the sacred and this religious sense are simultaneously positive and negative when it comes to recognizing Christian transcendence. They are negative in the measure in which the religious person runs the risk of being satisifed with a mythical transcendence. They are negative again in the measure in which the person is satisfied with a transcendence from which he expects nothing more than a response to his natural quest for human fulfillment.

When the God of Christian revelation intervenes and confronts us, it is precisely in order to call into question this very search for natural fulfillment—not in order to deny it, but to broaden it, purify it, and invite it to surpass itself on God's level. Not only does God want to help us excell in fulfilling our ideals, but he also reinforces the deep dissatisfaction of the human person by again placing before us the question of happiness, of human and collective destiny. Even if we did succeed in being satisfied on a completely human level of happiness, God would still have to speak to us, and faith would still have all its meaning, without any of the ambiguities of religious sentiment.

Thus the first Christians called themselves *believers* to distinguish themselves from the pagans who were often religious men and women. The Christians were convinced that faith in Jesus Christ inaugurates completely new relations with God.

So the Christian idea of God is contemporary with this adult faith which under the form of conversion constitutes the point of departure and the permanent source of sanctity. All the saints lived through their adult conversion to the God of Jesus Christ under the concrete form of the gospel absolute. Such is the story of Francis of Assisi seeking in God the glory he previously sought in men. It is the story of the mystical night of Pascal; "Your God will be my God. Forgetfulness of the world and of everything apart from God. He is to be found only in the ways taught by the Gospel . . . Joy, joy, joy, tears of joy." *The Christian idea of God involves a definitive choice of Jesus Christ. It means bearing witness to God's holiness and total commitment to evangelical perfection.*

If we are to raise up adult believers, we shall need educators who are true prophets of the God of Jesus Christ, prophets who in the name of faith will ceaselessly denounce the false images of God in their own lives and in the lives of others even within the Church—those false ideas of God which insinuate their way into the most ordinary expressions of our faith in God. We shall need prophets who will struggle for the purity of the motivating force of our faith against the current subtle temptations of magic, idolatry, and anthropocentric devotion, even as did the saints and prophets of biblical tradition. We desperately need this kind of prophet-educator in our seminaries and novitiates.

Being Able to Give a Reason for One's Faith

In a word, adult faith takes complete possession of the believer and is in turn possessed by him as a totality, a source of unity for the whole of his life.

The adult Christian must be able at all times to give a simple and confident answer to the question: "What does it mean to be a Christian? What do Christians believe?" Most Christians are embarrassed by such questions. They hardly even know how to begin to explain their beliefs. The catechism gave them a series of juxtaposed "mysteries." They generally have no idea of the relationship of the articles of faith one to another nor of the value and importance of each article in the ensemble. Their religious consciousness is an unfortunate bric-a-brac of dogmatic propositions and commandments.

Maturity in the faith has to give positive remedies to this kind of incoherence, for the Creed is a totality. There is only one mystery—Jesus Christ. Every article of the Creed expresses a single aspect of this unique mystery. The diverse aspects always have to be resituated in relation to their center: articles like God's love for us manifesting itself in the history of salvation; God's plan for creation; the Passover of Jesus Christ, the central event of history; the kingdom of God brought and preached by Jesus. It is faith alone that allows one to grasp the coherence of the various aspects of divine revelation. Everything holds together because God has acted with the coherence of love upon the history of salvation. Mature, adult faith supposes that one has begun to interiorize the mystery and that one has penetrated into the reality that lies within the dogmatic formulations.

Relative Importance of Doctrines

As a consequence of all this, the adult believer will be careful not to put everything in his profession of faith on the same plane. The kingdom is more important than hell, grace is more important than sin, the Holy Spirit is more important than the pope, Jesus Christ is more important than the Virgin Mary.

Faith such as this introduces the believer into the real world of the living God who has become present and active in history. It has nothing to do with any kind of mystical evasion nor with the morbid fear of primitive and romantic consciences.

This kind of faith includes a precise and definite awareness of the identity of Jesus Christ; it is not to be reduced to the theoretical or verbal "orthodoxy" of one who repeats a creed learned from a religion instructor.

This faith by its very nature involves a coherence of Christian conduct and action. Every aspect of revelation must introduce vital consequences into a person's life: the fatherhood of God is the basis of fraternal love; the resurrection of Christ determines the Christian use of the flesh; the Communion of Saints determines life in the Church; hell determines the seriousness of human liberty in the presence of God, etc. Baptismal life is nothing other than the progressive conversion of the whole of life to the reality of the mystery we contemplate in faith.

The proper milieu for the blossoming of such a faith is the assembly of the believers. Faith such as this is capable of bearing witness without any crusading spirit as well as without liberal tolerance. Being missionary appears to it as a need of its very nature.

Elementary Obligations of Christians

Certain pedagogical inferences manifestly derive from these reflections on the maturity of faith.

First, it is definitely not a question of learning a technique. What is essential is an interior life. Becoming an adult in the faith demands the effort of man's entire being and resources; it involves a serious dedication to Christ Jesus, a dedication that is renewed again and again. Mere moral generosity and religious observance are not enough. Not even a theoretical study of the basics of religion will suffice.

The most elementary requirement is constant meditation on the Christian message as contained in Scripture. I mean, the kind of meditation that brings a person to an ever more intense assimilation of the essential dialogue of God with men. It is not simply a matter of acquiring more religious knowledge. There has to be a rigorous struggle against spiritual laziness and the superficial habits of the do-gooder. A minimum of theological study is necessary, but it must be stimulated and prolonged by personal meditation. The adult Christian should be able to say, not "I have the faith," but, "I am *in* the faith; I *live* in the faith."

Another requirement is reflection on daily human experience and on the problems of the world in the direct light of the faith. A person has to reflect on his attitudes and his action. If he does this, action will nourish and deepen the personality of the believer. It is in doing the truth—and in knowing it—that one enters more and more into the light and the realism of the Christian world.

It is also in this kind of vital reflection on the Word of God that one's religious life rids itself of its impurities—its sentimental or sociological childishness, its formalisms, false mysticisms, human motivations, and non-Christian humanism.

Again, active and personal participation in the liturgical life of the Christian community is essential for fortifying adult faith (provided that it is a quality kind of liturgical life and not a "folklorish" or esthetic evasion). There can be no substitute for the liturgical mystery. This mystery ceaselessly reaffirms the essentials of the faith and grabs up the believer into its mystical realization.

Finally, a certain amount of interrogating of contemporary atheism can in some cases bring forth some maturity of faith. But guidance is necessary here. Some forms of atheism exist today which are indicative of a process suitable mainly to childish expressions of faith. The adult believer must be concerned that his personal religious life not only refutes but surpasses any kind of value that contemporary atheism might have to offer.

But always we come back to Christ—to our relationship with him. Who is Christ for us? How can we come to know him? How does he seek to enter our consciousness. How influential is he in shaping our lives? Our Christianity can hardly be mature unless we can answer questions such as these that will satisfy us personally. The next chapter will hopefully help the honest seeker to come to know Jesus better. But to know him fully—as he really is—is the joyous work, not of a lifetime, but of eternity itself. The next chapter may be a good beginning.

3

Jesus and the

Hunger for Happiness

If someone were to offer you what you most desire in all the world, what would you choose? And once you received it, do you think you would never again hunger for happiness? It seems that there are depths beyond depths of hunger in the human heart which through the ages poets, philosophers, theologians, and psychologists have sought to describe and analyze. After years of seeking satisfaction for his yearning heart in all manner of human gratification, St. Augustine concluded: "Thou hast made us for thyself, O God, and our hearts are restless until they rest in thee."

But long before Augustine, the Hebrew psalmists experienced and described their version of human hunger and desire:

> The Lord is my light and my salvation;
>   whom shall I fear? . . .
> Hear, O Lord, when I cry aloud,
>   be gracious to me and answer me! . . .
>   My heart says to thee,
> "Thy face, Lord, do I seek."
>   Hide not thy face from me (Ps. 27).
>   *   *   *
> O God, thou art my God, I seek thee,
>   my soul thirsts for thee;
> my flesh faints for thee,
>   as in a dry and weary land where

17

no water is.
So I have looked upon thee in the
sanctuary,
beholding thy power and glory (Ps. 63).

The whole business of advertising is constructed on and exploits mankind's hunger for happiness. Advertisements in magazines and newspapers, and especially on television, have but one message: buy and use our product and you will be happy. So happiness consists in using the right toothpaste, in smoking the right brand of cigarettes, drinking the right kind of beer, in using the right kind of face cream, having the right kind of car, in a vacation in Florida or Hawaii. And if you have a dog, you can make it happy with the right kind of dog food. We ridicule the simple-mindedness of the ads, but are we not subconsciously induced to buy the product we hear about most often? Even the most sophisticated of us has his ideal of happiness. It might be a long-dreamed of trip to Europe, or writing a successful novel, or getting a new and better job, or having no job at all, or just being young again.

The Basic Thirsts of the Human Heart

Long before he ever became a famous radio and TV preacher in 1930, Archbishop Fulton Sheen reduced the hungers and thirsts of the human heart to three: thirst for life, thirst for truth, thirst for love. The human person thirsts for the fullness of life: he wants to live forever; and the whole pharmaceutical and medical professions are built on this thirst for life—nourishing, protecting, and repairing life when it is threatened. We hang onto life fiercely, and no disease is so advanced that it can destroy hope for a cure even in the sickest of human victims. Friends and relatives die; newspapers are full of accounts of accidental deaths; but somehow we find it hard to imagine that it will happen to us.

Then there is the hunger for truth, the desire to know and learn more and more. The educational system, the news and communications media, all creative writing, all libraries, would pass out of existence if people ever lost their hunger to know truth, to know what has happened, what is going to happen, and what is the meaning of it all. The old retired university professor, with all his degrees and treasury of knowledge, and the child in kindergarten are both driven by the same hunger, the hunger for truth and knowledge. If or when that hunger for truth dies, the person dies.

Perhaps the deepest hunger of all is the hunger for love—the need first of all to *be* loved and at the same time the desire to give and share love, to be able to respond to proffered love with all the potentiality of our love-thirsty hearts. Poets, novelists, and counsellors explore and cultivate and elaborate on this hunger for love. The sense of failure they experience when they have finished one poem or novel drives them to try again and again to describe the dream of perfect love that haunts them. Apparently, no one can ever be satisfied that he has loved or has been loved to satiety. No hunger is more fragile and vulnerable, more in need of protection. It is well known that starvation kills millions of people every year across the globe, but no one could ever number the victims whose lives were blighted or even ruined and destroyed by the hunger for love that has gone unfulfilled. The need for love is the deepest of all human needs because we instinctively realize that love is creative, that in loving and being loved we become more than we were before, that we live on a higher level of life, that we can be free only in and through love.

So these are the basic human needs or thirsts, and everyone knows how difficult it is to safeguard and gratify them. The problem lies not only in the bottomless abysses of our thirsting hearts but also in that each human hunger is threatened by its own personal enemy. Thus, the thirst for truth is overshadowed by the presence of error and deception; the desire for life is threatened by disease, accident, and ultimately by death; and the hunger for love is undermined and too often destroyed by hatred, selfishness, neglect and hatred of self.

The Name of Our Desire

But the quest goes on, undiscouraged by failure. The restlessness of the quest, often its indistinctness, but ultimately its hope for complete fulfillment is beautifully expressed by Dr. José de Vinck:

> Along the moving paths of every sea, in raging storm or windless calm, in the blazing sun or under distant stars, the ancient mariners followed the songs of the sirens . . . and they drowned. We, too, have such dreams of sweet and silent paradise, of a green depth of delight, and we set sail for distant isles, and with pounding hearts and wide amazed eyes, we drown like the mariners of old without having been told the name of our desire.
>
> We often believe that happiness and peace are just beyond the bluest range of mountains; and because our heart is a wanderer and our spirit is a spirit of unrest, we leave the safe refuge of even days and stretch out our wings to follow the wild goose over the hills and far away. Alas, beyond the hills are other hills and seas uncounted. After many labors and after many days, we find ourselves returned to our familiar void, and still we do not know the name of our desire.
>
> So off we go to plumb the depths of life, seeking some food for what we cannot kill, seeking throughout the cities of the world that ecstasy that would be all in all. Down into the folds of our instinctive bodies we delve and dive and drown and drown again until we sink into the darkness of despair.
>
> O life, where is thy beauty? What of thy words and promises so fair? Where is the all-enfolding passion that quenches thirst and stills immortal hunger? Alas, we do not even know the name of our desire.

And all the while, along the sun's bright glory, along the silent wonders of the moon, there breathes one whose name is love, the long-forgotten name of our desire.

O Lord of seas and mountains, O Lord of love, have mercy on us who cry to thee. Perhaps the ways of our search were strange and tortured: often and most unwisely did we sin. But even though we did believe in other loves than thine, what is love outside of thee? Beyond the seas, over the mountains, more than power or wealth, more than the humble warmth of human flesh, was it not thee, O Lord, that we were seeking? Didst thou not hide among our earthly splendors, and did we not in our blind and clumsy way give our hearts to thee?

But now, O Lord, that thou hast spoken, now that we know the name of our desire, inflame our fragile love, clutch it between thy golden claws and lift us trembling to the splendor of thy sun.

The Quest, Epilogue of *The Yes Book*
(Allendale, N.J.: Alleluia Press, 1972).

Dr. de Vinck dramatizes the futility of man's search for happiness in worldly gratifications, a futility that the thinking person, after possibly running off in all directions in search of his heart's desire, eventually recognizes "Was it not thee, O Lord, that we were seeking?"

The Hunger of God

We are all more or less aware of this human hunger in our hearts. But we do not sufficiently realize that there is a corresponding hunger abroad in the world. It is God's hunger for our hearts, our love. Dr. de Vinck depicts man's effort to evade God's seeking, but already in the nineteenth century the English poet Francis Thompson, out of the fullness of his personal experience, wrote the poem "The Hound of Heaven" in which God is portrayed as a hound in eager pursuit of the sinner in his vain attempts to escape. We follow the runaway in his desperate struggle to find something that will take the place of God, and at the same time satisfy the yearning of his heart. He seeks every avenue of escape, but the hound relentlessly follows him. The first stanza reads:

> I fled Him, down the nights and down the days;
> I fled Him, down the arches of the years;
> I fled Him, down the labyrinthine ways
>   Of my own mind; and in the mist of tears
> I hid from Him, and under running laughter.
>   Up vistaed hopes I sped;
>   And shot, precipitated,
> Adown Titanic glooms of chasmèd fears,
>   From those strong Feet that followed, followed
>   after.
>   But with unhurrying chase,

And unperturbéd pace,
Deliberate speed, majestic instancy,
They beat—and a Voice beat
More instant than the Feet—
"All things betray thee, who betrayest Me."

Finally, exhausted by the chase, the sinner falls to the ground and presently the hound stands above him. But it is no longer a hound, but Jesus, who, in the final stanza, speaks gently:

"Ah, fondest, blindest, weakest,
I am he Whom thou seekest!
Thou dravest love from thee, who dravest me."

A modern poet, Catherine de Vinck, echoes both her husband and Thompson:

God
I pause and wonder:
am I not sought more than I seek
and are you not the hunter
and I the cowed prey
trembling in the dark?

A Book of Uncommon Prayers
(Allendale, N.J.: Alleluia Press, 1976,), p. 33.

Paradoxically, it seems that the human person can seek and run away from the true object of his search at one and the same time. The author of Psalm 139 caught hold of the paradox and put it into memorable verse:

O Lord, thou hast searched me and known me!
Thou knowest when I sit down and when I rise up;
thou discernest my thoughts from afar. . . .
Whither shall I go from thy Spirit?
Or whither shall I flee from thy presence?
If I ascend to heaven, thou art there!
If I make my bed in Sheol,
thou art there!
If I take the wings of the morning,
and dwell in the uttermost parts of the sea,
even there thy hand shall lead me,
and thy right hand shall hold me. . . .
Search me, O God, and know my heart!
Try me and know my thoughts!

One wonders why it is so difficult for human beings to learn that the wisest thing they can do is to slow down and—at long last—allow themselves to be captured. Unfortunately, too many of us do not learn the lesson until the end of our days when our legs (and hearts) are lame and tired unto death.

The Fascinating Presence of Jesus

And yet, history is full of people who did allow themselves to be caught by Jesus. No one has influenced more lives, satisfied more loves, fulfilled the human thirst for truth than he has. And fascination with him, especially among the young, is becoming more widespread today than at any time in recent centuries. When has the world witnessed more groups, people of all ages and denominations, gathering to pray and to praise Jesus than in our time?

Thousands of young women and men have freely and happily chosen to "leave all things and follow him." It is true, unfortunately, that many have been able to separate Jesus from the Churches and to devote their lives to him in communes and communities that have no connection with institutional Christianity. They make the claim (which may or may not be justified) that the Churches as institutions obscured Christ from them and that they have found more of the true Gospel spirit in their communes than they used to observe in their parishes. It is an accusation to which pastors and bishops could well pay serious attention. No one may ridicule the sincerity of these young followers of Christ. The truth is that most of these people have had some sort of personal encounter with Jesus which has changed their lives. Jesus is more real to them than anyone else in the world. He lives now and they follow and give their lives to him.

Yet this man lived more than 1,900 years ago. He was attractive then, as the Gospels indicate. His very presence fascinated and charmed men, women, and children. The evangelist John tells of the incident when two disciples of John the Baptist saw Jesus one day, followed him, and in answer to his question, "What do you seek?" replied, "Rabbi, where are you staying?" When he answered, "Come and see," they followed him and stayed with him. All of Jesus' disciples had a similar experience. They saw Jesus, experienced his charm, and when he said, "Come, follow me," they left all things—home, relatives, possessions, and professions, everything, to become his disciples. And so it has been ever since. The degree of the following and the manner of life to which he calls his disciples may differ, but Christ Jesus is the heart of the fascination.

The four Gospels, together with the Acts of the Apostles, make up a running account of the personal conquests of Jesus during his lifetime in Palestine. He challenged people then, and he continues to challenge us today to surpass ourselves, to become more than we are, to become "other Christs."

In the preface to American readers of his *Life of Jesus,* François Mauriac wrote:

I do believe that the reasons which account for the appeal of a *Life of Jesus* can disappear with time. Everything changes, except the need of the man without God for God, of the need of the Christian who has forgotten Christ for Christ . . . I wished to prove or demonstrate nothing save that the Lord, as He appears to us through the Synoptics and the Fourth Gospel, is Someone with human and consistent traits, a character in the most terrestrial sense of the word. Every one of us carries within himself a certain image of the Lord, exactly as we carry within ourselves a different representation of every other person. But it is the interest of a work like this, it seems to me, to show the meaning of Christ for the ordinary Christian, an ordinary layman, strongly bound up with the things of the world. "Here is the Man" as He rises up before the crowd with its single beating heart: that heart of Mauriac, among others, with its passions, its denials, its doubts, its needs, its miseries. Here is the Man who is (and this is sure) *the One I love the most in the world—and who for this reason is the One I have most betrayed* (emphasis added).

The Critic (September-October, 1972), p. 2.

I remember reading Mauriac's *Life of Jesus* when it was first published in the United States in the thirties. It may have been the last biography of Christ that I read, for after that authors gave up writing Lives of the Lord. The reason seems to have been: let the people learn about Jesus from the Gospels. When *The Critic* gave over its entire September-October 1972 issue to the republishing of the Mauriac work, I was puzzled, perhaps even a bit disturbed. Then, acting on some kind of impulse (another word for "grace"?), I read Mauriac again. Now I can make my own the sentiments of Raïssa Maritain's review on page 2 of the first American translation: "One cannot read this Life of Jesus without feeling grateful to the author of this work of humility and love which moves us to pray with the Good Thief, as does Mauriac himself: 'Good Thief, make us mad with hope.' "

Explaining the Fascination

How does one explain this "fatal" attraction Jesus had during his lifetime and continues to have now for people of all ages and on all parts of the globe? He fascinates us because he is God, he is God-with-us, to be sure. But perhaps most of all, because he is man, he is *the* Man, he presents the kind of ideal that people want to approach and imitate.

And yet instinctively we know that there is something special and extraordinary about him. Not only did no one ever speak like him (Jn. 7:46), but no one has ever been like him. He died, but he lives now. That alone makes him the singular being we claim him to be. He lives and continues to fascinate human hearts and to change their lives.

No one says this better than another French author, Alfred Fabre-Luce:

Jesus is a man who is at the same time in history and superior to history. . . . Christ after death has gone on living in the memory of human beings and, alone among the dead, lives more than any living man. That's a very important point. It is not like saying, Jesus is just like some Greek philosopher whom we still remember, who is still considered by intellectuals as living. You do not have people thinking of him on their death beds as they think of Jesus. It is not the same thing. A philosopher is not in their lives, he is not in their practices, they are not receiving Communion and thinking of him. . . . Christ guides us in our daily thoughts, and through him we participate in a great communion in living human beings. When I think of Christ I can feel something more or less in common with a long line of ancestors with whom I would have very little in common if there were not the element of Jesus. He also can be a link with the grandson of my grandson and so on.

Resistance to Christ

Then there is the other side of the picture. Though it is true that Jesus fascinated and attracted men and women during his lifetime and since, he failed with some whom he invited to come after him, and he attracted many enemies who sought to do away with him. Still many people today —as in every age—try to destroy him by depicting him as a perverse person, a charlatan, an immoral exploiter of the emotions and possessions of people. There were the Pharisees (not all, but some) and scribes who, out of revenge for his attacks on their hypocritical legalism, managed his condemnation and crucifixion, which they thought would rid humanity of his presence and influence. Jesus' resurrection did not prevent Pharisee Saul from giving vent to his hatred for Jesus and his followers by persecuting and bringing to trial and condemnation the Christians whom he apprehended.

I shall return to St. Paul shortly. It may be startling for us to realize that Jesus encounters a certain amount of resistance in most of his followers. We may not hate him to the extent of wanting to do away with him as did the Pharisees, but by our unwillingness and reluctance to say yes to the uncomfortable demands he makes upon us, our refusal to accept the Gospel ideal, all of it, into our lives, we manage quite well to keep him at a "safe" distance. He asks us to change from being self-centered to God-and neighbor-centered, and we put him off. He calls for the surrender of our lives to the Father. We resist. When he warns that we cannot be his disciples, we cannot truly love God, without at the same time loving and caring for our neighbor, we latch onto every possible device to explain away his command. He asks us to become like little children, i.e. totally dependent on the Father's love and care, trusting in him absolutely, being fully receptive to his gifts of love and grace. But we prefer to work out our salvation by our works, our full observance of the Law, as did the Pharisees.

"Oh that today you would hear his voice: 'Harden not your hearts . . .,' " the psalmist warns, but we take the warning as directed to another age, another people. It seems that most of us want our religion to give comfort. There is enough distress in the world and in life without allowing religion to add to it. If we have to take up a cross and follow Christ, why not have the cross padded with a Sealy postropedic mattress? Obviously, the way of Christ into our world and into our hearts is no easier for him than it was in his own day in Palestine. But with us, as with Saul, he never gives up. He cannot and will not impose himself and his grace on anyone. All he can do is keep on loving us and hoping that some day the love will be recognized for what it is and returned, as was the case with Saul.

The Experience of Saul

Something mysterious and extraordinary happened to Saul when he was riding to Damascus to carry out his vendetta against the Christians of that city. Here is his description of the event: "At midday, O king, I saw on the way a light from heaven, brighter than the sun, shining round me and those who journeyed with me. And when we had all fallen to the ground, I heard a voice saying to me in the Hebrew language, 'Saul, Saul, why do you persecute me? It hurts you to kick against the goads.' And I said, 'Who are you, Lord?' And the Lord said, 'I am Jesus whom you are persecuting" (Acts 26:13-15). All the world knows what happened after that—how the relentless persecutor turned into the most enthusiastic, the boldest, the most dynamic apostle the world has ever known.

This incident on the road to Damascus was for Paul a dramatic encounter with the living Christ, the like of which few other people have ever experienced. Hopefully, every follower of Christ has had or will have a personal Damascus. Meeting Christ in a definite way, really meeting him in the sense of experiencing his living presence, must surely be an unforgettable event in any person's life.

There seems to be some disagreement, however, on whether or not anyone can will it to happen by his own power alone. It is obvious that those of us who have had our faith handed down to us by our parents are in need of some kind of conversion to the living Jesus who is its content and meaning. Our faith will be meaningless, it will be a routine affair, unless and until at some point we say YES to Jesus, unless we commit ourselves to him deliberately and wholeheartedly. Whether or not this initial commitment will inevitably lead to a vivid *experiencing* of the Lord is not clear. It is even less clear that this experiencing of Christ in one's life is equivalent to "faith." If that were the case, what would happen to one's faith when one no longer "feels" or "experiences" him. As Catherine de Vinck says in a personal letter, "We know very well that darkness of spirit does not mean lack of faith; one should not rely on the felt experience of God, it is not centrally important. Faith is, and the daily perseverance in faith, no matter whether it is felt or not."

Concerning one's conversion to Christ, Father Weiler has written:

> The Christian's life involves an encounter with Christ, and the manner of the encounter can be different for every individual. The one thing certain is that no matter how it happens it must lead to a decision, for Jesus always summons us to follow him. Every individual must give his own very personal answer; in fact he must be ever more bent on answering. Perhaps our journey through life is leading us only slowly and painfully and in a roundabout way to a genuine encounter with Jesus? In any event, if we do what he says, if we mull over his words and never think they have no more to say to us, then as the years pass we will begin to realize what he can and wants to be for us in life and in death. *Jesus, Son of God,* p. 30.

I am quite convinced that, while every Christian needs conversion, needs to allow Christ to make him "a new creation" (Gal. 6:15), the vivid, dramatic conversion experience à la St. Paul is not essential. What we all have to come to realize is the absolute need to welcome Jesus into the center of our lives. The Danish philosopher Kierkegaard says, "We are always becoming Christians." And in the play *The Belle of Amherst,* Emily Dickinson writes, "I am sure that no person will ever be truly happy until that person can say, 'I love Christ.' "

Christ came to Saul on the road to Damascus. There is no limit to the number of ways Jesus can make his presence known to us *if* we are willing to see, if we are open to him with all our being. Most Catholics would probably understand and approve of the following testimony of Kenneth Woodward, religion editor of *Newsweek:*

> I was born into a sacramental tradition. The Catholic tradition says that you encounter Christ in everyday things like bread and wine, like the marriage bed, like in my brother. It is in these very human things that one finds oneself and finds Christ. And so, as much as I admit to liking an elevated sense of coziness with Christ, I think I will go with the bread and wine. I'll go with the everyday experiences and I won't necessarily wait for— although I would most certainly welcome—the personal experience. I prefer to be surprised by grace. *The St. Anthony Messenger* (March 1972), p. 40.

Openness to Christ

"I'll go with the bread and the wine," says Woodward. After the resurrection, two disciples on their way to Emmaus are drawn to Jesus, their hearts are warmed as he explains the Scriptures to them. When they come to the village, they invite him into the inn for a meal with them. "Stay with us, for it is toward evening and the day is now far spent," they plead (Lk. 24:29). Jesus accepts the invitation. While they are at table Jesus takes the bread, blesses it, breaks it, and gives it to them.

Their eyes are opened and they instinctively know that it is Jesus. He vanishes from their sight, and they rush back to Jerusalem with the good news that Jesus lives. They have seen him. And they came to recognize him, they say, "in the breaking of the bread," that familiar gesture that is still vivid in their minds from the Last Supper of a few days before.

The breaking of the bread in this case was a revealing sign of the divine presence. But again there is no limit to the number of signs whereby Jesus can and does reveal himself to sensitive people who are capable of seeing—really seeing—what is concealed in the world of nature as well as in the ordinary, familiar gestures of loving care that people manifest towards one another. Too many people see with their eyes but they do not grasp all that is concealed beneath the external appearances.

Jesus makes himself known to us also through the sacraments—all of them, but above all through the Eucharist and the sacrament of penance. Our faith tells us that Jesus acts now through and in the sacraments even as he acted during his earthly existence in Palestine. But here again, Christ cannot penetrate into a consciousness that is dull, unreceptive, uninterested. Contrast the mechanized way we often confess our sins with the "confession" of the "woman of the city, who was a sinner," who washed Jesus' feet with her tears and wiped them with her hair. "Her sins, which are many, are forgiven, for she loved much" (Lk. 7:47), Jesus commented. He can and does say the same conforting words to us, but too often we do not hear them or do not believe them, or having heard faintly, forget immediately.

The Supreme Importance of the Gospels

It is above all in the Gospels that Jesus lives and waits to be recognized and experienced by us. He waits there to be recognized as he really is. It is only a careful, prayerful study of the Gospels that will prevent our forming a false image of Christ for ourselves. It is evident from the many *Lives of Christ* that abounded in the nineteenth and early twentieth century that too many authors brought forth an image of Jesus that fitted their preconceived notions of him. For one Jesus was a social reformer, for another a revolutionary, for a third an emotional do-gooder. The same could be said about artists. The sentimental, pretty, "pious" pictures of Christ painted by some nineteenth-century artists falsified Jesus and contributed to a weak, sentimental, and emotional conception of Christianity in many Christians that had little or no relationship to the Christianity that derives from the Gospels.

I repeat, the only remedy for an overly subjective image of Jesus is to see him as the Gospels present him to us. But it is important that we study and read the Gospels in the right way. There are different kinds and ways of reading. You can read a page from a history book, a news-paper, a novel, or you can read a letter from (or about) someone you love very much. You read the letter with expectation, eagerness, joy. It is meant for you, it comes from the heart of a person who loves you. It stays with you so that you recall all its details, and you immediately begin to formulate phrases with which to answer the letter. Actually, the letter becomes an invitation to dialogue with the beloved.

A young man can see a young woman and be attracted to her. But he will never get to know her, will never fall in love with her, until he begins to speak to her, listen to her, answer her questions. So it is with the Gospels. They can be thought of as love letters from Christ to each one of us. If, according to Malcolm Muggeridge, there is such a thing as "creative listening," there can also be "creative reading." Writing of the Mary who sat at our Lord's feet and listened to him, Muggeridge says, "Mary possessed the gift of creative listening, of absorbing ardently not just words and ideas, but the ultimate sense of what someone they care for says, as a tree absorbs the sunlight in its leaves" *(Jesus* [New York, Harper, 1975], p. 97).

When the disciples heard and saw Jesus speak and act, they never hesitated to comment on the incident. They asked him questions, and they often asked him to explain himself. When we do the same thing while reading the Gospels, we are involved in "creative reading," we are praying and Jesus becomes more and more real to us.

To Know or to Know About

Studying and reading the Gospels creatively will help us not just to know about Jesus but to *know* him. Fr. Donald Senior, C.P., insists that there is a considerable difference between knowing and knowing about him. Hardly anyone anywhere in the world does not know something *about* Jesus. But knowing him is "something else." It is the basis of genuine Christianity:

> The urgency of the Christian mission since its beginning has been that people should come to know Jesus personally and, because of that rela-tionship, to transform their lives. To know someone in this sense presumes an intimate interlocking of lives and fate. We sense the mystery of another's person. We share with him some of the hidden richness of our own. We are present to each other, and we are able to communicate. Know-ledge of this kind is synonymous with friendship and trust. It means a mutual commitment to steadfastness and support. The language of a relationship like this is not curiosity or exploitation but love.
>
> This kind of language comes closest to describing the relationship between the believer and Jesus. The living presence of the Risen Lord in the world of today is unique, mysterious, even baffling. But the instinct of the Christian believer tells him or her that the living presence of Jesus is some-

thing more than the echo of his fame. It is even something more than the force of his example. The life of Jesus Christ tells us much more about what it means to be a human being. But the unique assertion of faith is that the presence of Jesus gives the believer the transforming power to *be* more human.

The reality of the living presence of Jesus is, in some ways, ineffable. But the experience of faith undergirds a conviction that is real—a surge of peace in a moment of prayer, the transforming power of genuine forgiveness, the infectious strength of another believer. These are the moments, however rare, when we touch the reality of the presence of Jesus.

Jesus: A Gospel Portrait (Dayton, Ohio: Pflaum, 1975), p. 6.

Conclusion

Hopefully, we are now better prepared to give a personal response to the question Jesus asks each of us: "But who do you say that I am?" (Mt. 16:15). No one can improve on Peter's answer: "You are the Christ, the Son of the living God!" (Mt. 16:16). And we can add our own conviction: "You are the answer to all the hunger, the thirst and the desire of the heart of every human being."

To sum up: coming to know Jesus and to be won over to him is primarily his work in us. He is the one who first calls us to intimacy; he is eager to meet us. However, there can be no "connection" between his heart and ours unless we are willing to listen and consent to his wooing of our love. Human love between a woman and a man is possible only when each realizes how much the one loves the other. It is only when Christ's personal love for me reaches my inner being and awareness that I am able and willing to love him in return. All of the New Testament, indeed, all of Scripture contains the story of divine love for human beings. One wonders why it is that so many never seem to have learned of that love . . . or respond to it. The next chapter attempts to answer that query.

4

The Holy Spirit:

Instructor of Hearts

Jesus Christ is known as the savior of the world. No one in all history has attracted and influenced human persons as he has. And yet he would be the first to admit that what he was, what he taught, and what he did needed to be implemented by someone else—Someone he calls "the Spirit of truth," the "Counselor," the "Holy Spirit." It is only the Holy Spirit who can bring home to us the full meaning not only of Jesus as Savior but of his Gospel and the implications of what it means to be a fully adult and mature Christian.

No one ever spoke or taught like the man Christ Jesus. Yet the Gospels remind us again and again how uncomprehending his chosen followers were both of him and his message. "Are you still without understanding?" he complained at the very moment of his ascension—some of them still wanted to think of him as a political leader who would restore the kingdom to Israel (Acts 1:6).

I shall shortly be indicating Jesus' associations with the Holy Spirit during his public life. It is appropriate here to go right to the Last Supper to see and hear his own teaching on what the Spirit will accomplish in the hearts of the apostles—in the Church:

> "I will pray the Father, and he will give you another Counselor, to be with you for ever, even the Spirit of Truth, whom the world cannot receive, because it neither sees him not knows him; you know him, for he dwells with you and will be in you" (Jn. 14:15-17).

* * *

"These things I have spoken to you, while I am still with you. But the Counselor, the Holy Spirit, whom the father will send in my name, he will teach you all things, and bring to your remembrance all that I have said to you" (Jn. 14:25-26).

* * *

"But when the Counselor comes, whom I shall send to you from the Father, even the Spirit of truth, who proceeds from the Father, he will bear witness to me; and you also are witnesses, because you have been with me from the beginning" (Jn. 15:26-27).

* * *

"It is to your advantage that I go away, for if I do not go away, the Counselor will not come to you; but if I go, I will send him to you. . . .

I have yet many things to say to you, but you cannot bear them now. When the Spirit of truth comes, he will guide you into all the truth; for he will not speak on his own authority, but whatever he hears he will speak, and he will declare to you the things that are to come. He will glorify me, for he will take what is mine and declare it to you" (Jn. 16:7-15).

The above helps us to recall a promise Jesus had made earlier in his public life when

> On the last day of the feast, the great day, Jesus stood up and proclaimed, "If any one thirst, let him come to me and drink. He who believes in me, as the scripture has said, 'Out of his heart shall flow rivers of living water.' "

And the evangelist comments:

> Now this he said about the Spirit, which those who believed in him were to receive; for as yet the Spirit had not been given, because Jesus was not yet glorified (Jn. 7:37-39).

Old Testament Foreshadowing

Most Catholics are aware of the manner in which Jesus *gradually* revealed the divine truth that God is one (in nature) but also triune (in persons). To be sure, Jesus never used the words *persons* or *nature* (which entered Christian theological vocabulary only after several hundred years), but he often spoke of his Father, shared with his followers his own prayer to the Father, and, as we have just read, he promised to send the Holy Spirit to his followers to complete his work. There is nothing particularly new about such a promise. The casual reader of the Old Testament will surely be astonished at the number of times the "Spirit of the Lord" is mentioned in its books.

Already in Gen. 1:2 we find these significant words: "The earth was without form and void, and darkness was upon the face of the deep; and the Spirit of God was moving over the face of the waters." The English poet Gerald Manley Hopkins captures this imagery in a memorable verse:

> The Holy Ghost, over the bent world broods with warm breast and
> Ah! bright wings.

The Hopkins verse may or may not be responsible for the note in the Jerusalem Bible: "Like a bird hanging in the air over its young in the nest." As the mother bird broods over her nest and warms the eggs till her chicks are hatched, so does the Spirit of God hover over the chaos of the primitive void and bring order and new life into that void.

There is further mention of the Spirit of God in other Old Testament books. Perhaps the best known of all the Old Testament references to the Spirit of the Lord is to be found in Joel 2:28-29:

> "And it shall come to pass afterward,
> that I will pour out my spirit on all flesh;
> your sons and your daughters shall prophesy,
> your old men shall dream dreams,
> and your young men shall see visions.
> Even upon the menservants and maidservants
> in those days, I will pour out my spirit."

The New American Bible has this note on the above text: "In the Old Testament the *spirit* is the gift of God bestowed on those acting as his agents. The promise of the spirit is quoted by St. Peter in Acts 2, 17-21 as fulfilled in an eminent way by the gift of the Holy Spirit, the Third Person of the Blessed Trinity, bestowed on the Apostles."

The Holy Spirit and the Virgin Mary

In the New Testament, Mary's "experience" with the Holy Spirit forms a sort of bridge between the Old Testament and the New. When the angel announces to Mary that she is to be the mother of Jesus, she asks, "How can this be, since I have no husband" (Lk. 1:34). There is tremendous significance in the angel's reply:

> "The Holy Spirit will come upon you,
> and the power of the Most High will
> overshadow you;
> therefore the child to be born will
> be called holy,
> the Son of God" (Lk. 1:35).

Anyone familiar with Old Testament history will immediately recognize the "cloud that covered the tent of meeting" when "the glory of the Lord filled the tabernacle" (Ex. 40:34). One of Mary's loveliest titles is "Bride of the Holy Spirit."

My confrere Fr. Kilian McDonnell, O.S.B., comments on the symbolism in the angel's words: "Luke uses the ark and the Presence as depicted in the book of Exodus to explain the function of Mary. The presence of Jahweh over the ark of the covenant is the model for explaining the Presence of the Most High over Mary. The consequences of this manifestation of the Presence are similar: the ark is 'filled with the Glory,' and Mary is filled with the presence of 'the Holy One,' the 'Son of God.' " And he points out how perfect is Mary's response to the divine Presence, namely, the Magnificat, her song of praise:

"My soul magnifies the Lord,
and my spirit rejoices in God my Savior,
for he has regarded the low estate of his handmaiden.
For behold, henceforth all generations will call me blessed;
for he who is mighty has done great things for me,
and holy is his name" (Lk. 1:46-49).

The Holy Spirit in Jesus' Public Life

The Holy Spirit is prominent in the public life of Jesus, especially at its beginning. When he was baptized the heavens opened and the Spirit descended upon him like a dove. The note of the New American Bible is again to the point: "The dove is the symbol of the Holy Spirit, derived perhaps from the image of the creative spirit of God hovering over the waters (Gn 1,2). The intimation is that Jesus, possessor of the Spirit, is the creator of the new people of God."

Each of the three synoptic evangelists mention how the Spirit led Jesus (Mark says "drove") into the desert where after fasting forty days and forty nights, he was tempted by the devil.

Luke relates how, when Jesus came back to Nazareth after he had acquired somewhat of a reputation as a miracle worker, he went to the synagogue on a sabbath and read from the prophet Isaiah:

"The Spirit of the Lord is upon me,
because he has anointed me to
preach good news to the poor.
He has sent me to proclaim release to the captives
and recovering of sight to the blind,
to set at liberty those who are oppressed,
to proclaim the acceptable year of the Lord" (Lk. 4:16-19).

And when Jesus closed the book, he told his fellow villagers: "Today this scripture has been fulfilled in your hearing." Jesus seems to indicate here that all of his messianic work—especially his preaching and healing —is being done under the impetus and inspiration of the Spirit of the Lord. But Jesus is rejected and threatened with death by the citizens of Nazareth, a situation that prompts some commentators to remark that Luke intends this entire scene to be prophetic of his ultimate rejection by his contemporaries.

There is no need to list the details of their rejection. It is more than enough to point out that the failure to see Jesus as the Messiah promised in the sacred books of the Old Testament lingered on in some of the disciples even after the resurrection. In Acts 1:3-6, Luke relates events that took place just before Jesus' ascension:

> To them [the apostles] he presented himself alive after his passion by many proofs, appearing to them during forty days, and speaking of the kingdom of God. And while staying with them he charged them not to depart from Jerusalem, but to wait for the promise of the Father, which, he said, "you heard from me, for John baptized with water, but before many days you shall be baptized with the Holy Spirit."
>
> So when they had come together, they asked him, "Lord, will you at this time restore *the Kingdom to Israel?"* (emphasis added).

There is infinite patience in the Lord's answer: "It is not for you to know times or seasons which the Father has fixed by his own authority. But *you shall receive power when the Holy Spirit has come upon you;* and you shall be my witnesses in Jerusalem and in all Judea and Samaria and to the end of the earth" (Acts 1:7-8, emphasis added).

All Filled with the Holy Spirit

After this final promise Jesus returns to his Father and the apostles go back to Jerusalem, to the upper room, where "all these with one accord devoted themselves to prayer, together with the women and Mary the mother of Jesus, and with his brethren" (Acts 1:14). Their prayer and waiting continued on to the Jewish feast of Pentecost, the day on which the Jews celebrated the bestowal of the Law on Mount Sinai. Again Luke gives the bare facts: "Suddenly a sound came from heaven like the rush of a mighty wind, and it filled all the house where they were sitting. And there appeared to them tongues as of fire, distributed and resting on each one of them. And they were all filled with the Holy Spirit and began to speak in other tongues, as the Spirit gave them utterance" (Acts 2:2-4).

The notes in the New American Bible provide us with the symbolism of the wind and the tongues of fire: "The sound of a great rush of wind would aptly presage a new action of God in the history of salvation. . . ." "Tongues as of fire: see Ex. 19, 18, where fire symbolizes the presence of God to initiate the covenant on Sinai. Here the Holy Spirit acts upon the apostles, preparing them to proclaim the new covenant with its unique gift of the Spirit (2, 38)."

Luke then relates the events following the apostles' being fired up by the Spirit. They rush out into the crowded streets of the city and speaking in a variety of tongues are understood by all the pilgrims from the different lands who had come to Jerusalem to celebrate the feast. "And all were amazed and perplexed, saying one to another, 'What does this mean?' But others mocking said, 'They are filled with new wine.' " (Acts 2:12-13).

Then it is Peter's turn to explain what has happened. With a touch of humor he corrects the impression that his fellow apostles are drunk because, he says, "It is only the third hour of the day," that is, only nine o'clock in the morning. A bit too early in the day for partying. The apostles are intoxicated all right, but the "spirits" in this case are non-alcoholic, it is the Holy Spirit. What actually has happened, Peter explains, is that the ancient prophecy of Joel (quoted above) has been fulfilled. God has indeed poured out his Spirit upon all flesh, and the people of Jerusalem are now witnessing the signs and wonders that were to accompany the event.

Peter then simply tells about Jesus; "A man attested to you by God with mighty works and wonders and signs which God did through him in your midst, as you yourselves know—this Jesus, delivered up according to the definite plan and foreknowledge of God, you crucified and killed by the hands of lawless men. But God raised him up, having loosed the pangs of death, because it was not possible for him to be held by it" (Acts 2:22-24). He goes on to claim Jesus as the descendant whose death and resurrection David had foreseen: "This Jesus God raised up, and of that we are all witnesses. Being therefore exalted at the right hand of God, and having received from the Father the promise of the Holy Spirit, he has poured but this which you see and hear. . . . Let all the house of Israel therefore know assuredly that God has made him both Lord and Christ, this Jesus whom you crucified" (Acts 2:32-33, 36).

No sermon has ever had a more powerful result. The people, cut to the heart, ask Peter and his compansions, "What shall we do?" And Peter tells them: "Repent, and be baptized every one of you in the name of Jesus Christ for the forgiveness of your sins; and you shall receive the gift of the Holy Spirit" (Acts 2:37-38). Luke then tells us that three thousand souls received Peter's word and were baptized. "And they devoted themselves to the apostles' teaching and fellowship, to the breaking of bread and the prayers" (Acts 2:42).

The chapter ends with a short but very complete description of the life of the primitive Christian community that came out of Peter's first sermon: fear came upon every soul; and many wonders and signs were done through the apostles: "And all who believed were together and had all things in common; and they sold their possessions and goods and distributed them to all, as any had need. And day by day, attending the temple together and breaking bread in their homes, they partook of food with glad and generous hearts, praising God and having favor with all the people. And the Lord added to their number day by day those who were being saved" (Acts 2:44-47).

The Effects of Pentecost

What actually happened on that first Christian Pentecost? The most obvious thing is that there has been a dramatic change in the apostles. The fear that had locked them in the upper room has vanished; they rush out into the streets to proclaim the Good News. It is hard to believe that the powerful preacher whose first sermon converted so many thousands is the same bumbling fisherman who just a few weeks earlier had thrice denied that he ever knew Jesus. The self-seeking men who had once vied for position in Christ's kingdom now share all their possessions with the community, and their example is accepted as the norm by all the new converts. Those same single-minded fishermen who up to then had been individual (and individualistic) disciples of Christ are now one body with him, they are the Church, aware for the first time of their identity as a Church, as a praying, praising, worshipping community.

The constitutive elements of the Christian life as we know it today are there in embryo: the teaching of the apostles followed and fellowship with one another enjoyed, above all, the "breaking of bread" (the earliest name for the Eucharist) and prayers.

In passing, we may note that Peter's style of preaching became normal for him and the other apostles, especially Paul, once he becomes an apostle. These men simply relate God's mighty deeds, the people hear, they are touched to the heart, and they ask for baptism. The message that comes through to them is that God loves them, and they respond to love with love.

Fr. Edward Farrell provides an excellent summary of the "communitarian" nature of the work of the Holy Spirit:

> The Holy Spirit is inclusive, all-embracing, community-creating. He comes upon us not for ourselves privately but to enable us to *be* for others, to build the Body. He builds up the Kingdom between us. He breaks down the strangeness, removes the barriers, and bridges the estrangement created by the cumulative sin of man. He enables us to perceive and discern the truth and light in each person. Our immediate, rash judgments of others are countered by his unconditional love and reverence for each person.
>
> *(Surprised by the Spirit* (Denville, N.J.: Dimension Books, 1973), p. 111.

But back to the event itself and what it did to and for the apostles. Now for the first time they fully understand Jesus and his message. All previous misconceptions about the nature and work of the Messiah give way to a realization of the true nature of the kingdom that Jesus had preached. During his public life of teaching the crowds and, above all, his forming of the apostles, he had instructed their minds and had informed them of the message he wanted them to hand on. But the instructing of minds had to be completed by the instructing *of hearts* as well. Some modern expressions made popular by young people give some idea of the condition of the apostles after the Holy Spirit had taken possession of their whole beings on that first Pentecost: they were "high," they were "turned on," they were "fired up."

Perhaps the word "enthusiasm" best describes the apostles' condition after Pentecost, and I do not hesitate to use it. Many bishops and priests are suspicious of enthusiasm in religion and of people who seem overly enthusiastic. There may, of course, be extremes of enthusiasm, and there may well be such a thing as false enthusiasm. But the enthusiasm of the apostles on that first Pentecost and that of the primitive Christian community thereafter was absolutely genuine. The word "enthusiasm" comes from the Greek "entheos," which means "in God." There can be no doubt that those first Christians were "in God" and God was in them, they were completely "inspirited," possessed by the Holy Spirit.

The Holy Spirit filled them with the desire and determination to share Christ with others. Christianity spread through the then-known world on the wings of their enthusiasm, their love for Christ and for one another. The Acts of the Apostles could well be called the Acts of the Holy Spirit through the Apostles and the Christian Community. For the apostles no one was a full-fledged Christian (even though he was baptized) unless the person had received the Spirit. A typical instance of their conviction is to be found in Acts 8:14-18:

> Now when the apostles at Jerusalem heard that Samaria had received the word of God, they sent to them Peter and John, who came down and prayed for them that they might receive the Holy Spirit: for it had not yet fallen on any of them, but they had only been baptized in the name of the Lord Jesus. Then they laid their hands on them and they received the Holy Spirit.

Again Acts relates how Paul and Apollos discovered some disciples at Ephesus, and when they asked the group if they had received the Holy Spirit when they believed, they replied "No, we have never even heard that there is a Holy Spirit" (19:2). They told Paul that they had been baptized in John's baptism, but now they consented to be baptized in the name of the Lord Jesus. "And when Paul had laid his hands upon them, the Holy Spirit came on them and they spoke with tongues and prophesied" (Acts 19:6).

The Eclipse of the Holy Spirit

The expression, "We have never even heard that there is a Holy Spirit," may well have been prophetic of a condition among Christians that has prevailed in certain eras of the history of the Catholic Church since those early times. Obviously, the Holy Spirit, once promised and sent by Christ, could never have departed from the Church. But it seems quite certain that the Spirit and awareness of the unquestioned need for the Spirit in order to be a complete Christian could well have vanished from the consciousness of the faithful and from their lives and piety. Most older Catholics today grew up in such an age.

When I was a seminarian and a young priest in the second quarter of this century (and before that when I was a child), one could rarely hear a sermon or read an article on the Holy Spirit. All we needed was Christ. There was one exception to that observation in my acquaintance. The bishop who ordained me managed to bring the Holy Spirit into almost every one of his sermons, and he actually wrote a book on the Holy Spirit. But everyone thought that he was a little "odd," to put it mildly. He was odd all right, with the "oddness" of God, of the apostles, and of the primitive Church. *

The "Return" of the Holy Spirit

That farsighted bishop would feel much more at home in our times when groups of Christians of all denominations gather together to pray, to read the Bible, and to ask for and receive the "baptism of the Spirit" through prayers and the imposition of hands of those who have already experienced that baptism. The modern "charismatic renewal" has met with some suspicion and opposition by many clergy and laity, and it is being "watched" by various national hierarchies. Nevertheless, it is the fastest growing "movement" in Christianity, its membership including

---

* If individual Catholics have not been wholly aware of the place of the Holy Spirit in their lives, the same cannot be said of the Church herself, especially since Vatican II. The ritual (i.e. the prayers and signs) with which all of the sacraments except matrimony and the anointing of the sick are administered now include the invocation of the Holy Spirit, along with the laying on of hands, the ancient sign of calling down of the Holy Spirit upon persons or, in the case of the Mass, upon the bread and wine which are to be changed into the Body and Blood of Christ. Here is the prayer for the Spirit in Eucharistic Prayer II:

> Let your Spirit come upon these gifts to make them holy,
> so that they may become for us
> the body and blood of our Lord, Jesus Christ.

The absolution which the priest pronouces as he extends his hands over the penitent's head in the sacrament of penance reads:

> God, the Father of mercies,
> through the death and resurrection of his Son
> has reconciled the world to himself
> and sent the Holy Spirit among us
> for the forgiveness of sins;
> through the ministry of the Church
> may God give you pardon and peace,
> and I absolve you from your sins
> in the name of the Father, and of the Son,
> and of the Holy Spirit.

countless numbers of priests and ministers, many bishops and at least one highly regarded cardinal, the Belgian Primate Leo Suenens. Pope Paul VI refrained from openly endorsing the movement, but it is significant that in 1975, on the occasion of the world meeting of charismatics in Rome, the Pope invited Cardinal Suenens to concelebrate Mass with him on the main altar of St. Peter's—an unprecedented privilege.

There seems to be plenty of evidence in their lives to back up the claim of the charismatics that their entire religious outlook has been changed, that they have enjoyed a genuine "experience" of Jesus and that they have been granted a fresh and dynamic vision of their faith. In the light of the evidence of the Acts of the Apostles, any obligation to justify the need for the Holy Spirit for a complete Christian life among the baptized would seem unnecessary. If such a justification is called for, the dramatic transformations in the lives of most of the charismatics constitute the best possible proof of the genuineness and effectiveness of the so-called charismatic movement. I doubt that any era in recent centuries has seen so many thousands of Christians of all ages and all denominations so unashamedly and so enthusiastically professing their faith in the Lord Jesus. According to *Our Sunday Visitor* (July 23, 1978), the charismatic renewal movement has about ten million members in one hundred countries, and it is hardly more than ten years old!

I am not a member of this movement, and I doubt that any of its adherents would claim that a person has to belong to a prayer group and receive the baptism of the Spirit in order to be a complete Christian. But I do insist that every Christian has to be open to the Holy Spirit, that the Spirit simply has to be a vital influence in our life of prayer and piety. If Jesus could insist that the Holy Spirit was necessary for the fullness of discipleship in his apostles, is not the Spirit just as necessary for us today? St. Paul is very explicit about this: "Any one who does not have the Spirit of Christ does not belong to him" (Rom. 8:9).

Why We Need the Holy Spirit

It is the Holy Spirit who makes it possible for the Christian to experience joy in his life, who grants the power to fulfill Christ's commands to love one another, to feel oneness with other members of a worshipping community. It is the Spirit who casts out fear, who gives vision, who helps us to see the meaning of life, who gives relish and the ability to savor the beauty of nature, of music, art, poetry. Above all, it is the Holy Spirit who enables us truly to praise and worship our Creator and to follow and dedicate our lives to Christ without hesitation or reserve.*

---

*Fr. Edward Farrell wonderfully enlarges our vision of the nature and work of the Holy Spirit:

The Holy Spirit is to our spiritual outlook on life what irrigation is to a dry, lifeless desert. The Belgian Louis Evely once wrote that "without the Holy Spirit, religion would be just a flat, barren code of obligations, empty prayers, fruitless sacraments and boring Masses" *(That Man Is You* [Westminster, Md.: Newman Press, 1965], p. 168.)

And he claims that "just as the Holy Spirit was the origin and the principle of Christ's incarnation in the womb of the Virgin Mary, so He's the origin and principle of Christ's incarnation in each Christian. His indwelling in us is as real as the Incarnation" (p. 170).

Judging by Acts 2 the Holy Spirit is available to any Christian for the asking. Receiving the Spirit is simply a normal part of the Christian experience, as the whole of Acts demonstrates. To be sure, the arrival of the Spirit in a person's life may not be as dramatic as on that first Pentecost or even as in the baptism of the Spirit experienced by many of the charismatics.

This truth is illustrated by the personal account of a woman who related her experience in an article in *The St. Anthony Messenger* several years ago. She told of her quest for the Spirit—her desire for a more vivid experience and awareness of the Holy Spirit in her life. She prepared herself, read her Bible, went to prayer meetings. Nothing happened. Then one evening she was walking along the river in her home town. The sun was setting, a slight breeze made the water ripple. And then "it" happened. She suddenly realized that she was striving to gain something that could not be earned, merited, or gained. She said to herself, "My pulse would not be beating—indeed, I would not exist were it not for the living, loving Spirit. The sun would not rise to set, nor the waters flow if it were not for the Spirit."

Then she thought of all the things she had been doing for her family, the healing of wounds, physical and mental, the love she had poured out on her family. She wrote:

> I had been looking high and low for an intangible mass of *truth*, failing to realize that truth is all around me. I expected something dramatic and sudden, like rushing winds and tongues of fire. Instead I found the Spirit while I was walking along the river bank . . . I realized that *I* do not make that awesome commitment; it has been made for me in his Love, when he chose to love *me*. I can only accept. What *new* Pentecost? Praise God that

The Spirit is inner transformation, being born again. The Spirit stirs up, prods, lifts up; never sleeps, is persistent, wears us down, ever returns. . . . He has His own way of revealing Himself. He is always *surprise*. When we least suspect it, He is breathing in us. He awakens us, recreates a forgotten appetite, stirs up a lost hunger and thirst, gifts us with an energy, a facility, a freedom and "unites us to the Lord to make with Him one Spirit" (1 Cor. 6:17). *Surprized by the Spirit* (Denville: N.J.: Dimension Books, 1973), p. 111.

the ever-present Spirit has never retired! We BREATHE by the Spirit, we LIVE by the Spirit, we LOVE by the Spirit.

What this lady experienced may or may not be accepted as a genuine example of "baptism in the Spirit" by the charismatics, but no one can deny that the Holy Spirit had become very real to her, that she had been enabled to see her own life and the world around her in a new and marvelous way. One may wonder if baptism in the Spirit has to consist in a ceremony or if the Holy Spirit can be confined to ritual acts.

Completing the Work of Christ

I may have overemphasized the usefulness, the potential power of the Spirit in the life of the individual Christian. Of course, this is not wrong, but I want to insist again that the main task of the Holy Spirit is to make the Church into a community of the redeemed, to make individual Christians aware that they are the Body of Christ (as were the apostles and their converts. As Yves Congar has written: "His [the Spirit's] task is not enlightening this man or that, but animating and building up the Body of Christ. For that reason His gifts and His works are essentially communitive. He operates through the mutual love of the faithful, a spirit of brotherly love and fellowship" (*See* Evely's *That Man Is You*, p. 177).

One more corrective may be in place. Necessary as the Holy Spirit may be both for the individual Christian and the Church, we may not forget that the full revelation of the Holy Spirit in our time, even as in the earliest days of Christianity, is necessary for the completeness and fullness of the revelation brought by Christ to the world. As long as ignorance of the Holy Spirit and his rightful place in modern Christianity prevails in us, we can hardly claim to be full-fledged disciples of Jesus Christ who know in truth what it means to be a Catholic Christian.

Openness to the Holy Spirit expressed in longing prayer is an essential element in the spirituality of the adult Christian. Many Catholics have found the Sequence for Pentecost a satisfying prayer not only on Pentecost but daily throughout the year. Fr. Roger Schoenbechler, O.S.B., of St. John's Abbey has translated this sequence, which is attributed to Stephen Langton (1155-1228):

> Holy Spirit, give us life!
> Spread your peace where there is strife!
>   Drive off darkness by your light!
> Come, O Father of the poor,
> With your Gifts make them secure;
>   Come, bring gladness to their plight!
>
> Be our honor'd Guest each day;
> Be our solace, Lord, we pray;

Free our restless hearts from pain!
Help us work with zeal apace;
Calm our passions with your grace;
Help us joy and peace regain!

Light from heaven, grace benign,
Flood our hearts with love divine;
Fill them to the brim with joy!
Share your wondrous Gifts with us
So that good may come from us;
Let not sin our souls destroy!

Drench our dried up lives with grace;
Wash us clean, our debts erase;
Heal our wounds brought on by sin!
Gently bend our stubborn will;
Warm the freezing hearts that kill;
May each day with you begin!

In you, Lord, we place our trust;
Help us to be truly just;
Guide us with your grace and light!
So that by our saintly life
We may conquer in the strife
And enjoy your Vision bright!

Amen. Alleluia.

Conclusion

This chapter was not intended to be a blueprint for bringing the Holy Spirit into our Christian life and daily experience. If someone were to ask me how to come more under the influence of the Spirit, I am not sure I could give a satisfactory answer. I do not believe that anyone can "program" the Spirit, as *The St. Anthony Messenger* article quoted a few pages ago indicates. The article describes a sudden awareness of a deeper meaning in the author's life than the lady had realized up to then. This sudden awareness was undoubtedly the work of the Holy Spirit in her.

I believe that the same experience is available to any sincere Christian who ardently desires the Spirit and who is fearlessly open to his sublime direction. I also believe that the Spirit is more active in the lives of Christ's followers than they generally realize. For example, that you are earnest about wanting to become a more mature Christian and are reading this book might well indicate that the Spirit is acting upon you now.

If, however, you would like to have a more vivid experience of the Holy Spirit in your life, or if you are undergoing a serious and painful trial, I would suggest that you join one of the prayer groups that are to be found in almost every parish or city, but again keeping in mind the experience of the author of *The St. Anthony Messenger* article.

My last suggestion comes from Scripture itself—from the example of the apostles and our Lady. After Jesus' ascension they returned to the upper room in Jerusalem where, no doubt in obedience to directives of Jesus, they "with one accord devoted themselves to prayer, together with the women and Mary the mother of Jesus, and with his brethren" (Acts 1:14). I am convinced that the Spirit—in some way or other, spectacularly or quietly—will not refuse to enter the lives of those who sincerely open their hearts to him in prayer.

> Come, Holy Spirit, fill the hearts of your faithful
> and enkindle in them the fire of your love!

5

The Church, Community of Faith

The main task of the Holy Spirit is to make the Church into the community of the redeemed, to build up the Body of Christ. We have to have clear ideas about the connection between Christ and the Church. There seems to be little doubt that the word "Church" has in recent years fallen upon bad times. Jesus is very real to a lot of people; they are on intimate terms with him. But mention "Church" and the conversation is likely to cool.

The Church and Christ

Nevertheless, one cannot read the Gospels without noticing that the idea of a Church is essential to Jesus' preaching. During the three years of his public life he carefully prepared the apostles for the task of carrying on his life and work after he would leave them. The idea of a body of people, a living community of his followers, who would keep alive his memory and the remembrance of all that he said and did and commanded, is explicit or implicit in all that Jesus said and did. He called a group of men to follow him. He lived on intimate terms with them for three years; he trained them, taught them by word and example, he formed them. And at the end of his ministry, after he had finished this formation and completed his work, which included not only dying and rising from the dead, but also providing for a living community which would continue and carry on his work, he commissioned the apostolic group: "All authority in heaven and on earth has been given to me. Go therefore and make disciples of all nations, baptizing them in the name of the Father and of the Son and of the Holy Spirit, teaching them to observe all that I have commanded you; and lo, I am with you always, to the close of the age" (Mt. 28:18-20).

Jesus himself used the term "Church" when he changed Simon's name and made him head of this new living community of his followers: "I tell you, you are Peter [rock], and on this rock I will build my church, and the powers of death shall not prevail against it" (Mt. 16:18). So the idea of a Church has excellent origin. The problem through the ages has been with the members of that body who have been so terribly "human," so subject to all the frailities of the weakest of her members. The Church of Christ has known periods of unbelievable corruption among its leaders, including the successors of St. Peter. We who live during a period of a strong papacy have no conception of the shame and sorrow the people of God has had to endure because of its leaders in some centuries of the Church's history.

The expression, "Ecclesia semper reformanda"—the Church is always in need of reform, reveals a true necessity in any age. The reason for this necessity is obvious to any person who is aware of his sinful past (or present). The Church is people, and people are vulnerable and sin-inclined. They are capable not only of the most heroic deeds of glory but also of dastardly and shameful acts of violence and evil. Their being Christian does not take away their freedom, their ability to choose between right and wrong, and often to settle for the wrong.

Possible Conflict Between Structure and Spirit

In our time the poor image attached to the word and idea of "Church" may come from what seems to be an overemphasis on bureaucracy, with a corresponding interference in the freedom of the people. There are some "Church people" who so stress Church as Church that they seem to lose sight both of Jesus and of people.

Christianity has long been aware of the potential conflict between "structure and spirit." Many Protestants (and not a few Catholics) have accused the Roman Catholic Church of placing too much emphasis on structure and organization and not enough on spirit. It is a temptation which any Church might succumb to, but the fact is, as our own government proves, it is difficult, if not impossible, to get along without structure when large numbers of people are involved.

But the Holy Spirit never allows the Church to forget that it is more than organization and structure, that it is the Body of Christ, the People of God. To forget this would be to risk losing her soul. The Church must always be Christ to the world. She must be the normal means whereby people can come to Christ, the living Christ. Apart from her divine vocation to carry Christ into the ages, to bring his word, his healing, his forgiveness, his sacrificial death and resurrection to people of all times, the Church has no reason for being.

The March 1972 *The St. Anthony Messenger* devoted an entire issue to "The Search for Jesus," which included articles on Jesus as Man, Jesus as Lord, Jesus as a great moral Teacher, with a concluding section on what Jesus has meant to a group of modern,people. To me it is significant that an article on the Church preceded the other articles on the humanity, the divinity, and the lordship of Jesus. Its theme was that "Jesus is the first fact of our existence as Christians. But our understanding of Jesus and our belief in him are intimately bound up with the community of faith—the Church" (K. Hurley's article, p. 13).

It may be surprising to many Christians to know that without the Church—the community of believers converted by the apostles—we would not even have the New Testament to provide us with our knowledge of Jesus. The Gospels were written long after Jesus ascended to the Father; the Gospels and the other books of the New Testament came out of the Church, they record the memory of what Jesus said and did, and they set down the early Church's growth in faith and understanding of who and what Jesus is (Wilhelm). "It is within this community of faith that I encounter the memory and meaning of Jesus alive in Scripture and tradition; it is within this community of love that I can personally encounter the risen Jesus in Liturgy and sacrament" (Hurley, p. 16). It seems to me that, if that is the way it was with the first Christians, that's the way it ought to be for us now.

Early Days of the Church

The Acts of the Apostles details the beginnings of the Christian community: the coming of the Holy Spirit in fulfillment of the promise of Jesus, the choosing of an apostle to take the place of Judas, and Peter's address to the people of Jerusalem on the first Pentecost, with the results recorded in our last chapter on the Holy Spirit.

Peter emerges naturally as the spokesman and head of the community, having been granted that position by Jesus himself. As already noted, he preached the first sermon and converted some three thousand persons. He said on that occasion: "You denied the Holy and Righteous One, and asked for a murderer to be granted to you, and killed the Author of life, whom God raised from the dead. To this we are witnesses" (Acts 3:14-15). He goes on to announce that it is by faith in Jesus' name that the lame man at the Beautiful Gate of the temple is cured.

Peter's speeches always ended with a call for repentance, persecution and death of Jesus. Though the apostles were persecuted for their faith and imprisoned, no one and no circumstance could stop them from witnessing to their belief in Jesus. And nothing could prevent the development of the infant Christian community. In desperation at the obvious growth of the Christian Church, some chief priests and Pharisees determined to kill the disciples of Jesus. Then a Pharisee named Gamaliel, "a teacher of the law, held in honor by all the people, stood up . . . and he said to them "Men of Israel, take care what you do with these men . . . keep away from these men and let them alone; for if this plan or this undertaking is of men, it will fail; but if it is of God, you will not be able to overthrow them. You might even be found opposing God!" (Acts 5:34-39).

Gamaliel's fellow Pharisees took his advice, at least in part. They beat the apostles, forbade them to speak of Jesus any more, and let them go. But the apostles left the presence of the council, "rejoicing that they were counted worthy to suffer dishonor for the name (of Jesus). And every day in the temple and at home they did not cease teaching and preaching Jesus as the Christ" (Acts 5:40-42).

I have already referred to the conversion of Saul, one of the most violent persecutors of the infant Church. Acts 8:3 details his history: "Saul laid waste the church, and entering house after house, he dragged off men and women and committed them to prison." "But Saul, still breathing threats and murder against the disciples of the Lord, went to the high priest and asked him for letters to the synagogues at Damascus, so that if he found any belonging to the Way, men or women, he might bring them bound to Jerusalem" (9:1-2).

The Church for St. Paul

The author of Acts goes on to relate how as Saul was riding to Damascus a light flashed about him. And when he fell to the ground, he heard a voice saying to him, "Saul, Saul, why do you persecute me?" And he asked, "Who are you, Lord?" And the voice replied, "I am Jesus, whom you are persecuting" (9:3-5). This is one of the most extraordinary events in history. The old Saul, the persecutor of the Church, is no more. He is replaced by a new man named Paul, who becomes the most zealous and successful of the apostles of the Lord Jesus Christ. Most of the remaining chapters of Acts relate the account of Paul's activities, his apostolic labors for Jesus and the spread of the Gospel.

There is meaning beyond meaning in this account of Saul's conversion. "Who are you, Lord?" asks Saul. "I am Jesus, whom you are persecuting," the Lord replies. Saul has never seen Jesus. He has been persecuting Christians, followers of Jesus. But Jesus claims that *it is he himself* whom Saul persecutes. Saul naturally concludes that there must be some identity between Jesus and Christians: Jesus and his followers are in some mysterious, but real, way, one.

It is a conviction that he will develop and perfect in his efforts to explain his new faith to the Christian communities he will establish at Corinth, Ephesus, and Rome. The analogy Paul uses is that of the human body. He writes to the Corinthians: "For just as the body is one and has many members, and all the members of the body, though many, are one body, so it is with Christ. For by one Spirit we were all baptized into one body—Jews or Greeks, slaves or free—and all were made to drink of one Spirit. . . . Now you are the body of Christ and individually members of it" (1 Cor. 12:12-13, 27).

From this doctrine Paul derives all manner of moral, social, and theological conclusions. Christ is the head of his body, we are the members. In the Body of Christ which is the Church, as in the human body, there are as many functions as there are members, each function being essential for the well-being of the whole. If one member is ill or functions badly, the whole body suffers. So also if one member is persecuted, Christ is persecuted. The good that one member does helps the whole body, just as the evil done by one member afflicts the whole unity. If all are baptized into the one body and share in the one Spirit of Christ, there can be no place for prejudice of any kind, no place for dissension or hatred. Since God so loved the world as to give his only Son to save that world, and since the Holy Spirit of love is the life-principle of the Body of Christ, the law of life in the body must be love. All the members must have at heart the welfare and well-being of the other members.

As the Body of Christ has its own way of life as a body, namely, mutual love and concern for all its members, so does it have its own special worship, the Lord's Supper, the Eucharist, wherein Jesus invites his members to make their own his entire redeeming act—his life, death, resurrection, and ascension. Is not the cup of blessing which we bless a participation in the Body of Christ. Because there is one bread, we who are many all partake of the one bread:

> For I received from the Lord what I also delivered to you, that the Lord Jesus on the night when he was betrayed took bread, and when he had given thanks, he broke it, and said, "This is my body which is for you. Do this in remembrance of me." In the same way also the cup, after supper, saying, "This cup is the new covenant in my blood. Do this, as often as you drink it, in remembrance of me." For as often as you eat this bread and drink the cup, you proclaim the Lord's death until he comes" (1 Cor. 11:23-26).

It all sounds very beautiful. The problem is (and Jesus recognized it himself) that the Body of Christ is not only divine, it is human. Its members are women and men who are not only capable of heroic acts of charity and sacrifice, but also of the basest criminal deeds as well. Becoming and being a member of Christ's body does not destroy or diminish a person's freedom—either to give love or to refuse it.

Paul's work was not finished when he established the Body of Christ in various cities of the Middle East in that first century. He had to keep the members together, prevent them from destroying or diminishing the power of the body of quarrels, feuds, and immorality of all kinds. In letters to these communities, he instructed and encouraged the members, but he often had to criticize and condemn the wayward and troublesome.

Perhaps Paul's greatest problem had to do with the demands to be made upon the Gentile converts from paganism. There were some Jewish Christians, including some apostles, who insisted strongly that the new converts adopt the practices of Judaism, submit to the law of circumcision, and observe the dietary laws which forbade the consuming of certain foods. It is not difficult to imagine what side Paul took. He insisted that his communities should not have to follow the old Jewish customs and rules. The problem was discussed by the apostles at the first general "council" of the Church in the year 48, and they decided in favor of Paul's position. If the decision had gone against Paul, it is likely that Christianity would never have become attractive to the Gentiles, it would never have become "catholic," that is, universal, it would have remained a small Jewish sect, confined for the most part to Palestine.

The Church's Names

Paul's designation of the Church as the "body of Christ" is, of course, not the only name that the Church has had during her history. Paul himself compared the Church to a building of which Christ is the cornerstone, the apostles the foundation, and the members the "living stones" of the construction. The Church has been called "mother," a name indicating her function of nourishing and caring for her children. One of the most expressive titles is that of "Bride of Christ," reminding us that, as husband and wife become one in mind, heart, body, purpose, and values, so should Christ and his members be one in every way.

Jesus' own "description" of the Church as the "vine and the branches"—like Paul's own analogy of the human body—brings out the unity of life that exists between Christ and his members. As branches of a tree grow out of the trunk and are filled with the same life-giving sap as is in the trunk, so are Christians one with Christ, filled with the same divine life that is in him. At the Last Supper, Jesus said to the apostles: "I am the true vine, and my Father is the vinedresser. . . . Abide in me, and I in you. As the branch cannot bear fruit by itself, unless it abides in the vine, neither can you, unless you abide in me. I am the vine, you are the branches. He who abides in me, and I in him, he it is that bears much fruit, for apart from me you can do nothing" (Jn. 15:1-5). It is a beautiful image of the Church, but while it stresses the intimacy of life between Christ and each member, it does not underline the interdependence of member upon member as the image of the Body of Christ does.

Since Vatican II the most popular name for the Church is "people of God." It is not a new title at all; the Jewish people were known as the people of God long before the coming of Christ. The term has value if it makes us think of the Church as a community of people rather than a hierarchical structure. It goes well with the description of the Church by Dr. Tad Guzie: "The Church is called to be a community of people who are conscious of grace and aware of the love of God made manifest in Christ Jesus."

To some, however, the name "People of God" seems to leave out the dimension of Jesus; therefore the reminder of Karen Hurley is well taken. She says that there is a distinctive way in which Christians are the People of God:

> We are the people of God who stand in a conscious relation to Jesus: Jesus is our Lord. It is in terms of Jesus that we define our relationship to God: Jesus' Father is our Father; and we believe that Jesus is the final and perfect Word that the Father speaks to us. It is in terms of Jesus that we understand the meaning of life. . . . We are a community of people bound together by our common desire to live our lives in the mystery of Jesus. Jesus is our reason for being together as a community, as a Church. The Greek word for Church, *ekklesia,* means a people called together by God *in Jesus' name.* It is in terms of Jesus that we live together in community: it is his Spirit that makes us all one. The Church *is* Jesus Christ today.
>
> Hurley, p. 14.

I think it is important not to confine one's preferences to a single name, but to keep them all in mind, since each emphasizes a particular aspect of the Church's richness and being. But more important even than a descriptive name is the *fact* of the Church being so essential in the lives of those who call themselves Christians. To maintain this emphasis is not always easy. But I insist: it is simply impossible to escape the New Testament foundations of the Church as they are found in the words and minds of Jesus and his apostles.

How Christ Saves Us

To sum up, in order to save mankind, to reconcile humanity to the Father, God became man in Christ Jesus. Jesus in turn placed that salvation in the hands of other human beings whom he appoints as human mediators between future human beings and himself. In their hands he places the sacraments, the signs of life, through which he acts upon, cares for and nourishes human hearts today and always. Karen Hurley says:

> To believe in Jesus means accepting the fact that I can't save myself; but believing in the Church means accepting the fact that it can never be just me and Jesus . . . To be Jesus people we must let go of our egocentric dreams that all that is needed is me—we must let *Jesus* save us. But we must also let go of our equally egotistical desire that it can somehow be just me and Jesus—we must let Jesus save us *in community*. If we want to live on Jesus' terms, we must also live in community, the community of his Church.   Hurley, p. 17.

Years ago I heard the great lay theologian and apologist Frank Sheed speak of his experiences while preaching in the streets and parks of London and New York. The purpose of the preaching was frankly apologetic, i.e. explaining and defending doctrines of the Roman Catholic Church, with the avowed purpose of making converts to that Church. He said that once the preachers had convinced the hearers that the Catholic Church speaks in the name and the authority of Christ, many conversions resulted. I would use the same reasoning today—not to defend doctrines so much as to insist that the *Church as Church is essential to the teaching of Jesus*. If lapsed or careless Catholics can be convinced of this truth, they are on their way to a better understanding of adult Christianity and its appeal.

New Testament: Book of the Church

As I have already insisted, if it were not for the Church, we would not even have the New Testament. The first books of the New Testament did not appear till several decades after Jesus' ascension. The earliest book is generally thought to be St. Paul's Epistle to the Thessalonians, dated around 50 A.D. The date of the earliest Gospel, that of Mark, is about 64 A.D. The other books of the New Testament came after that, with the Gospel of St. John closing the New Testament around the end of the first century.

The relatively late dates of the New Testament books resulted because the first Christians expected Christ to come again soon in glory to judge the living and the dead. They saw no reason for writing down what he did and said. This does not mean that the words and accounts of Jesus' deeds were unknown to the early Christians. On the contrary, the memory of his words and signs remained vividly alive in the Christian community. That memory was handed down, passed on to converts and to the children born into the Christian community. The decision to record in writing these accounts of Jesus' life came only after the Christian community realized that the date of the end of the world was unknown and that therefore it was appropriate to have written records of the life and deeds and words of the Lord as remembered by the eyewitnesses who lived close to him.

The fact is, however, that the Gospels existed in the Church as *oral* Gospel long before they were written down. There were other Gospels in addition to the familiar ones attributed to Matthew, Mark, Luke, and John. And there were other highly-prized writings as well. But since the Christian community, the Church, did not consider these writings to have been inspired by the Holy Spirit, they were omitted from the official list or "Canon" of the New Testament. It is important for our purpose here to insist that it was the Church that made this decision.

It was also the Church that decided how the Bible was to be interpreted. The Roman Church in particular insists that the meaning of the Bible is too important to be left exclusively to the private personal interpretation of the individual Christian. This is the case today as it has been from the beginning. There is too much evidence abroad today of the harm that results when individual Christians interpret the Bible according to their personal lights, without any recourse to consensus of the Church and its long-standing tradition.

Criticizing the Church

It is no secret that organized religion, and in particular the Roman Catholic Church, has had considerable bad press in recent years. As a result of changes in Church discipline and worship and the "modernizing" of the Catholic Church since Vatican II, many Catholics have become disillusioned with the old Church. A considerable number has given up the practice of their faith because of the changes or because they disagree with Pope Paul's reaffirming of the Church's traditional stance on artificial birth control. Some say that the Church has gone too far in modernizing, others that it has not gone far enough. There may be some non-practicing Catholics who take "a temporary leave" in order to arrive at a genuine reason for their belief in the Church. No one can seriously object to that. The Church does not want its members to claim to be Catholic just on the strength of what they have received from their parents, the sisters, or from catechism classes. The Church wants her members to come to terms with Catholicism themselves and to be able to give an account of and a reason for their faith. I am afraid, however, that many former Catholics just gradually slipped away from Catholic belief and practice without realizing what happened. Too many of them have also abandoned the pre-Vatican II doctrine they learned in catechism classes and have not replaced it with the new insights into theology that have resulted from Vatican II.

Criticism of the Roman Church has become more open and wide-spread than at any other time in recent history. In the last decade popular magazines have published articles declaring or predicting the demise of the Church. So far these predictions have not been fulfilled, and there seems to be no prospect that they will be. The professor-psychologist Eugene Kennedy asked his readers not to be discouraged by the harsh criticism of the Church at the hands of journalists: "We have words of life at a time when men desperately need them," he wrote. He declared himself to be optimistic about the future of the Church because he observed large numbers of Catholics working out their faith in an adult manner and accepting the personal responsibility for their faith.

A Realistic Attitude Towards the Church

Many Catholics resent all criticism and accuse critics of the Church of intolerant anti-Catholicism. For such Catholics the Church can do no wrong. To criticize the pope, the hierarchy, the clergy is to criticize Christ. They are offended at the very idea of any possibility of abuses in the Church—either the Church of the past or the present.

There is considerable tension between that kind of Catholics and another kind—those for whom the Church can do no right. This kind accuses the pope, the Roman curia, the hierarchy of being completely out of touch with the modern world. They say that the pope and bishops do not show leadership, do not speak with authentic voices to the needs of Catholics living in a modern world. There is no doubt that many Catholics are no longer listening to the Church, even though they may retain an external membership. The ideal attitude towards the Church is probably in the middle of these extremes. There is as much danger of expecting too much of the Church as of expecting too little. There is as much danger of thinking that the Church can do nothing wrong as that of thinking she can do nothing right.

It is terribly important to know something about history: to know, for example, that it was the Roman Catholic Church that was responsible for much of the glory of European civilization. It was the Church, and monasticism in particular, that copied, preserved, and handed on the great literature and philosophy of ancient Greece and Rome, to say nothing of the manuscripts of the Bible. The greatest architecture of the world is found in the cathedrals of Europe. It was the Church that founded Europe's great universities and hospitals.

But it is also important to know that the Church is made up of frail, sinful, corrupt human beings, and therefore there have been and still are abuses in the Church. There is no harm for Catholics to admit that there have been bad popes and bishops and that the Roman Church at the time of Martin Luther was in terrible need of reform, that indulgences were being sold, that superstition was widespread, and that many popes were the political tools of the great Roman families. Because the Church is people it is always in need of reform. The crucial truth is that the Church is not pope, nor bishops, nor priests, but people. We are the Church, and the Church is as good or as bad or as indifferent and as neutral as we are. We get the kind of leadership and administration as we deserve and want. We are not, or should not be, a flock of mute, dumb sheep.

The Church is not a supermarket or a filling station for our spiritual needs. The Gospel tells us that, in the intention of Christ, the Church is supposed to be and do for mankind what yeast is and does to the mass of dough. It is a movement for civilizing and humanizing the world, and we are all, or we should be, involved in that movement. Being involved is an essential part of our being Catholic, being members of a Church that is concerned not only with the spiritual needs and condition of mankind but also concerned about every aspect of the life of human beings—spiritual, social, and physical.

I have already referred to Professor Kennedy's optimistic evaluation of the Church's future. He makes an interesting observation about the difference between extrinsic belief (accepting doctrines and moral directives unquestioningly) and intrinsic faith (claiming a set of beliefs as pertinent to one's experience and necessary to one's humanity.) "Extrinsic belief," he said, "is concerned with the salvation of self. Intrinsic belief is concerned with saving others. Extrinsic belief closes its ranks. Intrinsic belief makes room for everyone. Extrinsic belief has answers for everything. Intrinsic belief asks questions." The Church needs members whose faith is intrinsic, and there seems to be growing evidence that more and more of her members do indeed profess that kind of faith.

Personally, I think a Catholic ought to be proud to be a Catholic, but he must never be either a complacent Catholic or a bitter Catholic. We must never be satisfied with our Church, just as we must never be satisfied with ourselves. What we and the Church constitute can always be and become better, more concerned, more vitally Catholic. It has been often repeated that the Church has too many unloving critics and not enough critical lovers. The unloving critic tears down and undermines; the loving critic builds and gives and sacrifices. We all need to know what category of Catholic we fit into.

The Church: Home of Sinners

Mayo Mohs, religion editor of *Time* magazine, has quoted Professor Kennedy's opinion that what the Catholic Church needs is not so much organization as a family where, when you go there, they have to take you in. Such a family, he said, fosters an atmosphere of growth rather than a domain of control. "It makes room for everybody because in the end it is the home of sinners."

"The home of sinners"—could there be a more appropriate name for the Catholic Church? The Pharisees complained about Jesus when he consorted with the tax collectors and other public sinners: "This man welcomes sinners and eats with them," they said, not realizing what a beautiful compliment they were paying him. Mohs believes that the long tradition of a sinners' Church is the most commanding reason for the survival of Catholicism. (Much as I like that idea, I prefer the promise of Christ that the gates of hell would not prevail against his Church.)

Mohs quotes the Belgian theologian Fr. Antoine Vergote, who believes that the young, searching for religion again, will increasingly find their answers in Catholicism because it perceives and preserves the tension between the immanent (God's closeness and oneness with us, his intimate presence to us) and the transcendent (the greatness, the infinite perfection and "otherness" of God), the human and the divine. And he says that nowhere is this tension better illustrated than in the continuing Catholic devotion to the Eucharist—that which Fr. Marc Oraison, the French psychiatrist, calls "the only essential, the only ultimately important reality."

There is much consolation and much challenge in these ideas for us Catholics. We used to have a slogan that "it is the Mass that matters." It is consoling to know that in these most modern of times it is still the Mass that matters. For it is Christ in the Mass who gathers us together as a people, a community of faith, who feeds us with his word and with his body and blood and then sends us back into daily life as a people on a mission, as a Church, made up of sinners, to be sure, but a Church ever young, ever enthusiastic, full of confidence in his words, "I am with you always, to the close of the age."

History, as well as the fragile nature of each Catholic, indicates how terribly human the Church is and always has been. But that same history undoubtedly proves that, having survived despite all the human frailty, it must be divine.

"The Church is Christ, Christ is the Church"—so went the old saying. I do not believe we can have the one without the other. Fortunately, we do not have to decide between the two. The more one exhausts the meaning of the one, the more perfectly one possesses the other. That is as it should be.

6

The Parish:

the Church Made Visible

The Church, the Body of Christ, the people of God, is made present, actualized, experienced in a parish community. Surely, this is the ideal. According to Peter S. Williamson, when St. Paul used the expression "in Christ" (which he often did), he meant "in the Church," that is a living part of a living Church. Baptism identified the new convert as a member of a Christian *community,* specifically a local church. "An individual was either 'in Christ' and in a specific, local church, or he was not 'in Christ' and not in the Church." That is a startling statement, but it indicates the crucial necessity not only of a parish being aware of its nature as a parish but also of the potential for spiritual vision and growth of its members.

The Need for Parish Renewal

Just as mature, adult Christianity is inconceivable apart from the Church, so also is it inconceivable apart from the parish. Largely because of the size of most city parishes (and even more basically, because of our failure to perceive our Catholic religion as essentially the experience of membership in a body, the Church) the majority of Catholics do not conceive of their parish as a family, a living community. The practice of their Catholic faith has little or nothing to do with the parish as a living community. In large parishes most people simply do not know one another, nor do they think it important that they do. I suspect that for most Catholics the parish is a place, a building, a plant where they can satisify their religious obligation of worship and renew their personal religious needs at sacramental sources. Because Catholicism has for centuries lacked the vital communal character that belongs to it by its very nature, its impact on the religious, moral, and social atmosphere of the wider community is likely to remain minimal (unless pastors, parish councils, and mature Catholics start doing something about this sad situation). The purpose of any parish is to allow Christ to become operative in and through the living parish community.

So every parish is in constant need of renewal. Every parish has a surplus of individual members who need—and are perhaps seeking—spiritual renewal and conversion. But the mature, earnest person who is converted to Christ and to a new vision of what it means to be a Catholic Christian will have difficulty remaining a convinced and fervent follower of Christ all by himself, apart from a loving, caring, open community which sees itself as the Body of Christ made visible. Parish renewal is or should be the chief and never-ending concern of every pastor and every parish council, indeed, of all the members. (For an ideal picture of what a parish ought to be as well as for valuable suggestions for implementing the ideal, I cannot recommend too highly the booklet *Spiritual Renewal of the American Parish* by Fr. Earnest Larsen, C.SS.R, Liguori Publications, Liguori, Mo., 1975).

What is needed is more than the old-fashioned parish missions, valuable as these missions have been in the past. The chief objective of the old parish missions was the renewal of the moral life of the people, bringing back strayed members of the fold. The appeal was largely to the individual Catholic. Unless I am mistaken, not much effort was expended on helping the people to a greater awareness of their being a family, a community of faith, the Body of Christ.

One wonders how it has been possible to lose sight almost completely of the teaching of Jesus and St. Paul on the nature of the Church as the vine and the branches or the Church as the living Body of Christ, with all members united one to another and mutually dependent, with all receiving common spiritual life from Christ.

In insisting on the communal nature of the Church and the parish community, I do not mean to diminish the strictly personal experience of Christ that is possible to each member, even apart from the community. The idea and ideal of the parish as the family or people of God does not destroy human freedom. It enhances it, but it also invites those favored with an experience of the love and grace of God to share their blessings with others.

Primary Task of the Parish

There are certain inevitable effects that will flow from parish awareness of itself as the Body of Christ, the community of faith. The first, of course, will be a universal concern for the quality of the community's obligations to God, its family worship. Nothing that the parish does can take precedence over the Sunday community worship, the parish Mass(es). One might even go so far as to claim that the parish exists primarily to give glory to God through communal worship.

Not that God needs the worship of anyone. He wishes us to worship him because he loves us; he wishes us to worship him *for our own good.* We simply cannot be human without it. As the fourth daily preface of the Mass prays to God:

> You have no need of our praise,
> yet our desire to thank you is itself your gift.
> Our prayer of thanksgiving adds nothing to your greatness,
> but makes us grow in your grace,
> through Jesus Christ our Lord.

If our worship makes us grow in grace, we can be sure it makes us grow as a community as well.

Pope St. Pius X is responsible for the statement "The primary and indispensable source of the true Christian spirit is active and intelligent participation in the public prayer of the Church." This principle inspired the efforts of all those who called for liturgical participation in the decades before Vatican II and the advent of the vernacular languages in worship. We promoted active participation by means of "dialogue Masses" and congregational singing of Gregorian chant. Everyone carried a missal, the English translation of the Latin Mass. We knew, of course, that missals were only a poor substitute for what we really needed—the Mass in the vernacular, with priest and people sharing the divine word and prayers with one mind, one voice, one language. Now we have had the vernacular—that undreamed of blessing—for almost a decade. Has it made much difference in "the true Christian spirit" of our parishes? (By the way, what is "the true Christian spirit?" I do not recall reading much on the nature of this spirit, but now I wonder if it might not be defined simply as the community's awareness of itself as the Body of Christ gathered together to worship the Father in and through Christ Jesus, our Head.)

Perhaps we are more realistic now. We now realize that there are no quick and easy solutions for the problem of parish worship and for the creation of community self-awareness. We have not given up the conviction that worship is its own reward, that God and God alone is the one who grants favor, grace, love, peace, community life, and sharing. But now we understand more fully that he grants his favors only to those who desire them and welcome them with open minds and hearts. The human element and above all the effort to worship with one heart and one mind may not be dismissed as trivial either for the well-being of the parish or for the influence of such a community on those who do not belong to it.

Need for a New Outlook

The German atheist and philosopher Friedrich Nietzsche is supposed to have said, "If you Christians want me to believe in your God, you'll have to learn how to look more redeemed, you'll have to learn how to sing better songs." Nietzsche put his finger on one secret of community-consciousness. Anyone who remembers his youth or who has ever participated in Masses in which children or young people joyously sing songs they can put their hearts into knows how such participation can create and intensify union and friendship. On the other hand, it is indeed sad to look out over an assembly and see the number of somber, frowning faces of people who refuse to join their voices to the common praise. One can hope that if they cannot carry a tune, they are at least "singing in their hearts to God."

A glad, joyous, radiant community, made up of members *who really know how to look redeemed* (without any artificiality) will sing joyous songs, and it will be one of the most effective missionary influences in any area. What is needed (over and above the personal conviction of each member that he has been redeemed by Christ) is a fresh outlook in the hearts and minds of parish members—a strong desire for unity—replacing the strictly self-centered vision of so many modern Catholics. Imagine the joy of a new convert or of Catholics who have moved from other cities or places on coming into such a community! They are simply swept into the life of the community (including parish social life) and made to understand that faith in Christ and the Church is not a transient thrill but the dearest enduring reality, a reality that has true meaning for people.

On the other hand, a convert entering a parish that is just a building full of individual Christians intent only on their personal "spiritual life" or their own Sunday obligation, Christians who refuse to enter into the spirit of the worship, a parish that does not understand that it is a family, a community of the redeemed, will discourage the newcomer, with the result that he may not even last as a Catholic. Humanly speaking, the convert has no greater human need than that of knowing himself to be accepted and genuinely welcomed and made to feel at home.

"Tell Them to Care About One Another"

The entire parish has to learn how to care, how to be open to new members, including passing strangers. But the concern of all the parishioners should be implemented by a special committee appointed by the parish council whose duty is to call on new parishioners, welcome them, and make them feel at home. This idea cannot be emphasized too strongly. Such a spirit of open friendliness not only benefits the newcomers, but it also builds community spirit as such. Parish social gatherings, either on a large scale on special occasions during the year, or more frequently, for example, after Sunday Mass or in connection with the baptism into the community of a child or the reception of a new convert can also be most helpful in increasing community self-awareness.

The unfortunate lack of an open, welcoming spirit in a Catholic parish is illustrated in an experience which Fr. Earnest Larsen, C.SS.R., had while attending a meeting of Alcoholics Anonymous. The main speaker was a black man who, as he spoke, continually watched the priest. Finally, he stopped and asked Father Larsen if he was a priest and if he was going to preach the next day. When father answered in the affirmative, the man asked if he would give his people a message. He told about how he had become an alcoholic, how he had finally decided that he was a slave to drink, and how, once he had made up his mind to stop drinking, he had cleaned up, put on the best clothes he had, and gone to a Catholic church. He told Father Larsen that he went to a dozen Catholic churches that morning, but he met no one in any of the churches who introduced himself and made the man feel welcome.

> All I got from your people, Father, were the kind of looks that I was too dirty or smelly or poor for them. It's not that I blame them. Being a Christian is no easy thing. If I hadn't found AA and people who knew what it meant to suffer and die that I might find a better way to live, I probably would have killed myself that night. They accepted me for what I was and could be. Father, if you would, tomorrow just tell them to care about one another. That's all—just to care. *Spiritual Renewal of the American Parish* (Liguori, MO: Liguori Publications, 1975), p. 20.

Father Larsen didn't say so, but I can well imagine that the black man had prepared his whole sermon for him. Every pastor who has ever preached to his people can be grateful to Larsen for sharing this story. But, if this situation is typical of Catholic parishes in this or any country, what a terrible indictment of Catholic parochial life everywhere.

It is obvious that everything I have said about making strangers feel at home in a parish needs to be applied even more emphatically when the newcomers belong to a minority group. Segregation of any group cannot possibly be justified, nor can it be reconciled with the spirit and practice of Christianity. St. Paul's word to the Galatians is surely to the point in this matter: "For as many of you as were baptized into Christ have put on Christ. There is neither Jew nor Greek, there is neither slave nor free, there is neither male nor female; for *you are all one in Christ Jesus*" (3:27-28; emphasis added).

Special Concern for the Elderly and Sick

A caring parish community must also be very much concerned about its own members, even though, or more precisely, especially when, they can no longer be active in parish life and worship. I refer to parishioners in hospitals, nursing homes, retirement centers, orphanages, and jails, not forgetting the many in any town or city who live all alone in houses or apartments. Concerned as most busy parishioners are with their own family and personal problems, all too few ever think of visiting the aged, the infirm, the unfortunate. Yet these are the ones most in need of attention, for theirs is a painfully difficult, even a heart-breaking vocation. Loneliness is the only companion for most of them, along with a feeling of being unwanted, of being useless now that their years of activity and productivity are at an end. The American way of life with its emphasis on productivity has so conditioned people that once they can no longer accomplish anything or produce anything useful they feel that their lives are without any value at all. Many are in danger of lapsing into a deadly defeatism, one of the most dreadful maladies of the human spirit.

It is this kind of defeatism that has to be overcome by the whole parish working together as well as by its individual members. The sick and elderly must be made to believe that they still belong to the parish family, that their lives are indeed worthwhile, that old age can be the most important and meaningful time of their lives. The only way to bring this truth home to them is to show them that it is not what one accomplishes that counts in the sight of God and in contributing to the life and value of the parish, but what one *is*. And what one is depends for the most part on one's ability to love.

It is the responsibility of the whole parish to see to it that these aged and infirm parishioners get to Mass if they are able. If they can no longer attend Mass, it is comforting for them to be informed both by the priests and by their friends that they have now arrived at the time of life when their prayer is the most powerful, that living bravely in their present condition is itself a most efficacious prayer, that the bed they lie on or the chair they sit in hour after hour, day after day, is an altar upon which they, as sharers in the priesthood of Christ, may offer the sacrifice of their loneliness, their pain, their weakened condition to the Lord for the parish, for peace, for vocations, for the missions, for fellow parishioners who suffer without their faith. This truth may be difficult for them to understand, conditioned as they are to believing that only an ordained priest can officiate at an altar and offer sacrifice. It will help considerably to inform them that St. Peter was writing to lay people when he recommended that they "be built into a spiritual house, *to be a holy priesthood, to offer spiritual sacrifices* acceptable to God through Jesus Christ" (1 Pet. 2:5; emphasis added).

Frequent Communion must be made available to them, and if the priests cannot always take care of this duty, the lay ministers of the Eucharist in every parish would surely be willing to take their turns helping out. However, one cannot emphasize too seriously that the sick and aged parishioners do need to see their pastor as often as his heavy schedule permits. Only he can comfort them with the important assurance that this Holy Communion in their homes is an extension of the parish Eucharistic sacrifice, that Christ and the parish have not forgotten them. In a parish that is aware of itself as a community of faith, there is no need for anyone ever to feel lonely or unwanted. We've been considering the meaning of mature Christianity. Of all the parish members the most mature and advanced in their faith ought to be the aged and the sick. They will be that when they are made to feel that they still belong to the community and have an essential role to play in its life and worship and missionary influence.

One of the greatest needs of the elderly is the companionship of young people and children. But the need is mutual. The young couple who moved from a large Eastern city back to their home state because they were convinced "that children need grandparents" was very wise. It is in the area of visiting and caring for the aged and ill that young people and little children can acquire their "basic training" not only in parish living but in living and growing in their faith. But they must be prepared with some serious instruction on the spiritual value of what they do when they visit the elderly. It would surely help for parents to read and explain our Lord's instruction, recorded in Mt. 25:31-45, "Truly, I say to you, as you did it to one of the least of these my brethren, you did it to me."

Little children must also have some preparation for their first visit to a nursing home. They may be able to cope with the appearance and mannerisms of a single grandparent, but a room or lobby full of the elderly and infirm may be a bewildering and distressing experience for them. To be told that "they are all somebody's grandmas and grandpas" may help the children to overcome any initial hesitation.

It is in contact with the children and young people that the elderly may be made aware of their own ongoing importance to their parish and to the Church. They must be made aware that they provide the very necessary continuity with the past when they tell children and young people about what it meant to be a Catholic "in the old days" before there were cars and freeways. Children will never be bored with the elderly who can relate interesting tales of their youth and who can teach a few useful skills as well.

And Then There Are the Singles

But loneliness and the sense of feeling unwanted is by no means confined to the aged and those in retirement centers. Every parish has its quota of women and men who live alone either as widows or widowers or those who have deliberately chosen to seek God in and through the single vocation. This vocation is discussed in chapter 8 on the variety of vocations, but some mention of the needs and potential of these parish members has to be made here. In just about every parish there are programs for families, for the young people, for the aged and children, but seldom, if ever, is there anything for the "singles." And they feel left out, neglected, even unwanted. The tragedy is that so many of them have great potential and could make valuable contributions to the well-being of the parish.

A sensitive Christian who understands the nature of his parish as the family of God, the Body of Christ, will have his eyes and heart open, his hand stretched out, to any and all of these "singles" in the parish. But more than that, the pastors have to be aware of their needs and their possible contributions. A parish simply cannot be said to live unless it does all that it can to bring every one of its members into the mainstream of its life, its worship, its growth. "Singles" must be the special concern of welcoming committees. No one—whether he or she is a stranger just passing through or a "native" who has lived in the area for any length of time—should be allowed to feel like an outsider in parish gatherings of any kind, above all the Mass. Parish members should introduce themselves and make special efforts to make all new members feel welcome.

More and more frequently one hears about Catholics who have left their Catholic parishes to join smaller, Protestant—usually Fundamentalist—parishes where they can experience a real sense of community, of belonging, of being welcomed with genuine Christian hospitality. Some Catholics feel badly and even angry at these departures, but I doubt that many of them question themselves on their own responsibility in the matter. This ought to be a special cause for self-examination by priests. We simply do not realize that the warm sense of belonging to a family is a Christian right; it is an essential part of our most ancient heritage. And when people do not find it, we must not be surprised or offended if they seek it elsewhere. These Protestant, Fundamentalist parishes are simply exploiting treasures that belong to Catholics by right, but which we have too often and too long neglected and forgotten.

Openness to Non-Catholic Christians

An attitude of friendliness and charity is especially important in parishioners' relationships with non-Catholics. Thank God the days are gone when suspicion and antagonism characterized the relationships between Catholics and Protestants. It was an attitude that was more or less encouraged by leaders on both sides. Now more and more Christians of all denominations are beginning to comprehend the shocking scandal of enmity between Christians. They are also beginning to recognize that the treasury of religious experience and wealth is not confined to any single denomination, that there is no denomination from which one cannot learn. Catholics must be friendly to Protestants, Jews, and non-Christians everywhere, but especially those living within their parish. They need not feel obliged to explain Catholic teaching to anyone (unless it is requested), but their very lives and attitudes ought to demonstrate that the teachings and example of Jesus have truly been a formative element in their lives.

Having taught at two Lutheran colleges for eight years and lived in those college and parish communities, I have personal experience of a praiseworthy change in relationships between Protestants and Catholics. I was invited to speak in several Protestant churches, and ministers were invited to speak in Catholic churches. I also spoke to groups of ministers. In one city I celebrated a "dry Mass"—that is, I went through and explained the actions and parts of the Mass, and a similar explanation of the Lutheran Lord's Supper (the name they use instead of "Mass") took place in the social room of the Catholic parish. There were also mixed study groups of Protestants and Catholics who discussed the doctrines and practices of their respective denominations. We have come a long way since the days when Catholics were forbidden to attend Protestant services, and, above all, take an active part in them. Today Protestants are generally made to feel quite welcome at Catholic services.

But we Catholics can well do without the old feeling that all Protestants are to be looked upon as potential converts. Too many Catholics fail to realize that most Protestants and Jews are satisfied and comfortable with their own religious practice and profession. If our Catholic religion is precious to us, as it has been for our ancestors, why should we not admit that Lutherans, Methodists, Baptists, Jews, and others feel exactly the same way about their religious traditions and beliefs? We have to learn to accept non-Catholics (as well as other members of the parish we do not particularly "like") for what they are—human persons whom the Lord loves and respects—regardless of denomination, social position, or education.

Importance of a Sense of Belonging

We keep coming back to fundamentals. When parish members begin to see their personal religious outlook in terms of their being members with others of a living organism, a family, then the parish is on its way to accomplishing its goal—allowing Christ to become operative in that area by acting in and through his new presence in this world, the Church.

In emphasizing the sense of community, I do no mean to imply that a deeply personal "I-Thou" attitude towards God and Jesus is to be discouraged. The sense of family does not preclude a private, personal relationship with the Lord. No one loses his individuality and selfhood by being immersed in a living body. Rather, it may very well be that the feeling for community, the sense of belonging, comes only after the "I believe that the Lord came to save me, the individual" feeling. In a word, it is important that "I feel and believe that he came to save *me,*" not just a generalized "all mankind." What is to be avoided, it seems, is that exclusive "me and God" kind of thinking that admits no one else into the relationship.

Closely allied to the sense of belonging, perhaps even its essential element, is a realization of one's dependence—on God, first of all—and on other members of the community as well. Everyone needs everyone in the community; we need one another both for our personal spiritual and psychological development and for the greater effectiveness of the whole parish in its worship and its work of witnessing to Christ.

It goes without saying that consciousness of membership with others in a parish family also includes an awareness of the need for growth in the body. Just as an individual Christian must be concerned with personal mental, spiritual, and intellectual growth, so too the parish community. No parish, no pastor can ever be satisifed that an ideal level of growth has been achieved. There are no limits to love's potential, either in the individual person or the community of faith.

Contributing much to this need to grow is the firm belief of parish members that every sacramental act and experience of any member involves the whole parish, benefits the whole parish. Every Mass, every baptism, every confession and every anointing of the sick—marriages and confirmations, too—affects the whole community. We are the Body of Christ, member for member. "If one member suffers, all suffer together; if one member is honored, all rejoice together," says St. Paul (1 Cor. 12:26). Not only sacramental acts, but all parish activities—the parish school (if there is one), the CCD program, parish council, choir, youth groups, prayer groups—everything must be the concern of the entire parish, not just those actively involved. If CCD is not working, all parish members worry and work for its improvement. Every parish activity aims at progressively establishing the parish as a community of faith, growing in faith. Everything in and about Catholicism involves sharing.

This parish consciousness will hopefully develop into a sense of mission, of apostolic commitment to carrying on the work begun by Christ and passed on by him to the apostles, to the whole Church. Consciousness of mission means much more than feeling an obligation to contribute funds or clothing to drives for foreign or home missions. It means also, perhaps especially, the idea of giving away the Lord, making him available to as many as possible, as Father Larsen recommends. And it means the influence on all society that results from the quiet witness of a community of Christians who work, pray, worship together and who care for one another.

The Task of Pastors

From all that has been said in this chapter, the supreme importance of a thoughtful, prayerful, "visionary" pastor in the parish community becomes more and more obvious. It is no exaggeration to say that it is the pastor and his associates who determine whether the parish will be a "filling station" for individual religious needs or a vital organism afire with the love and apostolic spirit of the early Church. But obviously the pastor cannot do anything by himself. He needs honest, generous, open-minded, open-hearted people as much as they need him. Together they can bring about a parish that lives; separated they are helpless.

The pastor's prophetic word from the pulpit, the divine word planted in his heart so that it can germinate into spiritual nourishment for others, must be accompanied by explanations giving the reasons for the changes in the Church and in the rituals of the sacraments and various parts of the Mass such as the Lord's Prayer and the Sign of Peace. The people must know also that it is not easy for any pastor or choir director to provide a liturgy that will satisfy all the parishioners. There is an unwritten rule in regard to liturgy that the particular kind of celebration, including the music and the instruments, will depend on the kind of congregation gathered at a particular Mass. The liturgical celebration for grade school children will differ from that of high school or college students. Each age needs and enjoys its own music.

The great number and variety of musical instruments mentioned in the psalms indicates that the Lord has no favorites among them and above all that the organ has no monopoly on providing accompaniment to the songs of the community. Tastes in music varying as they do, it is obvious that a parish Mass which includes people of every age will present a considerable problem. It is one that almost seems insurmountable without a great spirit of compromise by all groups. The mature Christian whose one concern is the quality (and quantity) of common worship will make adjustments and will certainly not try to impose narrow personal tastes on others. In the end it is not the instruments or even the songs that count: it is the love and enthusiasm of the community expressed by the music.

Public Nature of the Sacraments

Insofar as it is possible, the celebration of the sacraments ought to take place at a parish Mass or at some public service. Every sacramental experience of any parish member affects and benefits the entire parish family. Pastors miss an important opportunity to build parish spirit if they do not encourage parents to have their babies baptized in the presence of the whole community. After all, baptism is more than a private ritual that "cleanses an individual person of original sin." By baptism the child is baptized *into the Church,* the Body of Christ, which is made present in this particular parish. By baptism the child becomes a member of a priestly, a redeemed people. The parish often needs to be reminded of that truth.

So, too, in the sacrament of penance, the penitent is reconciled not only to the Lord, but to the Christian community. Public penance services are provided for in the new rite for the sacrament of penance, and there is no better opportunity than the public services for bringing home the "communal" character of sin. There is no reason why there should not be communal anointings of the sick at times when the entire parish can share the concern of Christ and the Church for these still valuable members of the parish. Such public ceremonies do more than anything else to convince the sick that they still belong, that they are not forgotten.

The same important lesson in belonging can be brought home to young people who receive confirmation, the sacrament of spiritual maturity, at the hands of their bishop, the chief pastor of the diocese. One of the great misfortunes of modern parish life is that the celebration of this sacrament is restricted mainly to the people to be confirmed, their parents, and the godparents. The parish at large has little or no part in this celebration, and the situation is not helped by the tight schedule of the bishop, who might confirm in more than one parish in a day, and it is usually not a Sunday. Every parish as a community can benefit greatly from celebrations, and there can be no better occasion for a celebration than the passage of a number of its younger members from the age of spiritual childhood to spiritual adulthood. Young people have as much need to feel wanted and to belong as the aged and ill. *

Happily, many young priests are now being ordained in their own parishes. And at weddings more and more pastors, at the end of the ceremony, present the young couple to the congregation with, for example, the words, "Brothers and sisters, I present to you Mr. and Mrs. _____." The congregation responds with a hearty clapping of hands.

I repeat: every sacramental act accomplished in the parish affects and concerns the entire community and gives it cause for celebration.

Crucial Importance of Preaching

It seems necessary to face a problem that many serious-minded Catholics are encountering in their parishes, namely, many of them get little and often no spiritual nourishment whatsoever from their priests' homilies. There may be a variety of causes for this sad and even tragic situation, the main one probably being a lack of preparation and the failure of the priests to read and meditate.

From the beginning the Church has considered the readings at Mass to be of crucial importance for all the people. The official *Instruction on the Roman Missal* states:

> In the readings, explained by the homily, God speaks to his people of redemption and salvation and nourishes their spirit; Christ is present among the faithful through his word. . . .
>
> The homily is strongly recommended as an integral part of the liturgy and as a necessary source of nourishment of the Christian life. It should develop some point of the readings or of another text from the Ordinary of the Mass of the day. The homilist should keep in mind the mystery that is being celebrated and the needs of the particular community (pars. 33, 41).

One commentator on this passage states that "the homily is not an extraordinary element added for solemnity, but an integral part of the Eucharistic ceremony, necessary for applying the Word to life" *(The New Order of the Mass* [Collegeville, Minn.: The Liturgical Press; 1970], p. 116).

---

* According to the recent *Rite of Christian Initiation of Adults,* Provisional Text, published in 1974 by the United States Catholic Conference (and based on the decree of the Congregation of Divine Worship, January 6, 1972), confirmation is to be regarded as the final step (just before the Eucharist) of Christian initiation of adults than as an adult passage rite for young Catholics. Here is a pertinent quote from the text:

> According to the ancient practice maintained in the Roman liturgy, an adult is not to be baptized unless he receives confirmation immediately afterward, provided no serious

There can be no doubt that without uncovering the meaning of the readings and applying the meaning to the lives of the faithful, the Mass—Christ's greatest gift to his people—fails to achieve its best possible effect. Considering the needs of the people as individuals and as a community, along with the inexhaustible potential of the readings for supplying those needs, it is evident that no preacher can spend too much time preparing his sermons. *Without a very serious reason,* it is wrong, it is an injustice to the parish, for a priest to go to the pulpit unprepared, trusting in the Holy Spirit to speak through him. The Holy Spirit does indeed often make use of the months of humble, honest, holy priests, but *not* if through neglect, pride, or a sense of superiority which looks down on the intelligence of the laity, the priest fails to pray, to meditate, and to study the texts of the Liturgy of the Word and commentaries thereon.

There is nothing that betrays this inexcusable lack of preparation more than a steady diet of negative "sermons"—having no connection whatsoever with the readings—on money, bad movies, and immorality in general and in particular.

The "Presidential Presence"

But bad preaching is a fact of life in many parishes. Very often it is joined to a total lack of what might be called the "presidential presence" of the priest. He simply does not know how to preside as the head of a worshipping community. His gestures are totally meaningless both to himself and to the people. He rattles off the prayers in a sing-song voice and rushes through the Eucharistic Prayer with no interpretation or understanding of the miraculous content of the prayer.

If a priest could see and hear himself on video tape, even he would be shocked (and possibly "converted" and decide to get some professional help from a speech instructor or a homiletic workshop). It is no exaggeration to claim that 95 percent of us priests simply have no idea how bad we look and sound to our people. There is nothing like a tape recorder (or even better, a video-tape recorder) for making us "honest" and terribly humbled. We simply do not realize that an excellent sermon, well-prepared and containing good material, can be ruined by an inadequate and careless delivery. One of the best pastors I ever knew, one who spent hours preparing his sermons, never realized how much he made his people suffer because of his bad delivery and his singsong rendition of the prayers of the Mass. We priests do not seem to realize

obstacles exist. This connection signifies the unity of the paschal mystery, the close relationship between the mission of the Son and the pouring out of the Holy Spirit, and the joint celebration of the sacraments by which the Son and the Spirit come with the Father upon those who are baptized (par. 34).

that our people have enough crosses without having another laid on their shoulders and hearts at the Sunday Eucharist. Along with the offense to their senses of sight and hearing and often their intelligence, many suffer from an awareness of what such a "performance" does to their children, many of whom simply give up on Sunday Mass and the practice of their Faith.

What can the mature lay Catholic do about thsi situation? Many possible solutions have drawbacks. Should one simply confront a pastor and tell him how bad his preaching and manner of celebrating are? Should the parish council assume that "duty?" It depends on their judgment of how "humble" the pastor is, how willing he would be to take the correction from the laity. I am not optimistic, speaking from personal self-knowledge. Correcting or suggesting improvement (a happier term) would be considerably aided if the people had evidence on tape. Should they send him a subscription to a homiletic service? It couldn't do any harm and might possibly do some good (although it would hardly correct or remedy a bad delivery). Should they complain to the bishop? Maybe, but if the bishop moves him, another parish would suffer. Besides they might get someone worse. *

It may be that there is no satisfactory solution for this problem apart from a miracle—which the Lord does not yet seem willing to bring off. Some of the blame certainly has to be assumed by seminaries that allow candidates to be ordained with insufficient training in the basics of public speaking and reading and worst of all without any convictions about the real necessity of the study, training, and meditation required for preaching well.

Assuming Personal Responsibility

In the end it seems that the mature Catholic has to face the problem in his personal way. And this could be the most difficult testing of maturity in one's faith. Almost every parish provides missalettes which contain the Sunday readings and prayers. Several new translations of the Bible have excellent explanatory notes for difficult passages in the readings (e.g. *The New American Bible* and *The Jerusalem Bible).* Also, The Liturgical Press publishes reading guides for both the Old and the New Testament books.

It seems to me that, with the help of the explanatory notes in these

---

* In this matter of preaching, the interview with Fr. James Scheuer in chapter 15 of this book is most instructive. I am more and more convinced that the chief purpose of the preacher *must be to make Christ more loved.* This may involve a complete turnabout in a priest's conception of the purpose and meaning of preaching. It is not easy to overcome the ancient understanding that moralizing or seeking our phrases or ideas from the readings and using them to scare or even

books, it should be possible and not too time-consuming for an individual and even a family to come up with a satisfactory and solid message from the Lord for each Sunday. And would not the mature Catholic and his family be more fitted for making practical applications to daily family life than the majority of us priests?

In the last analysis then, every Catholic has to assume personal responsibility for his growth in the faith, and this involves serious study and reflection. The study includes, of course, the weekly Bible readings for the liturgy, but also "spiritual reading" and study of new and contemporary insights into theology.

The chief topic for the 1977 Synod of Bishops in Rome was *catechesis*, instruction in the faith. In the past Catholics everywhere would never have thought of catechesis for anyone except children (or converts). But at the synod the possibility of serious catechesis of adults, of parents and families, was seriously considered. News reports stated that adult catechesis is spreading "in communist dominated countries because it is the sole means of reaching children where the Church is forbidden to conduct programs for the young" (Wilfred Paradis, *National Catholic Reporter*, November 18, 1977).

The Catholic Church has always held—at least in theory—that the obligation of instructing children in the faith belonged first of all to parents. In practice the obligation was assumed by parochial schools, and more recently by CCD programs, but now parochial schools are closing by the hundreds and CCD programs are meeting with doubtful success. The tragedy in the closing of parochial schools may well be diminished if Catholic parents are forced to instruct themselves in the faith so that they may once and for all take on the obligation that belongs to them by right (as well as by the very purpose of marriage, which, I was always taught, was not only the procreation but also the *education* of children).

The synod, says Monsignor Paradis, also strongly endorsed the concept that "catechesis is the responsibility of the whole Church, not just the clergy, religious and the relatively small number of persons who participate directly in catechetical programs." So we are back where we started—with the Church, the parish. Without any doubt, parish life, the awareness of what it means to live in and be a vital member of a community of faith, depends in the end on the responsibility which adult, mature Catholics assume for their own spiritual, intellectual, and theological growth.

urge the people to "be good" is what the sermon is all about. If this manner of preaching was effective in the past, it no longer suits the needs of present-day Catholics.

7

Prayer: The Indispensable Nourishment

There is probably no subject about which there is more interest and less satisfaction and understanding than prayer. Serious-minded people instinctively realize that prayer can hold the key to life's meaning. I have never met anyone who was completely satisfied with his prayer life, who did not feel that that prayer life could not be improved. One of the most poignant prayers ever uttered was one of the shortest, namely, the apostles' plea, "Lord, teach us to pray." Voiced or not, this is the instinctive prayer of all mankind.

As children we learned our prayers and recited them every night and, if we were not too much in a hurry, every morning as well. We said our table prayers before and after meals, and when we were in trouble or in some great need, we would "say" as many Our Fathers and Hail Marys as we thought necessary to elicit God's help. Was this prayer, even according to the old catechism definition of prayer as "the lifting up of the mind and heart to God, to praise him, thank him, glorify him, etc."? Was it communicating with God, conversing with him? In my own case, I am afraid that it was little more than a rote recitation of traditional prayer formulas, without their containing much of my heart and even less of my mind. My prayer was hardly an expression of my deepest self-awareness; it was a task to be fulfilled and gotten out of the way. I hope the situation has improved since that time.

Prayer: God Speaking to Us

Prayer has the strange quality of being man's highest or lowest human activity, depending on how it is entered into. I believe that the first need for most of us is to modify our old concepts of prayer and to think of it, not primarily as *our words to God*, but as *his words to us*. The author of the Book of Revelation depicts Christ saying to us: "Behold, I stand at the door and knock; if any one hears my voice and opens the door, I will come in to him and eat with him and he with me" (3:20).

The note in the New American Bible informs us that Christ is here inviting all men to the messianic banquet of heaven, but I do not believe I would be doing violence to the text to see in those mysterious words of Jesus a beautiful insight into the most elementary meaning of prayer. Prayer begins with God, with his desire to enter into the house of our consciousness, there to commune with our inner being and self, to make himself at home in us. In prayer God speaks to us before we speak to him. Our part is simply to open the door, to respond to his knock in a variety of ways, each according to the particular mood or need we feel at the moment. We may respond with praise, gratitude, adoration, abandonment, any expression of our creatureliness, and sometimes just silence. Prayer is the language of love, and very often lovers do not have to converse: they just rest and rejoice in one another's presence. If you enumerate all the different ways in which a lover communes with the beloved, then you can tell all the ways in which prayer is possible to us.

And that applies to God, too. Who can name the variety of ways in which he speaks to and is present to us? Of course, the most obvious of the Lord's words to us is the word of God, Sacred Scripture. When we read it, *if* we read it, and when we hear it in Sunday Masses, it too often comes to us as a message out of the past, with only the vaguest meaning for our hearts today. And yet it is no exaggeration to claim that every word of Scripture was uttered by God with us in mind as much as the Jews.

The Church understands this function of the word of God at Mass much better than we do. At the end of the first two readings, the lector announces, "This is the word of the Lord." And we respond, "Thanks be to God." The Church simply takes it for granted that we have just indulged in the most elementary kind of praying. God has spoken to us and we respond, not only with our "Thanks be to God," but also, after the first reading, with selected verses from a divinely inspired psalm which reflect on and sing about the basic meaning of the reading. And when Jesus speaks to us in the Gospel, we cry out, "Praise to you, Lord Jesus Christ!" He has spoken and we have answered.

From the very origin of humanity, God has been speaking to his children through the manifold voices of the world of nature, and man has been responding: he has been praying. This may be the most primitive kind of praying, and yet not the least important. Which reader of old western novels does not remember the great reverence that gripped the native Americans in the presence of the Great Spirit, whose presence and voice they perceived in the sun, the rain, the wind, the storm, the rhythm of the seasons?

God's presence and voice can be detected by any sensitive person who is capable of really seeing the world of nature as well as the familiar gestures of love and caring that people manifest towards one another. Too many people see what is around them, but they do not really see, they do not grasp the divine word that is calling out to them from that word. It is possible to imagine an insensitive person standing on the rim of the Grand Canyon or being bathed in the multi-colored light of a sunrise over Lake Superior and being completely unmoved.

Elizabeth Barrett Browning grasped the potential tragedy of such a situation in the quatrain:

> Earth's crammed with heaven,
> and every common bush afire with God;
> But only he who sees takes off his shoes.
> The rest sit around and pluck blackberries.

The reference is to the Exodus account of God calling to Moses out of the burning bush and saying to him, "Put off your shoes from your feet, for the place on which you are standing is holy ground. . . . And Moses hid his face for he was afraid to look at God" (Ex. 3:5-6).

The Basic Attitude: Reverence

Moses' action of hiding his face illustrates perfectly the most elementary human reaction to the presence of the divine, namely *reverence*. Reverence has been called "the mother of all virtues" by Dietrich von Hildebrand. It is a kind of holy fear, a combination of loving desire to remain in the Presence of the divine always, together with a deep sense of one's unworthiness. Consider, for example, the incident in Mt. 17:4-5 when Peter, James and John beheld Jesus transfigured before them on the Mount of the Transfiguration. Peter cried out, "Lord, it is well that we are here; if you wish, I will make three booths here, one for you, one for Moses and one for Elijah." Gripped by a holy fascination, Peter wanted to settle down. Then came the voice out of a cloud, "This is my beloved Son, with whom I am well pleased; listen to him." When the disciples heard the divine voice, they fell on their faces, filled with awe. The apostles illustrated the basic human reaction or response to God's presence. Perhaps without realizing it, they were praying.

It is necessary to point out that God can use music, poetry, literature, indeed every vehicle of beauty, to try to enter into our consciousness, to fill it with a sense of his presence, and to elicit a response from us? Everything that is—perhaps human love and friendship more than anything else—can carry God's voice, his goodness, truth, love, and beauty to us. But "only he who *sees*, takes off his shoes; the rest sit around. . . ."

The psalms are full of human reaction to the presence of God in nature, to his presence everywhere. God is. God is now. In God there is no past, no future; there is only the limitless Now of his vision and presence. The inspired psalmist cries out in response to this divine omnipresence:

> Whither shall I go from thy Spirit?
> Or whither shall I flee from thy presence?
> If I ascend to heaven, thou art there! . . .
> If I take the wings of the morning,
>   and dwell in the uttermost parts of the sea,
> even there thy hand shall lead me,
>   any thy right hand shall hold me.
> If I say, "Let only darkness cover me,
>   and the light about me be night,"
> even the darkness is not dark to thee,
>   the night is bright as the day;
>   for darkness is as light with thee (Ps. 139).

The Psalms—God's Own Prayers

The psalms are widely acclaimed as the universal prayers of all mankind. Coming from the Creator of the human heart, they express every possible human need, every mood, every hope and desire of men and women of all ages, of every century and land. The psalms also come out of the inner being of the people of God. In them God speaks to us and we can cry out to our God. Jesus prayed the psalms during his lifetime and on the cross. Today we have the privilege of making those same words and sentiments our own.

Unfortunately, the wealth of the psalms, their potential for expressing our needs, to say nothing of our most human response to God's greatness and love, are unknown to most Christians. Even those who pray them daily will miss the imagery, the poetry, the power of the psalms unless they pray deliberately, attentively and reverently.

To pray well is not easy. Prayer involves the human person in his highest self-awareness and attentiveness—awareness of God, of self, of membership in a human community. Maintaining attention for any length of time is difficult for most people. It frequently happens that one recites a psalm to the end and then wonders what he has said. I find that the psalm titles in many new breviaries which give the general idea of the content and purpose of the psalm help a great deal. But in the end the secret of praying these divine prayers profitably lies in the very fundamental, human ability to become and remain recollected. The opinion of some writers that "to want to pray is to pray" may fulfill one's obligation to pray, but it hardly satisfies the hunger of the heart for God. So we keep trying, striving for ever greater attentiveness.

St. Paul tells us: "We do not know how to pray as we ought, but the Spirit himself intercedes for us with sighs too deep for words. And he who searches the hearts of men knows what is the mind of the Spirit, because the Spirit intercedes for the saints according to the will of God" (Rom. 8: 26-27). These words are fulfilled above all in the psalms, but they have a further meaning, as we shall soon see.

Awareness of One's Own Worth

One of the greatest aids in praying well is an awareness of one's own worth and dignity as a human person, a child of God. Fr. Edward Farrell, perhaps America's most distinguished writer on prayer, tells the story about the encounter between an American priest and an old peasant in Ireland. They walk along together for a while till a storm breaks out and they have to take refuge in an abandoned building. After a few words, the old man takes out a small prayer book and begins to pray. Watching him the priest seemed to perceive a kind of glow or hallowedness about the old man and he remarked, "You must be very close to God." The man smiled and replied, "Yes, he's very fond of me." Father Farrell comments, "That's what prayer is all about: the discovery that God is fond of us, and it's something we discover in a way that is never-ending and always exciting."

There was no false humility in the old man. He had a deep sense of his own value in God's eyes, and therefore he could pray, he could receive God's loving word, he could respond to it out of the fulness of his own worth and goodness. Farrell remarks in this connection that too many people are unable to pray because they consider themselves nothing. To pray, he says, one has to be able to say, "I *am,* I am *myself,* and that is good."

This sense of one's high self-worth can very well co-exist with a deep sense of one's creatureliness which is so essential to prayer. When we pray we say, God is God and I am creature, I am totally dependent on him for everything—for my being, my life, my life-support—but I may never forget the chief message of the creation story in Genesis. After God created man and women, the inspired author says, "God saw what he had made and it was very good." God is indeed fond of every one of us, and that we exist is the greatest proof.

The Deepest Meaning of Prayer

The old Irish peasant illustrates another essential element in prayer, namely, the ability to receive gifts, especially the gift of God's love, his word, his truth, the ability above all to receive God's own life as the life of our inner being. Here we approach the deepest meaning of prayer. We have been speaking of prayer as God's word to us and our response to that word. But God not only speaks to us in Scripture and in the sacrament of nature, he speaks his WORD to us, the Word who is God, the Word who is with God, has been made flesh and dwells among us, he is one of us. He who is *the* Word becomes *our* Word, our prayer. This is the Good News of the incarnation, this is the heart of Christianity. In a variety of ways Scripture brings this truth home to us. Jesus himself at the Last Supper compares his solidarity and oneness with us to the oneness of a branch, alive with the life-sap of the tree trunk, with the trunk itself. "Abide in me, and I in you. . . . I am the vine, you are the branches" (Jn. 15:4-5). At that same Last Supper he said, "If a man loves me, he will keep my word, and my Father will love him, and we will come to him and make our home with him" (14:23).

As we have already seen, St. Paul compares the oneness of baptized Christians with Christ to a human body. Christ is the head of the body, we are the members. The same Holy Spirit who is in Christ the head is in us the members. In him we are all one. "I have been crucified with Christ; it is no longer I who live, but Christ who lives in me," thus did Paul phrase this extraordinary truth in Gal. 2:20.

Christ lives in me. The Trinity itself makes itself at home in me when I love Jesus. Would I not be praying simply by adverting to that divine Presence in me? This is precisely the point made beautifully by a modern teacher of prayer, Sr. Sylvia Rosell, O.P. She insists that the person who wishes to pray must make a special human effort to advert to God's presence in the heart of our being. She calls this human effort "centering down" and explains it as "concentrating on the life of God within you. It means letting yourself go and allowing yourself to be gripped by the Spirit, allowing God to reveal himself to you. To listen to God—or to another human being— you have to become very still and very quiet and center in on the presence of the other, forgetting your own ideas and judgments and your own expectations of what the other will tell you and just be actively passive. Listen" (*The St. Anthony Messenger*, [November 1977], p. 22).

But awareness of God's presence in me is only a beginning, great though it is. If God is present in us, may we not further conclude that the very prayer life of the Trinity itself goes on in us? that Jesus continues his communing with the Father in us? that his *Amen,* his *fiat,* his "not my will, but thine be done" is now being uttered by him in us and that we can make all his praying to the Father our own?

If Christ communes with the Father in us, is it possible for us to get into his mind, his consciousness? Surely, that would be an overwhelming experience, and we can wonder how much of his consciousness we could endure. Perhaps we underestimate ourselves. He himself was more than willing to share his consciousness; he even gave us the prayer formula that best contains that consciousness, namely, the Our Father, the "Lord's Prayer."

Understanding the Lord's Prayer—First Part

It might well be that the Lord's Prayer is more or less "worn out," that the majority of Christians have become too familiar with it. Perhaps if it were possible to take it away from us, if it were actually to disappear from our prayer life for a few generations and then rediscovered, its glorious meaning might come home to us. However, better than this drastic solution would be for us to reflect a bit on the meaning of the words and better still to learn about the original meaning of the words, the meaning that Jesus himself attached to them, for we must not forget that the Lord's Prayer is Christ's own prayer. It belongs to him, to his mouth and heart even more than to ours. Understanding the meaning that Jesus attached to the words and sentiments of the Lord's Prayer would be difficult for most Christians. But fortunately it has been done for us by such scholars as Joachim Jeremias and my confrère Fr. Godfrey Diekmann, O.S.B., who has researched the writings of the early Church Fathers on the subject.

Thus, we are told that in the Aramaic language that Jesus used the very name "Father" had the connotation of the childlike intimacy, dependency, familiarity, trust that we associate with the familiar "daddy." A child is very particular about whom he calls "Daddy." So too when we say, "Our Father. . . ." It is interesting to know, however, that by the time of Christ the Aramaic word for father—with all its connotations of intimacy—was no longer limited to children but was also used by adolescents and even grownups, who naturally added to the dimension of trust and dependency the special note of loving obedience to the Father.

When Jesus spoke of "my Father" and "your Father," and when he said to the apostles, "Pray then like this: 'Our Father who art in heaven . . . .' " (Mt. 6:9), he was sharing with them and with us a special and unique meaning that the Father had revealed to him as he had to no other being. Father Godfrey says that the joy and shock of this new revelation reverberates throughout the New Testament. This indeed is the Gospel, the Good News, that he came to bring to the world. Paul writes to the Romans: "When we cry, 'Abba! Father!' it is the Spirit himself bearing witness with our spirit that we are children of God, and if children, then heirs, heirs of God and fellow heirs with Christ, provided we suffer with him in order that we may also be glorified with him" (Rom. 8:15-17). This kind of relationship was completely new and original, and it is our prayer and our relationship now. But again, how new and how original is it to us? Actually, just to reflect seriously on those two words "our" and "Father" could be an act of highest contemplation—a complete prayer in its own right.

But when talking to their father, children usually do not stop with a salutation; they go on to tell their desires and needs. So too in the Lord's Prayer. Everything we say in the first part of the Our Father is God-directed, it is praise and glorification of the Father. The first three petitions obligate us who are children of the Father to act as true sons and daughters, to give him cause to rejoice in us so that it will be known to all who see us that we really do see him as our Father. "Hallowed be thy name," we pray. That is, may your name be hallowed in us, name, of course, meaning *person:* May you find yourself so at home in us that we become walking, rejoicing temples of the divinity on earth.

When we cry, "Thy kingdom come" . . ., we express the hope and prayer that the lordship of the Father will come to be established in the universal world of men, but most of all within our own hearts. May the Father be universally acknowledged as God of gods and Lord of lords, to whom all creation and every creature owes its existence, its origin and its sustenance.

When we pray "Thy will be done on earth as it is in heaven," we are making Jesus' own most personal and intimate prayer our own (it is also essentially the same prayer that Mary uttered when she replied to the angel's message asking her to become the mother of the Savior: "Be it done to me according to thy word.") In praying the Lord's Prayer during his lifetime, Jesus was anticipating the prayer he would utter in the Garden of Gethsemane: "My Father, if it be possible, let this cup pass from me; nevertheless, not as I will, but as thou wilt" (Mt. 26:39). In the light of all human rebellion of creature against Creator from the beginning, this petition could well be considered the heart of the Our Father. When we make it our own, we acknowledge our creatureliness in the presence of the Creator, we express fullness of obedience, we place our entire future in his hands.

In all of these God-directed petitions, we ask for the grace to *be* in our lives what we actually are as baptized children of the Father. What Jesus is by nature, we are by our baptism. If we call God our Father, then we ought to live as his children so that it may be known to all who observe us that we are indeed of noble birth.

Understanding the Lord's Prayer—Second Part

The petitions of the second half of the Lord's Prayer follow naturally from the initial salutation, "Abba!" or "Our Father." Children not only tell their father how great he is, they also tell him their needs. Living in this world, our first need is for daily bread, sustenance, the wherewithal to live from day to day. So we cry, "Give us this day our daily bread." We do not ask for a surplus, but only for the normal needs of each day for ourselves and for our families. After all, does not the Father care for us, will he not see to it that we have enough? But when we ask for "daily bread," we are thinking of more than material food for our bodies, important as that might be. We are also presenting our need for "super-substantial bread," the food necessary for our spiritual sustenance, the Eucharist; for unless we eat the flesh of the Son of Man and drink his blood, we shall not have life in us (Jn. 6).

We now turn to another basic human need—the power to forgive anyone who has offended us. This petition could be the most necessary of all: "Forgive us our trespasses *as we forgive* those who trespass against us. Apparently, we are asking for one of the Father's own prerogatives —the power to forgive faults and failings. Forgiveness is God's gift to us; we ask for the strength to pass on that gift to those who have hurt us. Father Godfrey quotes St. Gregory of Nyssa: "To forgive another's debts to oneself is to be the *ikon* (the image, the representation) of the divine nature." The Lord's Prayer asks us to take the initiative in forgiving others, but the way the petition is worded, it is essential to remind ourselves that if we refuse to forgive others, we are equivalently asking God not to forgive us. In Matthew's Gospel, immediately following the Lord's Prayer, we read: "For if you forgive men their trespasses, your heavenly Father also will forgive you; but if you do not forgive men their trespasses, neither will your Father forgive your trespasses" (6:14-15).

The Lord's Prayer concludes with the mysterious phrase," Lead us not into temptation, but deliver us from evil." We can readily understand the "deliver us from evil," but what about the "Lead us not into temptation"? Even the esteemed Jerome Biblical Commentary does not provide a very satisfactory explanation, so perhaps it is best to settle for the translation in the New American Bible: "Subject us not to the trial but deliver us from the evil one."

The beautiful conclusion to the Our Father, "For thine is the kingdom and the power and the glory for ever and ever. Amen," is not in the Gospel text of any of the evangelists. According to the Jerusalem Bible, it may have been introduced into the text through liturgical influences, and since 1974, it is now part of the Roman Catholic Mass.

Tertullian called the Our Father the epitome of the entire Gospel, containing as it does what is essential to the Christian life. It was an obligatory part of the initiation of new converts to the faith and was handed over to them in a solemn secret ceremony. Father Godfrey says that, like baptism it was a "mysterion," a kind of communion with the Father which God himself initiated. Christians in those early days saw it as a daily renewal of their baptism, and they took pains to pray it carefully at least three times a day. There is no need to emphasize that, if it is said earnestly and with deep attention to the meaning of the words, it can well take care of all the prayer needs of the Christian. It hardly seems necessary to remark, however, that any effort to add to the Our Father by other forms of prayer and meditation is praiseworthy.

Divine Reading

What about "meditation"? The word has become very widely used in the past few years. Strangely or not, the term "meditation" seems to have been preempted by what is more correctly known as "transcendental meditation," which, as I understand it, is not concerned with communing with God, but more with acquiring peace of mind through human effort.

Meditation in the traditional Catholic meaning is quite different. In the past meditation and mental prayer were somewhat carelessly used interchangeably and most often in contrast with spoken or sung prayer. Mental prayer or meditation was primarily an exercise of the imagination, the mind, and the will. And it usually followed a set method, the most widespread being the so-called "Ignatian method." Like all prayer, it aimed at spiritual freshness and renewal of intimacy with the Lord, and it undoubtedly formed a solid foundation for the prayer life of thousands upon thousands of priests and religious during the past five hundred years.

A much more ancient "method," going back to the early desert Fathers of the first centuries of Christianity was called *lectio divina*. St. Benedict mentions it several times in his *Rule*, insisting on it as essential for the prayer life of his monks, along with the Divine Office, of course. The term *lectio divina* is not easy to translate accurately or adequately. "Holy reading" or "divine reading" both leave something to be desired. We do know that it was called "divine" because it was thought to "divinize" those who engaged in it. Perhaps the full meaning will emerge from the explanation which follows (for which I am again indebted to my confrère Father Godfrey).

The word *lectio,* traditionally translated "reading," gives the main idea. But this is a special kind of reading. It is a prayerful, contemplative absorption of the word of God, a kind of savoring of the word. With the savoring comes the nourishing of the soul. St. Augustine spoke of the two tables provided by the Lord in his sanctuary for the nourishment of the people of God—the table of the Word and the table of the Bread, the Bread of the Eucharist.

It is not just any kind of pious book that can provide this kind of nourishing reading. It is primarily God's own book, Holy Scripture, and extending from that, the commentaries of the Church Fathers, such as Sts. Augustine, Ambrose, and Gregory the Great. I find myself wondering, however, if books by modern spiritual writers who draw their material from Scripture and record their own reflections on it may not also be material for "lectio divina." However, few of us have ever exhausted the riches of the Scriptures; indeed, how many have ever tried reading it at all?

It is important to consider *how* one reads. Father Godfrey recommends that one read slowly, deliberately, and aloud, so that the whole person can be involved in the practice. You read until you settle on a word or phrase which speaks to your inner heart, and this will then lead to the second stage of the *lectio* (reading), namely, the *meditatio* (meditation).

Meditatio results simply from repeating the phrase over and over until it becomes part of one's memory, one's entire being. But you do more than just memorize it. You exhaust its meaning by reflection, you turn it over in your mind, "taste" its sweetness, rejoice in its goodness. We can easily see how a treasure of such phrases stored in a person's heart can rise to his consciousness at any time of the day or night and recall one to prayerful awareness of God's constant presence.

The third step will again follow naturally and calmly, namely, the *oratio,* a word which is translated "prayer," but it is a very special kind of prayer. It is communing with the Lord in total surrender to him, after the spirit of Mary's "Be it done to me *according to thy word.*" It is a real tasting of the sweetness of the Lord, it is the "dessert" of *lectio divina.*

There is no special amount of time allotted for the exercise of *lectio divina.* The whole process, with the three steps, can take place in a few moments or for an hour. It goes without saying that this is not the only "method" of mental prayer or meditation, but it is one that seems easiest to learn, one that is most available to the greatest number of people.

Avoiding the Extremes

It might well be that there are two "extremes" with regard to prayer. Some Catholics, both lay and religious, think that they do not have to set aside any specific time for prayer, mental or vocal, since as members of Christ their every breath and deed is prayer. I have already indicated that simple awareness of the indwelling of the Godhead in us can indeed be a high form of prayer, but to use this truth as an argument for excusing one from following any kind of regular routine in praying seems dangerous and presumptuous. Friendship and love between lovers is in serious danger of being lost when communication between them is diminished or lost sight of. Without a regular routine of prayer, we run the risk of losing all touch with God.

The other extreme is demonstrated by those Catholics, especially among the laity, who succumb to a strange kind of inferiority complex with regard to the higher forms of prayer. Too many of them think that they are incapable of aiming for any degree of prayer beyond the memorized prayers they recite morning and evening, their Sunday Mass, with an occasional rosary on the side.

And yet most of them can become totally absorbed in any number of tasks such as cooking a meal, rocking a baby to sleep, counselling a patient, teaching a class, ploughing a field. Being absorbed with God, with something Jesus said or did, with a passage from a spiritual book can be contemplation. As Sister Sylvia says: "Contemplation is simply a matter of allowing myself to be caught up. I'm silent and I'm caught up in God's presence. . . . Ultimately what I want is union with God—a personal God who walks with me and says, 'Don't worry. I will lead you to salvation, to wholeness and to enlightenment' " *(The St. Anthony Messenger,* November 1977).

The "Jesus Prayer"

One of the means she and countless other modern Christians have found most conducive to maintaining loving awareness of God's presence is the "Jesus Prayer." I first learned of this prayer more than twenty-five years ago in one of Dorothy Day's columns about the great Russian spiritual classic *The Way of the Pilgrim.* Hardly a year has gone by since then without my running across some reference to the prayer, and in our time it seems to be more widespread than ever.

The practice of the Jesus Prayer goes back to the early Desert Fathers of the fourth century, but its true origin is to be found in the Gospels themselves, in the pitiful cries of the sick to Jesus for help and mercy. The modern version is simple and short: "Lord Jesus Christ, Son of God, have mercy on me, a sinner." It is easy to synchronize the prayer with one's breathing: you breathe in "Lord Jesus Christ, Son of God" and breathe out "Have mercy on me, a sinner." It can readily become second nature to any person, in any walk of life, in any situation, whether it be working, walking, waiting, riding. The net result of its use is the fulfilling of St. Paul's recommendation that we pray always. It is not just a pious exclamation. It is, or should become, a way of life whose aim is to endow the person who says it with Christ-consciousness. I recommend it enthusiastically.

The Rosary

No chapter on prayer would be complete without a reference to the Rosary, the saying of which is a precious tradition to countless older Catholics. The Rosary is a series of meditations on the main events of the life of Jesus, such as his conception in his mother's womb, his birth, his being condemned by Pilate, his carrying of the cross, his resurrection and ascension, the sending of the Holy Spirit to the apostles, and, finally, two mysteries referring to Mary—her assumption and glorification in heaven. Each meditation concerns the redemptive work of Christ, sometimes more explicitly as exemplified in Mary, his mother.

Each of these events is called a "mystery," and there are three such groupings—the "Joyful," the "Sorrowful," and the "Glorious." As one ponders the central meaning of each mystery, one first recites the Lord's Prayer, then ten Hail Marys, and the doxology. The Hail Mary is made up mainly of the greeting to Mary by her cousin Elizabeth, as recorded in Luke 2.

The word "rosary" also refers to the string of beads which aids its recitation. The beads are divided into sections of ten small ones, one for each Hail Mary, interrupted by one large bead for the Our Father. It also has a pendant of three small beads formed by two larger ones and ending with a crucifix—the pendant being for the recitation of the creed and the prayers for faith, hope, and charity. One fingers the beads while reciting the prayers and thinking about the events of the mysteries.

It is a very consoling and enriching way of praying for many Catholics, especially older ones. As is true of all kinds of praying, there is danger of thoughtless routine recitation, of saying the prayers without thinking about the mystery. But this is the danger in any prayer and does not cancel out the great benefits that can derive from its use.

A final word about a form of prayer that seems strange and even "risky" to many Catholics, especially when they are with others. I refer to "spontaneous prayer." Members of charismatic prayer groups move quite easily into the practice, but most Catholics feel much more at ease with the prayer formulas they grew up with.

The very term "spontaneous prayer" describes its nature. You are in a particular situation, you experience a special need, you feel like praising and thanking God, and you spontaneously break out into the kind of prayer—petition, thanks, praise or regret—that fits the situation. At least for beginners, it is a kind of adventure into the unknown, requiring an act of faith both in God and in oneself, but springing as it should from the depths of the human heart and addressed to the Lord God, it can be of inestimable benefit to the one who prays in this manner. The given situation may be considered God's word to you. You respond to that word with your word. In a word, you pray.

How to Think about God

Before ending this lengthy chapter, I want to emphasize what seems to me to be the most essential element in praying—the way in which we think of God. Years ago I quoted the French theologian Louis Bouyer, as follows: "If it is *truly* God whom we seek, we have to seek him as a person. Martin Buber . . . has expressed this very adequately: 'a person is only sought as a person, in dialogue. It is only in the "I to Thou" relationship that the person remains personal for us. Someone of whom we get into the habit of speaking as "he" is no longer a person for us' " *(The Meaning of the Monastic Life,* New York: P.J. Kenedy & Sons, 1955). Our whole attitude towards God changes when we stop thinking of God as "he" or "it" (third person) and start thinking of him as "you" (second person). One can dialogue and commune with the "You" but not with "Him." This kind of conversing or dialoguing with Jesus is what I tried to do in my book *A New Meditating the Gospels,* The Liturgical Press, 1977.

There may seem to be a great deal about methods, of ways, and means of praying in this chapter. The way you pray, the means or method you use, is important, but it is not of the essence. What is important is the goal of prayer—personal, loving union with God. Use whatever method or means that best brings you to that goal. If others find satisfaction with a different means, leave that to them. As it is impossible to limit God's approaches to our hearts, so too is it impossible to limit our approaches to his.

As I said earlier, the number of books on prayer seems to indicate that there is more interest in prayer than ever before. It is good to read about prayer, but it seems that the time has to come in each of our lives when we stop reading about how to pray and start praying. The "how" is a matter of free choice.

8

"Here Am I: Send Me"—Vocation

Among the constantly recurring themes of both Testaments of the Bible—God's choosing the Jews to be his people, the covenant he formed with them, the themes of promise, kingdom, exile, and community—the one that stands out most vividly is that of vocation, of God's call and man's response to that call. It is not for human beings to try to find reasons for the divine call; their part is to hear and to respond.

The basic call issued by the Lord was to a people, to the Hebrew people. The Book of Deuteronomy quotes the Lord: "You are a people holy to the Lord your God; the Lord your God has chosen you to be a people for his own possession, out of all the peoples that are on the face of the earth. It was not because you were more in number than any other people that the Lord set his love up on you and chose you, for you were the fewest of all peoples; but it is because the Lord loves you" (7:6-8).

The Scriptural Idea of Vocation

Here is the way the prophet Isaiah describes Israel's vocation:

> Listen to me, O coastlands,
>   and hearken, you peoples from afar.
> The Lord called me from the womb,
>   from the body of my mother he named my name....
> And he said to me, "You are my servant,

87

Israel, in whom I will be glorified." . . .
"I will give you as a light to the nations,
   that my salvation may reach to
     the end of the earth" (49:1-6).

The universal divine call to a nation is also narrowed down to individual persons within the nation. Thus the first and greatest of all vocations was to the father of the Jewish nation himself, Abraham, whom God called to leave his old country and to launch out into a new life in a new land so that in him all the nations of the earth would be blessed (Gen. 12). God called Moses to lead his enslaved people out of Egypt into the Promised Land. He called the prophets to give up their old lives and to go forth among the people proclaiming God's word and recalling the sinful people to the covenant Jahweh had made with them. He called David to be the greatest of the kings of his people and the ancestor of the Messiah. God called Mary to be the mother of his Son, the Savior of his people; and he called Joseph to be her husband and the foster father and protector of his Son. Jesus in turn called the apostles to give up everything—profession, families, possessions—to follow him and become the foundation pillars of his Church. And since those ages God has continued to call women and men to leave their past behind and to launch new lives of service to his people and to the world.

I have already quoted Isaiah's description of Jahweh's call to Israel. His account of his own call to the vocation of prophecy is even more striking. God first gives him a vision of the heavenly court in which he hears the angels crying out: "Holy, holy, holy is the Lord of Hosts; the whole earth is full of his glory." At first the prophet is terrified at his own unworthiness in the presence of the Divine until he is reassured by one of the Seraphim who touches his lips with a burning coal and takes away his sin. Then Isaiah hears the voice of the Lord saying, "Whom shall I send, and who will go for us?" And without hesitation Isaiah responds, "Here am I! Send me," and the Lord immediately commissions him to go and recall the people to fidelity to the covenant. In obedience to the call of the Lord, Isaiah becomes one of the greatest of the prophets (chapter 6).

The Human Element

Every vocation begins with God, but the divine summons remains sterile unless there is a free human response from those who are called. In almost every case there is initial resistance of greater or lesser degree, based in part on a poor self-image because of past sins, on fear of the unknown, reluctance to give up former security, or just plain lack of interest. But in the end, at least in most of the scriptural vocations, God has his way, and the person called heeds God's voice and goes off into the new life, into the unknown. It is this launching out into the unknown —into an adventure the details of which are known only to God—trusting completely in the Lord and his call, that constitutes the nobility of vocation.

The call that we as a people and each of us as members of a people receive from God may not be as dramatic as were most of the prophetic vocations in the Old Testament, but it is imperative that we truly believe that even as he put his finger on the Jews, on the Old Testament prophets, on the apostles, so does he put his finger on us now, giving assurance that he knows and trusts us, despite our human weaknesses. In its most basic sense vocation is a call to awareness of who and what we are in the overall plan of God, above all of who and what we are as members of the people of God.

In the New Testament, as in the Old, the first and most essential divine call is to a people—the people of God. Everything the Lord said to Israel as quoted above is now applicable to the people of God, to us. "I have set you to be a light for the Gentiles, that you may bring salvation to the uttermost parts of the earth" (Acts 13:47). This is the first step in the establishing of our personal identity. God has called each of us into membership in his people. The words of St. Peter are meant for us today: "You are a chosen race, a royal priesthood, a holy nation, God's own people, that you may declare the wonderful deeds of him who called you out of darkness into his marvelous light" (1 Pet. 2:9). God has called us to membership in the community of the redeemed, whose universal vocation is to praise and thank him as a community and so be a light to the nations. And in this community of those called by the Lord, each member is important, each has a special function to fulfill, each has a vocation.

It is now time to consider some of these special vocations within the people of God. Unfortunately, for most people the term "vocation" has too restrictive a meaning. A priest or a sister will say to a young man or woman, "I think you might have a vocation," and the young persons concerned know that they look like likely candidates for the priesthood or the religious life.

It is only in recent times that writers and preachers ventured to speak of marriage as a vocation or to the various professions in society as "vocations within a vocation," especially the vocation of marriage. Now we no longer think exclusively of the priesthood or the religious life when we use the term "vocation" as including God's call to men and women to do his work in a particular walk of life, or when we think of God calling people to holiness in and through and because of their choice of a particular way of life to which they give the fullest exercise of their talents.

The Vocation of Marriage

Surely the vocation to which God calls the great majority of men and women is marriage. It is truly a divine call to do God's work, and by that I mean much more than the spouses' continuing God's creative work by bringing new life into the world, important and necessary though that may be. The wonder of marriage is that a man and a woman do become God's instrument for bringing into the world those particular human beings to whom God wills to give existence. No human person is an "unplanned accident," not at least from God's standpoint. The Lord can say to each of us, even as he said to Jeremiah: "Before I formed you in the womb I knew you, and before you were born I consecrated you" (1:5).

A New Catechism captures the beauty of this truth:

> The beginning of a new human life is a sacred moment in which this creative power is particularly evident. After all, my parents could not have wanted "me." At best, they wanted a "boy" or a "girl." Only God wanted "me". . . . Hence the power to cooperate with God is bestowed on parents as they give new life to a child. This cooperation does not end at the birth. It is completed in the education of the child. God nourishes, loves and guides the new human life through its parents. They have a serious and joyful responsibility. (New York: Herder and Herder, 1967), p. 382.

It is crucial to emphasize this responsibility. Apparently, for normally endowed human beings it is all too easy to effect the birth of a child. It is after the child is born that the real work and the never-ending sacrifice begin. It is the raising of children that demands inexhaustible patience, genuine creative thinking, and, above all, trust.

Then, of course, there is the daily life together with all its problems, its personality conflicts, its worries—financial and personal. It is the most intimate kind of union on all levels. And it is from the raw material of that kind of intimate living together that God expects spouses to shape a marriage that will in turn shape them, as well as their children, into greater maturity and wholeness as human beings *and* as Christians. In and through and because of every aspect of marriage, including sexual intimacy, God calls men and women to holiness.

Their ideal is to build a home where not only the members of the family but God himself will be at home. A home is much more than a house, important as the physical dwelling place might be. To make a home requires the same amount of creative and sacrificial effort that it takes to bring up a child, and both husband and wife must work at it fulltime. The Christian home has been called an *ecclesiola,* that is, a "little church." And again, I do not mean the dwelling but the people, God's people in miniature, God's people learning to love, to grow in responsibility, to develop their talents, to sacrifice, to suffer and above all to learn how to worship and praise the Creator whose blessed idea it all has been.

To do this kind of creative "work" for the Lord is the main challenge of the holy vocation of marriage. As I have said, it is the vocation to which God summons the majority of his children. Obviously, it is no vocation for the immature, for weaklings, for the thoughtless, the selfish, the escapist, or the irreverent.

The chief theme of this book is maturity—growth into the fullness of one's Christian profession. It is wholeness, fulfillment. But these goals are identical with the goals of marriage. Marriage is one of the divinely appointed paths to adulthood—human adulthood and adulthood in faith and religion as well. Marriage, like religion, requires selflessness, a consuming willingness to live for others rather than for self. Above all, marriage, like religion, requires reverence for the person of the beloved, the kind of reverence that resembles the adoration reflected in the old Anglican marriage ceremony in which the groom says to the bride, "With my body I thee worship." Above all, marriage, like religion, requires faith, trust in one's partner, the same sort of faith and trust that the Lord has in each of us. Finally, marriage, like religion, requires forgiveness—the ability to receive it as well as the graciousness to grant it.

The following quote (regretfully, I cannot give the author's name) seems to me to express perfectly the possibility for adventure, satisfaction, and challenge that every marriage can and should provide: "Every human person is a mystery that must be learned slowly, reverently, with care, tenderness and pain, and never learned completely." The ideal proposed here requires that husband and wife *be present to* one another always—which means never being oblivious to the presence of the other, never taking her or him for granted. The ideal also implies that husband and wife *be good for* one another, which is much more difficult and demanding than being good *to* one another. To be good for one another requires a depth of personality and an all-round attitude of caring that results only from years of practice in self-giving.

I could go on and on, but there are other vocations to be considered in this chapter. I hope that the above convinces the reader that marriage is a true vocation—a genuine call from God to men and women to come to him in and through this most intimate of all relationships. I also hope that the above pages will help married people realize that it is the vocation of marriage more than any other influence that conditions their maturing as Christians. This vocation, perhaps more than any other, brings a deeper realization of dependency on God and of the need for his grace, and that realization is an inevitable pre-condition for growth in the likeness of Christ, who—may they never forget—is an active partner in their marriage. A marriage can hardly fail if—at the beginning, during, and at the end of their union—the spouses can pray: "Here am I, Lord. I come to do your will."

The Single Vocation

In society, in the Church, there is a special vocation that few persons ever think of as a vocation, i.e. a special call from God. I refer to the vocation of the fifty million women and men in the United States who, though they may follow one of the professions, are neither married nor priests, nor members of a religious Order. They are single people, living alone "in the world." The fifty million includes men and women who are divorced or widowed, but twenty-four million have either chosen not to or have never had the opportunity to marry. To my mind these are the most neglected, unchallenged, and unsung heroes of the Church. The saddest fact about them is that no one ever tells them that the single life in society is a true vocation, just as much as is the priesthood or religious life or marriage.

What is worse, people feel badly about them and sorry for them. They make remarks like, "She's such a nice person. She would have made a wonderful mother. Too bad she never married." Or, "With a heart as big as his, it's a shame he never got married and had kids." And judging by the lack of interest in the "singles" in most parishes, it seems that even the Church neglects them. Most parishes have programs for married people, for young people, for the aged, for children, but what parishes ever consider doing anything for or inviting the help of the unmarrieds?

All in all, it could be that this is the most difficult of all vocations, the one that demands the most faith, dedication, and sacrificial spirit. In marriage, in the priesthood, and especially the religious life, the human hunger for close companionship with others is always readily gratified. But single people—while it is always possible to find satisfying companionship with other "singles" and friends—must go back "home" after work to lonely apartments and rooms.

In addition to loneliness, their worst enemy might well be a poor self-image, a sense of inadequacy, of usefulness, and this in turn can easily turn into self-centeredness. (It has to be pointed out, however, that it is easy to become selfish and self-centered in marriage and the religious life as well. And in these vocations others suffer as well as the one who is guilty of self-centeredness.) So self-acceptance, so essential in any vocation, is especially necessary for those called to live alone in the world. I've got to be convinced in my own mind that I am accepted by God as I am, not as I think I should be, and therefore I must accept myself. And the best reason for a good self-image is the firm conviction that the single life is a true vocation; it is God's choice—permanent or temporary—for me here and now. It is in and because of this vocation that he calls me to maturity in my faith.

I must accept myself, not for what I achieve or accomplish, but for what I am. Father van Breemen says that self-acceptance is the essential condition for being accepted by others, and acceptance by others is the essential condition for fulfillment as a human being (*As Bread That Is Broken* [Denville, N.J.: Dimension Books, 1974], p. 9 ff.). Many people have the impression that a husband or wife or a community are the only way for anyone's growth into fullness of personality. Far from it. Some of the most fulfilled, whole and wholesome people I have met have been singles, and some of the most immature have been married or religious.

Helps Towards Self-Fulfillment

In addition to acceptance by self and by others, we are brought to perfection as human persons by our creative efforts, by our work, our intellectual curiosity (and its satisfaction), by friendship, by helping others, and, above all, by our prayer and sacramental and parish life. For me personally reading is very important, and I have always considered the encouragement of good reading habits as one of the essential lessons I could leave with my students. (In some vocations, above all, the priesthood, there is simply no substitute for it; the priest, whose duty it is to preach, who does not read defrauds his people of their basic right to the understanding of God's word.) But since not everyone has an inclination and taste for reading, some other interests have to be found. One does not have to look far in any parish for opportunities to help persons in need of being loved and cared for. Every community has more than its share of elderly, lonely people to whom one can bring Christ by bringing oneself. (The possibility of bringing Christ in Holy Communion could also be looked into.)

Perhaps the greatest need for an unmarried person is for understanding, loving friends. Long ago St. Augustine said that a friend is someone who knows all about you and still accepts you. In every vocation, but above all in this one, friendship is of the essence for human and humane living, as well as for maturing as a human person and a Christian. I am reminded of the lasting impression made on me many years ago by one of Gerald Vann's first books. He wrote in *Of His Fullness:*

> It is worth reminding ourselves . . . that the creative instinct, which finds its normal mode of expression in human love, cannot be repressed without disaster; it must find some outlet somewhere. Celibacy without creativity is a terrible danger. If every man should find the work suited to his creative abilities, it is more than ever necessary that the celibate should do so. And

let us not, in this context also, forget the enormous importance of friendship, which is one of God's most precious gifts; and if we reject it we are not only despising a divine gift, but are again endeavoring to repress and dry up those very instincts which our nature needs if it is to be whole, generous, sane, and free. If we want to be barren, self-centered, crusty, uncharitable, let us choose a life of friendless celibacy. That is not holiness.

(New York: P.J. Kenedy & Sons, 1939), p. 37.

Most singles who are physically capable have positions in society. It should be obvious that any person (married or unmarried) in any position should be as competent as possible in his position. Nor may anyone neglect the work required in order to pursue religious exercises. Holiness is no substitute for competence. One's first obligation is to one's employer. (Just as it would be wrong for a married person to neglect his spouse and family in order to do works of piety or charity in the parish or in society.)

But one does not, should not, lose sight of who and what one is as a member of the Body of Christ. You do not have to be a visionary to believe that because of your presence in a particular place or task, Christ is present there. You can say: "If I were not here, Christ would not be here. If I were not here, no one would be offering thanks and adoration to the Lord in this spot."

This conviction alone can supply the foundation for the attitude of *quiet* joy (emphasis on "quiet") that ought to characterize every Christian everywhere. In fact, joy can well be the ultimate indication of maturity in religion. Surely there is no better sign than joy of the genuineness of one's faith, just as lack of joy in one's heart and appearance is the worst possible scandal to the non-believer that a Christian can give.

The Priestly Vocation

I have already mentioned that when most Catholics hear the term "vocation," they think automatically about a call to the priesthood or the religious life or both. I hope that this chapter will provide a wider and deeper understanding of the term. However, a chapter on vocations would hardly be complete without some treatment of the special call which the Lord extends to some members of the Church to serve him and his people in the priesthood and the religious life or both.

The priests most American Catholics are most familiar with are diocesan priests who serve the majority of the parishes of the country. Their immediate superior is the bishop, the chief shepherd or pastor of the diocese. When a priest is ordained, he makes a promise of obedience to his bishop and his successors in that office. It is the bishop who assigns priests to particular parishes (or to other diocesan positions). However, in these post-Vatican II years few bishops would make any appointments without consulting the personnel board of the diocese. Contrary to the custom in most Protestant churches (in which a person is called to a parish at the end of his/her seminary training and then ordained), the Catholic bishop calls his seminarians to Holy Orders and only then does he ordain them and give them an assignment.

What is the priesthood? Perhaps the best way to describe this vocation is to draw on the *Decree on the Bishops' Pastoral Office in the Church* of the Vatican Council II. This decree treats not only bishops and their duties but also those who share the bishops' pastoral work, the parish priests. Number 30 of the decree lists the priests' duties as so fulfilling "their duty of teaching, sanctifying, and governing that the individual parishioners and the parish communities will really feel that they are members of the diocese and of the universal Church" *(The Documents of Vatican II,* Walter M. Abbott, S.J., ed. [New York: America Press], p. 418.)

To me it is most significant that the document lists preaching as the first and most important of the priest's duties: "In the exercise of their teaching office it is the duty of pastors *to preach God's word* to all the Christian people so that, rooted in faith, hope, and charity, they may grow in Christ, and that the Christian community may bear witness to that charity which the Lord commended" (Abbott, p. 418; emphasis added).

The document then instructs pastors on the primacy of worship in the life of the parish: "In discharging their duty to sanctify their people, pastors should arrange for the celebration of the Eucharistic Sacrifice to be the center and culmination of the whole life of the Christian community. They should labor to see that the faithful are nourished with spiritual food through the devout and frequent reception of the sacraments and through intelligent and active participation in the liturgy" (Abbott, p. 418).

Finally, the pastor's office as shepherd will be best fulfilled only if the pastors know their people: "Since they are the servants of all the sheep, they should foster growth in Christian living among the individual faithful and also in families . . . they should visit homes and schools . . . they should pay special attention to adolescents and youth, devote themselves with a paternal love to the poor and the sick, and have a particular concern for workingmen. Finally, they should encourage the faithful to assist in the works of the apostolate" (Abbott, p. 419).

What Is Vocation?

In the light of efforts on the part of some theologians and some recent popes to define the essence of the priestly vocation, it may seem strange that the Vatican II *Decree on Priestly Formation* makes no such attempt.

The footnote to number 2, chapter II of the document admits that some Council Fathers wanted a theological definition, but "The Council preferred to describe in a very general way how vocations are discerned and fostered. In keeping with the new stress on the involvement of the whole People of God in the mission of the Church, the responsibility is placed in varying degrees, but in a real way for all, on the entire community" (Abbott, p. 440).

The document does take pains in chapter III, number 6, however, to enumerate the requisites of a vocation that were formerly listed by theologians who wrote on the matter: "Depending on the age of each seminarian and his state of progress, careful inquiry should be made concerning the *rightness of his intention and the freedom of his choice, his spiritual, moral,* and *intellectual fitness, the suitability of his bodily and mental health* . . . His ability to bear priestly burdens and exercise pastoral duties must also be weighed" (Abbott, p. 443).

To aspire to the priesthood at present in the Catholic Church of the Latin (Roman) rite, it is necessary for a man to make a special vow of celibacy. And it would probably be a serious mistake for a young man to consider a priestly vocation if he judged that it would be too difficult for him to live a chaste life. The requirements of celibacy do not, on the other hand, necessitate any kind of fear of or dislike for members of the opposite sex. A man who fears or dislikes women does not belong in the priesthood (and he should have his head examined!)

Diocesan priests do not make a special vow of poverty, as do those who belong to religious Orders; this means that diocesan priests may own property and spend their meager salaries as they see fit. Compared to men in other professions, and even to their brethren in Protestant parishes, priests are not well paid. To be sure, they do not have the family expenses incumbent on a Protestant pastor.

Who, what, is a priest? He is called to be for his people all that Christ was: a man of God, a shepherd, a prophet, a father, a comforter, a healer, a sanctifier, a mediator. He stands between his people and God. God acts in and through him, and he in turn is to lead his people to God. Such is his dignity, but such also his responsibility. And yet he is human —sometimes too human. No person could fulfill such obligations by his own power alone. This is the reason why the Roman Catholic Church believes that Jesus instituted a special sacrament, Holy Orders, in and through which he enters into priests' lives, gives them the same powers he had, and the grace and strength to carry out the duty of being Christ to their people.

In his article on vocations in the *New Catholic Encyclopedia* (vol. 14, p. 735), C. A. Schleck lists the following indications that a person does not have a vocation to the priesthood or the religious life: extreme difficulty in remaining continent; an habitually ill-regulated temper which would make community life and obedience difficult; habitual lack of docility; an over-bearing disposition; jealousy—all of which faults are so deeply rooted and pronounced in the personality as to preclude the serious probability of their being overcome with available means; and finally, lack of at least the minimum judgment necessary to accomplish the duties of the priestly or religious vocation (one can imagine the difficulty of a person's being a suitable marriage partner if he or she possesses any of these personality problems!)

According to the present discipline of the Roman Catholic Church, the priesthood is limited to males. Such, too, is the case with permanent deacons.

The Permanent Diaconate

Most Catholics do not realize that many changes in the Roman Catholic Church introduced by Vatican II are little more than a return to or a recovery of some very ancient customs in the Church. Such, for example, is the recently-introduced manner of receiving Communion in the hand. And such, above all, is the restoration of the permanent diaconate. This order had its origin in the early Church when the apostles decided that they could not do justice both to preaching the word of God and serving food to the growing number of converts. So they said to the Christian assembly: "Pick out from among you seven men of good repute, full of the Spirit and of wisdom, whom we may appoint to this duty [of serving at the table]. But we will devote ourselves to prayer and to the ministry of the word" (Acts 6:3-4).

The assembly picked their men and presented them to the apostles who "prayed and laid their hands upon them" (Acts 6:6). Eventually these men came to be known as deacons; their chief duties were to assist the apostles in caring for the spiritual and physical needs of the Christian community.

In the course of centuries the diaconate ceased to be permanent and came to be considered only as the final order leading to ordination to the priesthood. For a variety of reasons the Fathers of Vatican II saw fit to restore the permanent diaconate to Church practice. In the United States several thousand men have already been ordained deacons and a growing number of laymen are undergoing a period of theological, scriptural, and pastoral preparation with a view to being ordained as deacons for service in their parishes or dioceses. Theirs is strictly a ministry of service.

The United States Bishops' Committee on the Permanent Diaconate lists these essential elements of a deacon's vocation:

The invitation of the Spirit, the manifestation and realization of this call through sacramental ordination for the benefit of the universal Church, the special fraternal sharing of accountability for the kingdom with all ordained ministers, the acceptance of the community he is called to serve, and the complete commitment of self to serve the name of Christ and His Church.

Permanent Deacons in the United States (Washington, D.C.: United States Catholic Conference), p. 7.

Deacons can proclaim the Gospel and preach at Mass; they assist the priest in the celebration of the Eucharist and distribute Communion; they can be ministers at a solemn baptism and can officiate at marriages. They are ministers of charity to the needy of the parish and help with the religious instruction of children and converts.

Permanent deacons may either be married or single, and they exercise their service in their parishes in addition to holding down the regular positions and vocations they have in society. At present, the minimum age for being ordained a permanent deacon is thirty-two.

That a growing number of men are becoming interested in the permanent diaconate in the United States is an excellent sign of growing maturity in the American Catholic community.

The Vocation to the Religious Life

If the priesthood and permanent diaconate are presently limited to males, the same cannot be said of the religious life, thank God! Very few religious Orders and congregations do not have both male and female branches. The religious life is defined in the *New Catholic Encyclopedia* as: (vol. 12, pp. 287, 288):

a particular expression of the love of God through a following of Christ that is characteristically originated, approved by the Church as a public state of life and characterized by a commitment to a group or community (ordinarily including life in common); by a profession of evangelical poverty, chastity, and obedience through public vows (or other similar bonds); and by some form of separation from the world, practiced, however, for the sake and service of the world.

This exact, if somewhat cold, description hardly hints at the heart of religious life which involves a very special espousal to Christ. Christ enters the life of a woman or a man, he extends an invitation ("Come, follow me"), and the invited person leaves all things behind and goes off to follow him. The vows of poverty, chastity, and obedience form a framework which conditions the human response to Christ's call.

The vows are called "evangelical counsels," and the word "counsel" is essential for understanding their nature. They are not commands and are definitely not of the essence of Christianity. Christ *invites* some women and men to follow him more closely, and by means of these vows they freely give their consent. Out of love for Christ and the Church, they renounce certain basic human rights for the sake of the kingdom of God.

Thus the human person has an inalienable right to own property, to call certain possessions his own. Freely, out of love for Christ, he or she gives up that right by taking the vow of poverty.

Again, men and women, naturally endowed in mind and body for marriage, deliberately choose to give up the rightful exercise of sexuality and vow to remain unmarried.

Finally, each person is born with free choice, with the native right to follow one's own initiative and make personal decisions about the manner and style of his or her life. By the vow of obedience the person gives up that right and hands over its direction to a superior.

It is to be emphasized that these are basic human values that are renounced, and they are renounced, not because they are lesser values or because there is anything wrong with them (on the contrary!), but precisely because they are good, their renunciation becomes a loving gift to God. The profession of vows has to be motivated by love. If that motivation is lacking—or if it diminishes along the way of religious life—the vows, besides being emptied of worth, can become a sham and an obstacle to the following of Christ. The purpose of the vows is to liberate a person from human anxieties and so enable that man or woman to give undivided dedication and devotion to the Lord.

The vows form a framework that conditions the human response to the call of Christ. This framework lasts as long as religious life lasts and it can never be taken for granted. It obligates the religious to an unceasing growth in detachment from the values renounced which must result in a corresponding growth in union with the mind and heart of Christ.

The definition of religious life given a few pages earlier mentions another characteristic that deserves comment, namely, "commitment to a group (ordinarily including life in common)." Community life can be a blessing or a burden, depending on the degree of sacrifice and the ideals of the members of the community. If the members are concerned about making theirs a community of the praise of the Lord, if each member is deeply concerned about "building community" (one of the main purposes of religious life, according to some authorities), the religious house can become a vivid, living witness to the riches of Christianity. It can become missionary simply by its existing in a particular locale. It can likewise become the perfect answer to the hunger for community life for which countless numbers of young people are seeking satisfaction in the communes of the nation.

The Variety of Religious Orders

Every religious Order or congregation seems to have been founded for a special work in the Church—for meeting a need that may have appeared and expanded according to the developing requirements of a culture or a society. However, most Orders and congregations do not limit themselves rigidly to one particular kind of work. For example, an order best known for its missionary character might also run schools or hospitals.

Sisters are all religious. Some teach, some nurse, some are in administration, some are catechists or are involved in the social apostolate or are hospital or college chaplains. Men who join religious Orders may choose between serving God, the Church, and the community as priests or as brothers. They all make the same vows of poverty, chastity, and obedience, and that profession, rather than whether or not they are ordained to the priesthood, is what makes them Benedictines or Franciscans or Dominicans.

Just as there is a religious Order (as well as the diocesan priesthood) for every need in the Church and in society, so it seems safe to claim that a particular religious Order or a particular religious community within an Order will respond to the particular needs and talents of a particular candidate. It is entirely possible that a person who feels frustrated or out of place as a Jesuit or a Dominican might very well find satisfaction and happiness as a Maryknoller or a Redemptorist. Those who are deeply desirous of leading the contemplative life will surely do better as Trappists or Carmelites than as Paulists or Christian Brothers. It is up to a counsellor to take a person's personality, talents, and religious inclinations into account in directing that individual to the Order or congregation best fitted to satisfy those needs and inclinations.

So it is perfectly natural and praiseworthy to want to find an Order or a community where one can find self-fulfillment through the use and development of one's particular talents, but if a person makes personal fulfillment his or her only goal and purpose and does not see the religious life as the best means to serve Christ and society, there is good reason to doubt the authenticity of that particular "vocation." There can be no substitute for the desire to *serve* as an essential ingredient in any vocation, but that service need not be only with one's hands or voice. They also serve who pray and suffer for the welfare of humankind.

It would definitely be wrong to look upon the religious life as a "cop-out," as an effort to escape the difficulties of life. One does not "leave the world" in order to cast aside or forget the cares of the world. Nor does the dedicated religious look with disdain or superiority on the world and the people who bear the heat of the day by working in the world. Most religious come to the healthy conclusion that there is more heroism among Christians living in the world than in convents and monasteries. The religious vocation is a divine summons to growth in humility.

A Priestly People

The crisis in vocations that is evident in the Catholic world today is alarming. Many priests and religious have left the priesthood and religious life and replacements are not arriving in the same numbers as in pre-Vatican II times. It is fruitless to try to determine the causes of the departures or to make accusations. What is more important is to encourage what seems to be the latest trend back to seminaries and religious Orders. Too many young men and women never consider the priesthood or religious life because they feel unfit or deficient in talent or because no one ever suggests it to them.

What is crucial, of course, is the Church, its needs, the needs of the people of God. It is obvious that without priests and sisters the people are deprived of necessary spiritual care and nourishment. On the other hand, if the shortage of priests and religious brings home to everyone that the entire Church is a priestly people and that every baptized Christian has priestly duties resulting from his baptism, we may have a healthier Church than we had when there was a priest for every parish church, very often with a parochial school attached. No one may forget the powerful words of St. Peter: "You are a chosen race, a royal priesthood, a holy nation, God's own people, that you may declare the wonderful deeds of him who called you out of darkness into his marvelous light" (1 Pet. 2:9).

So the entire Church is the assembly of those who have been called, those who have a vocation to be followers of Christ carrying on his work in our world. The Church has a variety of calls from God. Every age means a different call, a call to a new adventure, following the development of mankind. But always it is the same call: to go forward in a new effort to bring Christ and his word to the people and to society. The Church may never rest in the past, never bask in the security of her glorious history. In every age the call comes to leave the past and to strike out anew like Abraham. A new world is constantly in formation. It is the duty of the Church to be a leaven in the world in every age. Being a Catholic is not primarily a matter of saving one's own soul. It is doing one's personal part in creating a world in which it will be possible for all peoples to live as normal, decent human beings. That personal duty never ends.

The Ultimate Vocation

I have tried to point out that within the assembly of those whom God has called there is a great variety of vocations, so much so that no one can be said to be without a vocation. There is a special vocation that very few people would think of as a vocation at all: it is that of retirement and old age. This could be the most difficult, the most demanding, and the most important of all.

It is a difficult vocation, not only because of the physical limitations old age places upon a person, the hardships and suffering that eventually become the lot of every aged person, but also because of that recurring old enemy, a poor self-image, that often results from having to give up the active, productive, "useful" life and in some cases to settle for doing nothing. The old American work ethic takes its revenge, and it is hard to tell the aged that the worth of a person is not measured by what he produces but by what he *is.* If there ever is a need for self-acceptance, it is in the case of those who because of age or infirmity no longer seem able to do or produce anything worthwhile or measurable in terms of a salary.

These people have to be convinced that they are specially chosen and beloved members of the Body of Christ, that now, even as in the lifetime of our Lord, they are the special objects of his concern, his care and love. And they have to remind themselves again and again of the beautiful and consoling truth contained in St. Paul's mysterious words: "Now I rejoice in my sufferings for your sake, and in my flesh I complete what is lacking in Christ's afflictions for the sake of his body, that is, the church" (Col. 1:24).

We wonder what could possibly be lacking in the sufferings of Christ? Was his passion and death not sufficient to redeem the world? Of course, it was, but Paul is telling us that by some mysterious divine "transaction" each of us is privileged to join our sufferings to those of Christ for the sake of bringing him and his Good News to those whose lives have been deprived of his presence.

The greatest vocation (and adventure) of all is the call to leave this world and go back home to the Father. This vocation seems completely unreal to us now. The call comes to everyone else, but somehow or other we seem to feel that we will go on forever. But nothing is more certain than that the day will inevitably come to each of us, the day when the cycle of calls from the Lord will be ended and the final vocation will come. We shall each hear the voice of the Lord saying, "Whom shall I send? who will be my messenger?"

If all through life we have been generous in answering God's calls and have given our all to the best possible fulfilling of those calls, we are sure to answer the final one with the words, "Here am I, Lord. Send me." And we shall go forth into the greatest adventure of all, the adventure of rejoicing forever in the fulfillment of all our hungers and thirsts for inexhaustible truth, life, and love. But it will not, I am sure, be an adventure devoid of labor and concern for our world.

9

On Coming to Terms with Suffering, Pain, Dying

There may be a certain brashness in such a chapter heading. One could ask if it is possible to come to terms with suffering and death? It would be easier to go along with those authors who consider the problem insoluble and so make no effort to arrive at the understanding that is possible, but that would be taking the easy way out of a problem that for most people is the most difficult one they face in their lifetime.

Perhaps one reason for our reluctance to face suffering is its mysteriousness. We seem to feel that there is no possible explanation for suffering, no meaning in it, so we try to escape even thinking about it. I do not deny there remains an element of mystery even after some meaning has been discovered. My point is that the impossibility of finding a completely satisfying meaning in suffering should not prevent us from finding whatever meaning is available. My chief concern in this chapter is related to the concern of the person who wrote, "The great tragedy in suffering is not that it exists but that so much of it is wasted."

It hardly seems necessary to establish the universal fact of suffering. Quite simply, no one escapes it. The main question has to be: how do people react to suffering? Does it crush and defeat them, does it embitter them, destroy their faith in God? Or do they face it calmly and courageously, determined not just to refuse to let it defeat them but much more importantly to come to terms with it and utilize it for their own personal growth and for the good of mankind.

It is difficult to pinpoint what it is in a person that will determine how suffering will affect him, whether it will crush or recreate the person. For some it might be sheer courage, it might be strength of character, and for others it might be religious faith and hope. Hope above all. Without hope the sufferer is doomed to defeat. Everyone who suffers needs to discover meaning in it for his life. No one wants to suffer and die for little or no cause. Useless and misdirected suffering is sterile; no one benefits by it, neither humanity, nor the individual person, nor society.

Lessons of the Holocaust

The April 1978 TV mini-series "Holocaust" brought some one hundred and twenty million Americans face to face with the most inexplicable, most frightening massing of suffering, torture, and dying ever inflicted by human beings on a group of their fellow human beings, the Jews of Europe. How does anyone "explain," much less try to find any justification for or meaning in the murder of six million Jews and Christians and the imprisonment of many millions more? While the columnists and even so distinguished a writer as Elie Wiesel (himself a survivor of the concentration camps) disagreed whether or not the program ought to have been aired, no one made any effort to try to understand or explain how such a thing could have happened. The columnist who, to my mind, best grasped the enormity of the mystery was Ellen Goodman of the Boston *Globe*. She wrote: "The Holocaust, experienced even vicariously in a shallow TV program, is inevitably a confrontation with Evil. Pure Evil. Irrational Evil," and she claimed that few of us are even willing to confront the problem. "We fear that if we 'understand' evil, we will be accepting it, condoning it, perhaps even paving the way for it to happen again. . . . The sheer difficulty of accepting evil in the world, in humanity and in ourselves leaves us, as it did last week, silent. But not unaware" (Minneapolis *Tribune*, April 25, 1978).

Surely, there is one truth the "Holocaust" did illustrate, namely, there is a vast difference between the evil and suffering brought about by natural causes (earthquakes, storms, tornadoes, etc.) and the much worse evil caused by sin and human perversion. This is the evil that can and has to be diminished and eventually rooted out of the human heart.

The depression that came over me after viewing the first segment of "Holocaust" reminded me of the book of Dr. Viktor Frankl, a survivor of the camps. The main portion of his book is autobiographical, relating his day-by-day experiences in the camps. Dr. Frankl is a well-known psychiatrist and has been president of the Austrian Medical Society for Psychotherapy. The original title of his book was *From Death-Camp to*

Existentialism. I find it fascinating that he later changed the title to *Man's Search for Meaning,* with the sub-title *An Introduction to Logotherapy.* Frankl does not spare details of the suffering and dying of the savaged prisoners, but his main emphasis and determination is to discover the meaning in it all in terms of the future of humanity. In the end one's only conclusion is that Frankl has written a magnificent hymn to the indestructibility of the human spirit.

The will to live that prevailed in most of the prisoners depended in large part on their hope for survival and deliverance, on the memory (amounting in some cases to a vivid sense of presence) of loved ones, but more than anything else on their determination to find meaning in, and to make some sense out of, their apparently senseless suffering. "It is here," says Dr. Gordon Allport in his preface to Frankl's book, "that we encounter the central theme of existentialism: to live is to suffer, to survive is to find meaning in the suffering. If there is a purpose in life at all, there must be a purpose in suffering and dying. . . . Frankl is fond of quoting Nietzsche, 'He who has a *why* can bear with almost any *how*' . . . But no man can tell another what this purpose is. Each must find out for himself, and must accept the responsibility that his answer prescribes. If he survives *he will continue to grow in spite of all indignities*" (p. xiii; emphasis added).

This might sound like a healthy kind of that old pagan Greek virtue, stoicism, meaning courage and endurance in the face of pain, or even indifference to pain (also to pleasure). There are worse defects a person could be accused of than stoicism. But Frankl is no pagan; he is a believing Jew whose faith in God and whose religious belief grew rather than diminished during his incarceration. Allport's observation is again to the point: "Unlike many European existentialists, Frankl is neither pessimistic nor antireligious. On the contrary, for a writer who faces fully the ubiquity of suffering and the forces of evil, he takes a surprisingly hopeful view of man's capacity to transcend his predicament and discover an adequate guiding truth" (p. xiv). Strangely or not, Frankl often uses the Christian expression, "bearing his cross."

Hope: The Sustaining Power

Hope is the sustaining force in Frankl, as in the other prisoners who refused to go down to defeat. The story Frankl tells of a young woman whose death he witnessed could be true of him as well:

> This young woman knew that she would die in the next few days. But when I talked to her she was cheerful in spite of this knowledge. "I am grateful that fate has hit me so hard," she told me. "In my former life I was spoiled and did not take spiritual accomplishments seriously." Pointing through the window of the hut, she said, "This tree here is the only friend I have in

my loneliness." Through that window she could see just one branch of a chestnut tree, and on the branch there were two blossoms. "I often talk to this tree," she said to me. I was startled and didn't quite know how to take her words. Was she delirious? Did she have occasional hallucinations? Anxiously I asked her if the tree replied. "Yes." What did it say to her? She answered, "It said to me, 'I am here—I am here—I am life, eternal life' " (p. 109).

Frankl comes back again and again to the truth that it is possible for man to transcend his predicament and to discover an adequate guiding truth through it all. "One could retain human dignity even in a concentration camp." One could go on and on, with mounting admiration for Frankl and his fellow prisoners. He quoted with approval from Dostoevski: "There is only one thing I dread: not to be worthy of my sufferings." Frankl and his companions bore witness to the fact that the last inner freedom, that of freely choosing "one's attitude in a given set of circumstances, the ultimate freedom," can never be lost. *They* were indeed all worthy of their sufferings. And this was their free choice. "It is this spiritual freedom—which can never be taken away—that makes life meaningful and purposeful" (p. 106).

Woe to anyone who saw no sense in his life. What Frankl found tragic was the attitude of a man who said, "I have nothing to expect from life any more." His comment to that was: "We had to teach despairing men that it didn't really matter what we expected from life, but rather what life expected from us. We needed to stop asking about the meaning of life and instead think of ourselves as those being questioned by life" (p. 122).

It is astonishing that there is not a single word of hatred for their oppressors either in the account of the author or in the attitude of the prisoners. Towards the end of his ordeal, he is asked one night to speak to the rest of the men in his hut. "Finally, I spoke of our sacrifice, which had meaning in every case. It was in the nature of this sacrifice that it should be pointless in the normal world, the world of material success. But in reality our sacrifice did have a meaning. Those of us who had any religious faith, I said frankly, could understand without difficulty" (p. 132).

Finally, when liberation comes Frankl tells of walking in the green meadow outside his camp:

> Larks rose to the sky and I could hear their joyous song. There was no one to be seen for miles around; there was nothing but the wide earth and sky and the larks' jubilation and the freedom of space. I stopped, looked around, and up to the sky—and then I went down on my knees. At that moment there was very little I knew of myself or of the world—I had but one sentence in mind—always the same: "I called to the Lord from my

narrow prison and He answered me in the freedom of space."

> How long I knelt there and repeated this sentence memory can no longer recall. But I know that on that day, in that hour, my new life started. Step for step I progressed, until I again became a human being (p. 142).

It is truly a magnificent story, the best evidence I have ever seen of the potential contained in suffering for re-creating the human person and making a man or woman a better, more developed, more rounded human being. This surely can provide at least a partially satisfying understanding of the problem of suffering. And yet, there must be more meaning in suffering than this re-creative potential, important though it may be.

Creation in Labor

It is that deeper meaning that I shall try to discuss here, using ideas borrowed from one of my favorite writers, Fr. Michel Quoist. In chapter 7 of his book *Christ Is Alive* on the mystery of redemption, Quoist has some very satisfying ideas about the meaning and purpose of suffering in the life of the Christian. Following St. Paul, Quoist sees suffering as an essential element in the redemption of the universe. Not just the spiritual element in man, but the whole of creation is in the need of salvation:

> I consider that the sufferings of this present time are not worth comparing with the glory that is to be revealed to us. For the creation waits with eager longing for the revealing of the sons of God; for the creation was subjected to futility, not of its own will but by the will of him who subjected it in hope; because the creation itself will be set free from its bondage to decay and obtain the glorious liberty of the children of God. We know that the whole creation has been groaning in travail together until now; and not only the creation, but we ourselves, who have been the first fruits of the Spirit, groan inwardly as we wait for adoption as sons, the redemption of our bodies. For in this hope we were saved" (Rom. 8:18-24).

I concede that this idea of the whole of creation being "in labor" in the hope of arriving at better things may not be very thrilling for most Christians. To be sure, they want to see meaning and purpose in their suffering, but the evolution of the universe into a higher spiritualized creation which is so dear to St. Paul is much too unreal for them. But it is a tempting and as yet quite unexplored idea.

I admire Father Quoist's ability to provide correctives for some popular ideas about suffering. He does not believe that God sends us suffering in order to punish us or even to make us better persons. Nor does God "try those he loves." "God does not act out of emotion, or illogically, or imperfectly. He does not spank his children. On the contrary, he comforts them and helps them to bear the hurt" (p. 97). Quoist does not approve of those Christians who can "bless the will of God." "We do not need people who are resigned and submissive. We need men; men who will fight against suffering. And when suffering refuses to submit, when evil refuses to change, then man must make use of the grace of Jesus Christ to convert it into good" (p. 97).

This does not mean that Quoist would disagree with Frankl's thesis that suffering can and does help us to grow and develop into nobler personalities. On the contrary. He accepts that comforting possibility, but he insists on going further. I gather from Quoist's use of St. Paul that our human view of suffering has to begin with Christ—in his mind and his heart, rather than in our own particular circumstances. In other words, it is impossible for us to have any satisfying concept of our human suffering until and unless we see Christ taking upon himself not only the sins of the world but also the sorrows, the pains, the deaths of us, his members, his brothers and sisters.

Quoist does not quote him, but I was reminded of the prophecy of Isaiah:

> Surely he has borne our griefs
>   and carried our sorrows. . . .
> But he was wounded for our
>   transgressions,
>   he was bruised for our iniquities;
> upon him was the chastisement that
>   made us whole,
>   and with his stripes we are healed.
> All we like sheep have gone astray;
>   we have turned every one to his
>   own way;
> and the Lord has laid on him
>   the iniquity of us all (53:4-6).

Is it too unrealistic to claim that Christ died six million times in the Nazi concentration camps and that he continues to die with every human death until the end of time?

The Redemptive Power of Suffering

"When we love, we suffer with the suffering of the one we love," says Quoist (p. 100); and he applies this to Jesus on the cross—to the nature of his suffering. "In a very real sense, he was a victim of his own love. His Incarnation was a success. He had incorporated all of humanity into himself. On Calvary, all of mankind was joined together in him. The whole of his Body was nailed to the cross." And when Jesus cried out, "Father, into your hands I commit my spirit," that spirit was enriched with all of humanity, past, present and future. "It was all of man, all of human history, and all of creation, now reoriented by Love towards

Eternal Love. It was the redemption of the world." Three days later the Father gave life back to his Son, not only his own life, but the life of all mankind, a life now purified and recreated by love. And that is ultimate redemption.

I can well understand that for the prisoner in a dank jail cell or for a pain-wracked victim of disease on a hospital bed, or the worry-ridden parents of a strayed teenager, such ideas may sound alien and irrelevant. Perhaps we have not yet sufficiently trained ourselves to feel personally and to accept the great love that Christ has for each of us. Perhaps that experience is one of the special "graces" of a "happy death." The article "Living With Dying" in the May 1, 1978 *Newsweek* pointed out that the greatest need of the dying is relief from pain *and* closer contact with loved ones. It might well be that the availability of loved ones to the dying person is the only way that the love of Christ for him can be brought home to the dying patient.

The key to the discovery of meaning in suffering, the element that alone can make it endurable, is the conviction that one's suffering can and will bring about greater good for one's loved ones and even for the world. For the person of faith, what greater proof can he have that his suffering is worthwhile than the conviction that he shares in the very redemptive act of Christ himself? It is a redemptive act that is going on now in the suffering of this particular Christian, having had its beginning with the Lord's death on Calvary. "It is the Spirit himself bearing witness with our spirit that we are children of God, and if children, then heirs, heirs of God and fellow heirs with Christ, *provided we suffer with him in order that we may also be glorified with him"* (Rom. 8:17).

One does not have to "accept" or "be resigned" to suffering. I insist that we can and must do all that is humanly possible to overcome it and to seek cures for it by every natural and medical means possible. But there comes a time in everyone's life when the inevitability of suffering and eventually dying must be faced. Then it is that our human freedom is faced with the decision either to accept or to rebel. Quoist agrees with Frankl in insisting that the worth and effectiveness of suffering becomes operative in a person only when he gives it his free and loving consent. Then and only then does the mystery of redemption belong completely to the suffering Christian.

When this free and loving consent is given, the Christian is ready to make his own the tremendously satisfying and joyous meaning of St. Paul's mysterious comment: "Now I rejoice in my sufferings for your sake, and in my flesh I complete what is lacking in Christ's afflictions for the sake of his body, that is, the Church" (Col. 1:24). We, who are trained to think of Christ's redemptive death and resurrection as the greatest deed ever accomplished by any being, can ask ourselves what possibly could be lacking in Christ's sufferings. The only possible answer has to be simply that the only element that is missing in Jesus' suffering is our free acceptance of it together with the grateful, loving gift of our own suffering to be made part of his universal, redeeming deed, keeping in mind all the time that "it is not suffering that redeems, but only love redeems."

The Way of The Cross Now

It has been said more than once that Christianity is not a spectator sport. It calls for participation, for the personal involvement of each member. Once we express our willingness to suffer, the Way of the Cross made by Jesus along Jerusalem's streets to Calvary ceases to be just a pious memory for us. The Way of the Cross is going on now in our world, and we are the ones bearing the cross:

> The Way of the Cross is being followed by the whole of humanity, by all the members of Jesus Christ. This Way of the Cross comprises all the streets of humanity, all the paths of history and of time. It runs through man's torn body, through his divided heart, through his convulsed being. . . . The cross dominates the world and time as it dominated Jerusalem. For sin too remains and unfolds in time, just as Redemption is a living and continuing action—an uninterrupted mystery of love which shall last as long as the race of man.   Quoist, p. 104.

Every person's sickbed is an altar, and the one suffering on it is both priest and victim, as was Christ himself. So too, the figure on the crucifix is Christ, priest and victim, but it is also the Christian who suffers with Christ.

It is not true, as I have said, that Christ tries those he loves, as even the great St. Teresa seems to have believed (she is said to have complained to the Lord, "That's why you have so few friends!") But the fact is that if we really want to encounter Christ, the surest meeting-place is in the midst of suffering.

A Young Woman's Experience

This truth, as a matter of fact, is not just a pleasant conjecture. It was verified in a remarkable article called "Pain: Meaning and Purpose in the Life of a Christian" by a twenty-two-year-old Luther College senior who died of Lupus in the fall of 1977, just shortly after she finished writing the article for the National Lutheran Youth Encounter newspaper. The article is reminiscent of the acts of the early martyrs, and like the Frankl book it is a beautiful testimony to the power and potential of suffering in bringing a young woman to the perfection not only of human personal expansion but also of theological and mystical depth of meaning.

Kristi Hermeier does not pretend even to begin to solve the enigma of pain, since this enigma "reflects the mystery of God. It begins a journey of trust." But she does have extraordinary insights into that mystery. She says it is only when our efforts to rationalize and eradicate seemingly useless pain are exhausted, and we reach the end of our rope that Christ's strength becomes available to us. If the mystery were fully explained or explainable, there would be no crisis. But most of all, there would be no need for our faith walk with God. "Pain and suffering are not some type of Cosmic Character Builders sent by the Almighty. They are, however, used by Him to strengthen and cleanse our relationship to Him and to each other." She agrees with Frankl and Quoist, without, I am quite sure, ever having read them.

Kristi believes that fear, and all the other "negative" emotions that follow it, can be healthy, normative, and even creative forces in our lives:

> They become evil when we allow them to immobilize and blind us to the lessons we *could* be learning. Personally, I have chosen to concentrate on my life as it is now. I cannot wish the pain away, or ignore it. It has become a very real part of who I am. But what I can do, whether I am suffering or not, is to concentrate on the health that exists inside of me. *The acceptance of my human condition, in the light of God's promises, leads to a fresh hope, and a new peace of mind.*

In studying the Bible she became amazed at the incredible sensitivity of Jesus towards humans. She says that we all need that same kind of sensitivity for those who suffer, remembering always that the suffering Christian lives with a constant reminder of his frailty. There is no question that God heals, she maintains, but we just do not always understand how he does so:

> Ours is not a total theology of glory. We live, as Martin Luther puts it, 'in the shadow of the Cross.' We must take this cross seriously, with *all* its implications. There is no victory without defeat, glory without shame, or health without suffering. I cannot say that I have been healed of my disease (not yet anyway). I can say, however, that *I have been healed of many other things through my disease"* [this idea is so remarkable that I added the emphasis]. I've never felt as loved as when I discovered I had Lupus. I saw Christ alive through the caring of his Church, and I experienced first hand the sensitivity of His followers. Healing with suffering . . . victory in the shadows.

She admits that, simply because she is human, it is impossible for her to accept the pain and to trust all times. "When I am in pain, I'm constantly reminded of my mortality. But I'm also reminded that in the shadow (or light?) of the cross, and God's promise of redemption through Christ, *there is hope."*

Kristi has valuable advice for the friends and loved ones of the stricken person. What they need more than anything else is honesty:

A person is rarely alone in their pain. If there are people around who care, they will be suffering also. If you find yourself in that boat, don't be afraid to admit you're afraid. Be honest about your feelings, hurts, and fears. If you're angry or confused, talk about it, it helps. Be supportive of the suffering person, but don't pity them. Let them know you care by being yourself, that is after all who they love and need. Accept the ills of those you're dealing with as part of themselves. A very real part. Most of all, don't underestimate them. They will fight the pain, fear, and desperation hand in hand with you, and with our Lord.

She ends with the wish and hope that her reflections on her experience of pain will help her loved ones and friends with their pains when they come. "I hope it [the article], helps the next time you hold me, or someone like me when they cry. I hope most of all, you use your experience in suffering to grow in sensitivity, and that our God will burn into your conscience your need of Him in health as well as in pain. . . . May you be guided *by the tender compassion of our bleeding Savior.*"

What remains to be said after that? She surely must know in her new existence that the meaning in suffering that she glimpsed so delicately in her last days is now a reality greater and more glorious than in anticipation. I've spoken of the redemptive element in human suffering that everyone yearns for. Only God can know how many persons of all ages whose lives she touched during her short lifetime, and only he can know how many now possess insights into the value of suffering that without her they might never have discovered.

Facing the Mystery of Death

Until a few years ago very few people talked or wrote about death—the old conspiracy of silence idea. Death may have been the most ordinary fact of daily life, but generally death competed with the hope of relief from suffering and was submerged in a conspiracy of silence. The person who first began to speak and write openly about death was the psychologist Dr. Elizabeth Kübler-Ross, her book *On Death and Dying,* published in 1969, having become a best seller. Through her study and observation of hundreds of dying persons, she concluded that a terminally ill person goes through five stages in the course of facing his "end-time."

It is quite evident that each of these stages seems perfectly natural from the human psychological point of view. The dying person's first reaction to the news of terminal sickness is *denial*—No! This may have happened to others, it can never happen to me! Denial is usually accompanied by a sense of *isolation,* the desire to be alone. Then almost immediately *anger* sets in. This in turn gives way to a kind of *bargaining* —the effort to "make a deal," to exchange the death-sentence for some less definitive, though possibly costly, remuneration. When this effort comes to appear fruitless, the natural reaction is likely to be *depression,* which, however, usually proves to be temporary. It is only after the sick person has gone through those five stages that he arrives at the final stage, *acceptance.*

Some, if not all, of these stages—and especially the final one of acceptance—are evident in the Kristi Hermeier story. The psychologist Charles Garfield also speaks of the low-level fears experienced by the dying—of "bodily deterioration, separation and loss of family and friends. But beyond all that is the absolute terror of ceasing to be" *(Newsweek* [May 1, 1978], p. 53).

Surely, for the believing Christian that absolute terror can be tempered and even hopefully obliterated by what Fr. Robert Morneau of Silver Lake College, Manitowoc, Wisconsin, proposes as a sixth stage in the Kubler-Ross list, namely, that of *expectation* or *anticipation.* In this article "Beyond Death and Dying" in the April 1978 *Sisters Today,* Father Morneau vehemently rejects the materialist-rationalist, existential attitude that death is the end of the ball game, that it is the supreme evil, that is is meaningless and that life is therefore absurd.

He proceeds to illustrate his thesis of the sixth stage of expectation or anticipation by quoting from the lives and teachings of Socrates, St. Paul, Jesus, and C. S. Lewis. In each of these men Morneau senses an initial rebellion and reluctance to exchange life in this world for that of the next world; and, like Frankl, Quoist, and Kristi Hermeier, he emphasizes the need for a free choice of death by the one facing it. To arrive at the stage of expectation, it is absolutely necessary for the sick person to be able to say YES to death, even as did St. Paul and Jesus. Morneau shows how the whole experience of the "Paschal mystery"— of participation in the death-resurrection of Christ—permeates the history of Christianity. "To live in Jesus is to accept the whole package of sorrow and joy, death and life, the cross and the crown" (p. 523).

C. S. Lewis, the popular English writer and radio speaker of several decades ago, frequently referred to the need to look forward to unending happiness. His first reaction to tragedy in his own life caused by the death of his beloved wife was one of almost overwhelming grief. Full of self-pity, he soon found that there is a great difference between writing *about* suffering and experiencing it himself. Fortunately, he recorded his personal reaction to the tragedy, and the latter part of his journal (published later under the title *A Grief Observed* shows him emerging from self-pity "into the realization of joy that his wife had attained all that both she and he had hoped and longed for. In Lewis' experience we witness a person who, because of the cultural conditioning of our times, passes through all the stages from denial to acceptance, and yet, because of his faith perspective, adds the sixth stage of expectation" (Morneau, p. 525).

Each of the four men quoted by Morneau—Socrates, Paul, Jesus, and Lewis—loved life and took great satisfaction and joy in working for others. St. Paul was passionately concerned with preaching the Gospel of Christ. Love for Christ impelled him. Yet he eventually concluded that death was the most desirable of all human experiences. He longed to suffer and die with Christ so as to be able to share his glory. Here are some quotes:

> For to me to live is Christ, and to die is gain. If it is to be life in the flesh, that means fruitful labor for me. Yet, which I shall choose I cannot tell. I am hard pressed between the two. My desire is to depart and be with Christ, for that is far better. But to remain in the flesh is more necessary on your account (Phil. 1:21-24).

*   *   *

> [All I want is] that I may know him [Christ] and the power of his resurrection, and may share his sufferings, becoming like him in his death, that if possible I may attain the resurrection from the dead (Phil. 3:10-11).

*   *   *

> For I am sure that neither death, nor life, nor angels, nor principalities, nor things present, nor things to come, nor powers, nor height, nor depth, nor anything else in all creation will be able to separate us from the love of God in Christ Jesus our Lord (Rom. 8:38-39).

Morneau concludes his beautiful article with a quote from the book *Spirituality for Religious Life* by Fr. Robert Faricy, S.J.:

> But by His death and resurrection, Christ has transformed death from a blind alley into a passage to glory. At my death, I will be completely fragmented, torn apart, disintegrated. And, on the other side of death, Christ will put me together again, this time completely centered on Him" (p. 75).

The Ultimate Meaning: The Resurrection

This brings us to the ultimate meaning of suffering and dying, namely, the resurrection. Kristi Hermeier says that "ours is not a total theology of glory," and she quotes Luther to the effect that we live in the shadow of the Cross. But we know that for Jesus, his Cross, his Good Friday, was followed by Easter Sunday and resurrection. For the Christian to find satisfaction and a sense of the worthwhileness of life only in suffering and to forget about the resurrection of Jesus is to be but a partial Christian. Christ died and rose again from the dead. So with the Christian. The mystery of suffering and of redemption must also include the mystery of the resurrection.

And it is good to emphasize that the resurrection is indeed a mystery about which we know very little. This includes the very way in which we look at our personal resurrection. We have been trained to think about the resurrection of our bodies only on the last day; and until that last day our souls have to languish in heaven, yearning for reunion with their bodies. But St. Paul seems to indicate that our personal resurrection has already taken place. He writes to the Ephesians:

> But God, who is rich in mercy, out of the great love with which he loved us, even when we were dead . . . together with Christ (by grace you have been saved), and raised us up with him, and made us sit with him in the heavenly places in Christ Jesus, that in the coming ages he might show the immeasurable riches of his grace in kindness toward us in Christ Jesus (2:4-7).

The preface of the Mass of the Dead has a fascinating statement:

> Lord, for your faithful people life is changed, not ended.
> When the body of our earthly dwelling lies in death
> we gain an everlasting dwelling place in heaven.

It is difficult to conceive of existence in heaven from now until the general resurrection on the last day as being that of disembodied spirits. Perhaps speculation on the matter is a waste of time. The essence of the Christian idea of the resurrection is the hope that our personal Way of the Cross will inevitably bring us to full participation in the glory of Christ's victory, his resurrection.

Because of the Christian's belief in the resurrection, the greatest suffering and the greatest joy can co-exist in one and the same life; they can be intimately interconnected with one another (Quoist, p. 115). And this joy is no transient pleasure nor blind optimism, but rather it is "calm, the interior serenity, and the profound peace which permeate and emanate from a man who, notwithstanding a torn heart and body, and despite the suffering of mankind and the world, believes with all his strength in the victory of the Savior. And he believes this without for an instant forgetting or denying the existence of suffering and sin, and without giving up the fight against them" (p. 115).

In a word, through suffering and dying, the words of St. Irenaeus are finally and completely verified: "The glory of God is man fully alive." In death the human person reaches the ultimate stage in his communion with the mystery of Christ and his own personal development. As in life he shared in the mystery of creation, of the incarnation and the redemption, so in death he achieves the highest degree of glorification, the sharing in the mystery of Christ's resurrection.

Value of the New Funeral Ritual

No Christian ritual better illustrates the full meaning of suffering and dying better than the new funeral and burial rite given to us by the Vatican Council. It is so beautiful and full of meaning, even of excitement, that I tell my students with only a hint of facetiousness that I can hardly wait for my own funeral. In contrasting the new rite with the old, with its black vestments and, above all, the somber Gregorian singing, especially of the *Dies Irae* ("O Day of Wrath") that came out of the gloomiest period of the Middle Ages, I do not mean to deny beauty to the old rite or to indicate that its tone was wholly lugubrious. In fact, the funeral Mass preface just quoted (we now have a choice of several) was the only one formerly used. And the Gospel of the old Masses can be used now, as well. I simply want to indicate that the emphasis in the new burial ritual is no longer on death, no longer on judgment *(Dies Irae—*"O Day of Wrath"), but rather on victory with and in Christ. Rather, the emphasis is on the resurrection of Jesus and on the pledge of resurrection which Christ's victory has provided for this follower of Christ who has reached the goal of his pilgrimage. There is no note of sadness or grief in any part of the ceremony, but rather of joy, of triumph, of victory.

In the Catholic burial ceremony the priest greets the coffin and the funeral party at the entrance of the church, praying: "Praised be God, the Father of our Lord Jesus Christ, the Father of mercies, and the God of all consolation! He comforts us in all our afflictions and thus enables us to comfort those who are in trouble, with the same consolation we have received from him." This greeting sets the tone for the whole ceremony.

As the celebrant blesses the body with holy water, he recalls the dead person's baptism in which he (she) was inserted into the death and resurrection of Christ—a theme that continues when a white pall, a remembrance of the baptismal robe, is spread over the coffin with the words, "On the day of his (her) baptism, N. put on Christ. In the day of Christ's coming, may he (she) be clothed with glory." A short prayer for a welcome reception into the company of the saints follows and then the procession up the aisle of the church, headed by a person carrying the Easter candle—chief symbol of the risen Christ. This candle stands at the head of the coffin throughout the entire ceremony.

There is a wide choice of readings from the Old and New Testaments and the Gospels. Again, the theme of most of the readings is that of resurrection, victory, triumph. In the Eucharistic Prayer of the Mass (the priest has a choice of several), after the consecration of the bread and wine the prayer is interrupted to commemorate the deceased. In Eucharistic Prayer III is the following:

Remember N.
In baptism he (she) died with Christ:
may be (she) also share his resurrection,
when Christ will raise our mortal bodies
and make them like his own in glory.
Welcome into your kingdom our departed brothers and sisters,
and all who have left this world in your friendship.
There we hope to share in your glory.
when every tear will be wiped away.
On that day we shall see you, our God, as you are.
We shall become like you
and praise you for ever through Christ our Lord,
from whom all good things come.

Again, there is considerable choice in the prayers and readings that conclude the burial ceremony. Here is a sample of the prayer for the final commendation which takes place in church:

Our brother (sister) has gone to his (her) rest in the peace of Christ. With faith and hope in eternal life, let us commend him (her) to the loving mercy of our Father, and assist him (her) with our prayers. He (she) became God's son (daughter) through baptism and was often fed at the table of our Lord. May the Lord now welcome him (her) to the table of God's children in heaven, and, with all the saints, may he (she) inherit the promise of eternal life.

Let us also pray to the Lord for ourselves. May we who mourn be reunited one day with our brother (sister). Together may we meet Christ Jesus when he, who is our life, shall appear in his glory.

There is a song of farewell (again, several choices):

Choir
I know that my Redeemer lives, and on the
last day I shall rise again;
in my body I shall look on God, my Savior.
All repeat:
I know that my Redeemer lives, and on the
last day I shall rise again;
in my body I shall look on God, my Savior.
Choir
I myself shall see him; my own eyes will gaze on him.
All
in my body I shall look on God, my Savior.
Choir
This is the hope I cherish in my heart.
All
in my body I shall look on God, my Savior.
All repeat:
I know that my Redeemer lives, and on the

> last day I shall rise again;
> in my body I shall look on God, my Savior.

The church commendation and farewell concludes with a choice of antiphons, typical of which is:

> I am the resurrection and the life.
> The man who believes in me will live
> even if he dies,
> and every living person
> who puts his faith in me
> will never suffer eternal death.

At the cemetery, after the blessing of the grave, the body is again sprinkled with holy water and incensed, after which the priest may say:

> Let us pray for our brother (sister)
> to our Lord Jesus Christ,
> who said:
> "I am the resurrection and the life.
> The man who believes in me will live
> even if he dies,
> and every living person
> who puts his faith in me
> will never suffer eternal death."

The theme of the resurrection characterizes the rest of the prayers at the cemetery, as it has the entire ceremony, the final words being:

> We commend our brother (sister) to the Lord:
> may the Lord receive him (her) into his peace
> and raise up his (her) body on the last day.

Songs filled with alleluias and rejoicing characterize the entire ceremony from beginning to end. As I have said, the contrast between the old Requiem Masses and the new Catholic Burial Rite is dramatic. There may be objections to some of the changes in the liturgy of the Church since Vatican II, but I have never heard anyone complain about the new Burial Rite or express a preference for the old one. The Easter candle, the alleluias, the constantly recurring theme of the resurrection, the joyous songs, and the readings in the Mass all combine to create such a joyous mood of celebration that one rarely sees tears any more.

The title of this chapter is "Coming to Terms With Suffering, Pain, Dying." The dominant impression here might have been that "Coming to terms" is a difficult, if not impossible, achievement. I do not intend now to diminish that impression nor to soft-pedal the difficulty. To suffer is to die a little, and most of us die daily by degrees. Nevertheless, I would like to conclude with the strong conviction that, if there is any experience in the Catholic repertoire that can make any sense out of the mystery and pain of suffering and dying, it is the experience of being present at a Catholic funeral—either as a spectator or as the guest of honor whose victory over suffering and death has just been so joyfully celebrated!

10

The Christian in the World

The Christian does not live in a vacuum. He should not think of his religious life as having no bearing on his daily living. On the contrary, his religion should contribute to the quality of his daily living, and daily living in turn should enrich his religion. If one does not help the other, there is something wrong either with a person's conception of daily life and work or with his understanding of religion.

Daily living is a composite of a person's vocational, professional, social, political, and religious life. It involves coming to terms with wealth and possessions, sexuality, leisure, pleasure in all its varieties—in a word, with anything and everything that in any way conditions the human person for better or for worse. To present guidelines to cover all the problems arising from these areas of life is a difficult and dangerous task.

On the face of it, there seems to be considerable incompatibility between one's relationship with God (religion) and one's "secular" life in the world. I quite firmly believe that the incompatibility is only apparent, that it is possible to believe in and serve both God and man, and that there can be rightful and salutary relationships to all the areas just mentioned without any diminution of one's religious life. To propose an either-or choice between God on the one hand and man and daily life on the other is to propose a false alternative.

There is a variety of vocations, as we have already seen. It is obvious that God calls the majority of his children to the vocation of being his disciple and witness while living as a layman or laywoman "in the world." The lay person is not a monk or a religious who seeks God within the context of community life in a convent or monastery, and it would not be right or healthy for a lay person to aspire to the spirituality and the lifestyle of a monk or a nun. To be sure, some characteristic practices of the religious life, such as retreats, periods of silence and solitude (when possible), a disciplined prayer life, including spiritual reading, can and should be cultivated by the lay person, but only a condition that these practices help to enrich and provide new and refreshing purpose and vision to his life.

Work

Happy the woman or man whose work is indeed work and not a "job." It seems necessary to make the distinction, even though it may be offensive to some. Understood in the ideal sense, work implies creative and personal effort by the worker. It is a constant challenge to one's attention and to whatever creative talent and skill a person possesses. The result of work in this sense is satisfaction and joy that something new and original has been brought into the world. But not everyone can be an artist, a discoverer, a teacher, a musician, a carpenter, a doctor, cook, inventor, farmer (add whatever other profession you desire).

It is not possible for modern society to exist without factories, mines, railroads, etc. where the employee simply puts in time and effort, but not much more of himself. There is little that is creative and satisfying about a job on an assembly line other than drawing one's paycheck. And yet this is the way millions of Christians make a living.

The jobholder need not, however, feel any inferiority simply because he has a job instead of work. Both a job and work in the creative sense can and must be "redeemed." With regard to a job, the best approach is to stress that it is not what is done that is important but rather the person who does it—the attitude, the motivation of the person who does the job. There may or may not be much satisfaction in the old saying that "work can be redeemed by love," but I think we have to accept that possibility or run the risk of utter boredom and possible despair. In addition to love, every person working on a job ought to be able to put enough personal attention and creativity into the task to avoid becoming a mere robot.

Working at a job with love as a motivation (love for God, for one's family) surely makes it possible for a person to find God in the daily routine of the job. The best reason for God's being present might well be precisely because the effort required is "merely" a job. But the person working on a job needs to find some other creative work or hobby that can occupy his leisure. To neglect or allow one's creative instincts to diminish or disappear is to run the risk of becoming dehumanized (which is or can be equivalent to being de-Christianized).

I confess that I have mixed feelings about the old notion of "offering it up." On the face of it, it seems like a kind of unhappy acquiescence to a bad situation which in turn is made into a reluctant gift to the Lord. What the Lord wants of us is not the giving up or the gift of things and situations. He wants the gift of our selves, our hearts. Working at a non-creative job may better be understood as part of the hardship of life, the cross that the Christian is invited by Christ to bear daily. And surely any difficult, boring, and tiresome work can be seen as redemptive in the sense that St. Paul indicated when he wrote to the Colossians: "Now I rejoice in my sufferings for your sake, and in my flesh I complete what is lacking in Christ's afflictions for the sake of his body, that is, the church" (1:24).

On the other hand, why not "offer it up?" Catholic theology, rooted in St. Peter's first letter, indicates that every baptized Christian shares in the priesthood of Christ, enabling him "to offer spiritual sacrifices acceptable to God through Jesus Christ" (2:5). It undoubtedly requires considerable faith to see a non-creative job as a gift worth giving to the Lord, but no one may downgrade or diminish the tremendous value and dignity inherent in being a member of Christ's Body and a sharer in his priesthood (which makes everything a person is and does redemptive and beneficial to the entire Body of Christ.)

It is much too easy to forget that members of Christ's Body share in his very own life and work, that therefore there is nothing a member of the Body does that is unrelated to the Father and to the entire Body of Christ. It is not merely an act of "offering work and suffering up to God," but it is realizing that Christ is with one in the actual accomplishing of the work or suffering. One's work is therefore redeemed by the very fact that a member of Christ's Body, one with him by a bond of life and love, is doing the work.

The appreciation of this truth will surely bring considerable satisfaction to the worker and will also prompt him to give his best to carrying out the work. Carelessness, ineptitude, reluctance to grow in one's skill or craft, slovenliness—all these assume a particular degree of wrongdoing in the light of one's membership in Christ. To be unwilling to grow in one's professional skill and work is to begin to die. We die soon enough without that!

Coming to Terms with Wealth and Possessions

I recall being happily surprised many years ago when a successful lawyer told me that he did not feel that he *owned* anything, but that he considered himself to be only a steward of whatever wealth and property his profession had brought him. It seemed then, and even more now, to have been a beautiful ideal, straight out of the Gospels, but one wonders how widespread such an ideal is among Christ's followers today. The right of private ownership of property is surely sanctioned by the Roman Church, sometimes almost to the extent of diminishing the ideal of stewardship just mentioned.

In the Beatitudes, Jesus laid down a principle that corresponds perfectly with the ideal of stewardship: "Blessed are the poor in spirit, for theirs is the kingdom of heaven" (Mt. 5:3). Fr. Bruce Vawter writes that the Sermon on the Mount, of which the Beatitudes are a part, "is not a collection of idealistic poetry but a proclamation of Christian values . . . a realistic exhortation to a standard of virtue that is possible only through the power given by the Spirit of God" *(The Four Gospels* [Garden City, N.Y.: Doubleday, 1967], p. 119).

When Jesus called the poor in spirit "blessed," he was surely not proposing poverty in the literal sense as the desirable social condition. Far from it. Thank God the time is past when priests used to try to console the poor on the grounds that they would get their reward in the life to come. And I doubt that any modern priest would dare to preach a sermon "On the Eminent Dignity of the Poor" (as Bishop Bossuet did to the well-fed nobles of Louis XIV's seventeenth-century French court), praising poverty because it provides the rich with the very special opportunity to practice charity!

"Blessed are the poor *in spirit,*" Jesus said. What does "poor in spirit" mean? Father Vawter says that it means having the spirit, the mind, the attitude of standing before God naked and defenseless, trusting in him and in him alone. And this kind of poverty of spirit is the indispensable quality of being a Christian. "It is a quality far more easily asserted than lived, and far more embracing than to be, or to think that we are, 'detached' from worldly goods" (p. 120).

Such language may sound somewhat frightening to any Christian, lay or clerical. Who can reach and live on such a lofty level? A satisfactory answer is not readily forthcoming, but we can surely remind ourselves that growth towards an ideal of Christlikeness and progress in that growth is primarily the work of divine grace. But we can surely help it along with a spirit of "detachment." This is the kind of mentality that refuses to allow anyone to be *possessed by his possessions* to such an extent that one is in danger of becoming miserly and avaricious.

Although the wealthy might seem to be in special danger of succumbing to such a condition, it is by no means confined to that class. The poorest of the poor can become overly possessive of the little they own. It is entirely possible to be poor in actuality—to possess little or nothing— but not to be poor in spirit. If a Christian is in earnest about avoiding the vice of possessiveness, the best test and cure is sharing one's possessions. In the Beatitudes, Jesus counsels his followers to seek and find happiness, not so much in having as in giving and sharing. It is only in giving and sharing that one can attain genuine inner freedom.

This ties in again with the idea and ideal of stewardship. God shares his riches with us so that we can act as his agent in caring for the needy. But when we mention the poor and needy and the right Christian attitude towards them, we have to be careful not to feel that we have met our obligations towards them when we give alms. There is the further and perhaps even more difficult task of working for the ideal social conditions so that the poor can get jobs and help themselves. However, to work out and propose a program for achieving that goal is beyond the scope of this chapter.

How Much?

A New Catechism makes an excellent observation that we are never done giving: "Jesus said that we must love our neighbor as ourselves, and this is an endless process" (New York: Herder and Herder, 1967, p. 435). When Jesus was asked, "Who is my neighbor?" he replied with the well-known parable of the Good Samaritan. This man definitely went out of his way to give both of his time and of his money to care for the unfortunate man who fell among robbers and was so desperately robbed.

The parable of the Good Samaritan provides us with a lofty standard in giving. What he gave even more than his time and money was his concern for the unfortunate victim—a Jew whom he did not know and who, if he were true to the prevailing unfriendly attitude towards the Samaritans, would have undoubtedly scorned him. If Jesus presents the Samaritan to us as an ideal model, it was not only for his generosity, but for his "heart," his caring attitude. This is the least we can strive for in our lives.

It is also the extent of Christ's guidance for the question, "How much?" He simply does not tell us how much. He leaves that to our own judgment as persons of faith, charity, and trust. Surely one does not have to give and give to the extent of endangering the livelihood and the future of his family. A husband and father certainly has the right to provide for the education of his children and to look to the future when his earning power will be ended and he has to rely on what he has saved through the years.

But whether or not it is proper for me to ask the question, it does seem appropriate to wonder if anyone needs to live extravagantly. Could we not all get along on a more reasonable and frugal manner of living, eating and housing? Do we need—and how much real good do we receive from— expensive cars, boats, homes, clothing, furniture, and food? Do we always have to have the latest and best of the products we see and hear advertised so enticingly on TV?

So, in giving to the poor (including the missions and all the vast variety of good and praiseworthy causes whose appeals we receive), it is important to avoid the danger of feeling that one's obligations of giving alms and practicing charity are ever satisfied. It is all too easy to write a check; it is also all too impersonal. (And if the amount is large enough, it can qualify as a tax deduction!) Again the example of the Good Samaritan can give needed guidance for us all. He did not see the robber's victim as a "tax deduction," but as a brother human being. I once met an old Jew who greeted me with the friendliness of an old acquaintance. When I asked him if he knew me, he replied, "Do I have to know your name? You're a human being, aren't you?"

Of course, I am not opposed to writing checks in response to the appeals we receive. But we have to be careful not to feel that we have fulfilled our obligation by writing the check, that the check does not absolve us from more direct and more personal confrontations with the poor. We may never forget the true identity of the unfortunate person whose hand is held out to us. Christ tells us: "I was hungry and you gave me food, I was thirsty and you gave me drink, I was a stranger and you welcomed me. . . . Truly, I say to you, as you did it to one of the least of these my brethren, you did it to me" (Mt. 25:35, 40). The Good Samaritan was probably not aware of this magnificent truth; nevertheless, he acted as though he did. May we all do as well!

"If You Would Be Perfect. . . ."

It seems necessary to say something about the "charism" of poverty. The evangelist Mark relates the incident of the man who knelt at Jesus' feet and asked him:

> "Good Teacher, what must I do to inherit eternal life?" And Jesus said to him, "Why do you call me good? No one is good but God alone. You know the commandments: 'Do you kill, Do not commit adultery, Do not steal, Do not bear false witness, Do not defraud, Honor your father and mother.' " And he said to him, "Teacher, all these I have observed from my youth." And Jesus looking upon him loved him, and said to him, "You lack one thing; go, sell what you have, and give to the poor, and you will have treasure in heaven; and come, follow me" (Mk. 10:17-21).

Then Mark makes one of the saddest observations in the New Testament: "At that saying his countenance fell, and he went away sorrowful; for he had great possessions" (10:22).

Instead of Jesus' comment in Mark, "You lack one thing," Matthew has him saying, "If you would be perfect, go, sell what you possess . . ." (19:21); to which the Oxford Annotated Bible adds this observation:

> Jesus consistently turned men's attention from concern over their own religious standing, calling them to involve themselves in the basic, vital interests of others. Neither wealth, poverty, nor formal piety was so important as sharing in the working out of God's design for all men. Eternal life will be found through utter dependence on God, not through a ritual that wealth makes possible. Oxford University Press,
> (New York: Oxford, 1965), p. 1196.

But back to the Gospel text. Both Mark and Matthew have Jesus reacting to the young man's sad departure in terms that must have been even more troubling and startling to the Jews than to us: "How hard it will be," he says, "for those who have riches to enter the kingdom of God. . . . It is easier for a camel to go through the eye of a needle than for a rich man to enter the kingdom of God" (Mk. 10:23, 25). We have to understand the prevailing sentiment about riches as a sign of divine favor in order to appreciate the astonishment of the disciples when they ask, "Then who can be saved?" And we may doubt that our Lord's response relieved their anxiety: "With men it is impossible, but not with God; for all things are possible with God (Mk. 10:26-27).

The New American Bible in the note to Mt. 19:23-26 states that "Jesus replies that the rich as well as the poor are dependent on God for their salvation." And it seems we'll have to settle for that. History has rejoiced at some of the saints who have taken Jesus' invitation literally and followed it, the best known having been St. Francis of Assisi. In our own day Dorothy Day and her Catholic Worker houses, also Mother Teresa and her followers, have come as close as anyone to a literal living out of the Gospel ideal. But it still remains a charism, a special grace from the Lord, that he hardly seems to expect every disciple to take literally. "If you would be perfect, go, sell what you possess and give to the poor," he says.

And so it seems that the "poor in spirit" mentality is the only workable way of looking upon the ideal. I don't suppose all this means that the rich have to feel guilty about being rich, but perhaps it would be spiritually good for them to worry a little, and perhaps even feel a bit uncomfortable, about their riches. No one has ever quite succeeded in explaining *away* Christ's ideas about the danger of riches. Concerning the disciples' question "Who then can be saved?, *The Jerome Biblical Commentary* says: "The paradox is not softened by the saying that what is impossible with men is possible to God, and this does not mean that it is possible by a miracle for the rich to retain their wealth and still be saved. It means that God makes possible what man finds impossible — the renunciation of riches" (Englewood Cliffs, N.J.: Prentice-Hall, 1968, p. 97).

Everyone—rich, middle class, and the poor—has to be on constant watch for the ever-present danger of becoming possessed by possessions, of succumbing to the vice of avarice which has been described by the modern American author Henry Fairlie, as:

> the love, not so much of possessions, but of possessing. To buy what we do not need, more even that we need, for our pleasure, and for our entertainment, is a love of possessing for its own sake. . . . Avarice is a form of death in life. It is put high among the sins, and we cannot lightly dismiss the severity of Christ's words: "It is easier for a camel to go through the eye of a needle, than for a rich man to enter into the kingdom of God!"
>
> "The Seven Deadly Sins Today," *The New Republic* (October 1, 1977), pp. 23-24.

Coming to Terms with Pleasure

In our world, conditioned as it is by the universality of advertisements aimed at convincing us that we need products and ideas that will satisfy our appetites for amusement and sense-enjoyment, this may seem like a strange and totally irrelevant section. "What's wrong with this author?" you may be tempted to ask. "What's wrong with enjoyment and pleasure?" I can list a lot of things wrong with me, and I can answer the second question in this way: "There's nothing wrong with pleasure, unless. . . ." Or, "There's nothing wrong with pleasure, if. . . ." Hopefully, the conditions contained in the "unless" and the "if" will become specified in the pages to follow.

Readers must surely be aware of the at times sad and unhealthy attitude towards pleasure that many Christians have held through the centuries. There have been followers of Christ who interpreted their discipleship as including abstention from and the condemnation of pleasure of any kind. Some even went so far as to condemn marriage because marriage normally includes the exercise and enjoyment of sexuality. Most of them admitted that intercourse between husband and wife was necessary if the human race was to carry on, but because of sexual pleasure, continuation of the human race depended on a kind of "necessary evil." There have actually been some Christian moralists in past ages who insisted that unless the sexual act was intended for procreation, it was wrong and sinful.

The fruits of this dangerous and heretical thinking persist to our day in the attitude that many parents bequeath to their children, namely, that the human body is shameful and dirty and to be feared. (It must be admitted, on the other hand, that the reaction to the old "puritanical" attitude is not very healthy either; I refer to the widespread and increasing nudity in films, magazines, and even TV programs).

The heading for this section is "Coming to Terms with Pleasure," which is quite a different way of looking on pleasure than thinking of it in terms of "What am I allowed? How far can I go?"

It seems to me that our consideration has to begin with the beginning itself, with the Book of Genesis, where chapter 1, after detailing the story of creation, climaxed by the creation of Adam and Eve, makes the significant remark: "And God saw everything that he had made and behold, it was *very good"* (1:31; emphasis added). (After the creation of the earth with its vegetation, etc., then all the beasts of the earth and the "cattle according to their kinds," the author's remark was simply, "God saw that it was good" [1:25].) The earth and all that is in it reflects the goodness and beauty of God, its Creator, which ought to mean that grateful appreciation of God's creation and the correct use of any of its elements can bring us closer to God.

So there is a very good historical and scriptural basis for the traditional Christian conviction that the world is good, that man, the human being, as a human being (body and spirit, if you will) is good. The Word was made *flesh*—God's own Son became one with us, one of us.

The Right Christian Attitude

I have long believed that the theologian who has best understood the true Christian attitude towards the world with all its goodness and "goodies" was the Dominican Fr. Gerald Vann, whose books were very popular during and immediately after World War II. He in turn had been well trained by an excellent master, St. Thomas Aquinas.

Vann writes:

> We believe that earthly reality is not an illusion, with which we can have no concern if we are to come to God; but on the contrary a sign of His goodness and beauty, which may lead us to Him if we view it aright. It is the whole man, and his environment, that we have to offer to God and in that offering we do not renounce the world, but with Christ, and by the grace of Christ, discover and sanctify it. Rightful contact is indeed *implemented by renunciation; our love of earthly reality grows deeper, stronger, purer, only in so far as it is a growth also in detachment rightly understood, for love*

increases only as self decreases.

Of His Fullness (New York: P.J. Kenedy & Sons, 1939),
p. 26; emphasis added.

Vann is saying that pleasure is good; it can bring us closer to God by reminding us that if things can be so good, how much better must be the Author of all things. Moreover, the gratitude we experience for the Author of all things is also very much a part of the process of arriving at greater union with God through the right use of things. But Vann also implies that there is an element of "danger" (for want of a better term) in an *immoderate* use of things. Food is good, but it can destroy a person if one's hunger for it is not controlled by a higher power in the human person than his appetite. This is above all true of drink. People can be possessed by their appetites—and destroyed—as much as by their possessions.

Accordingly, Father Vann insists: "There is the world-renouncing, and self-renouncing, element; for the picture of engraced man we are here considering cannot leave the fact of sin out of count. *There is in us a bias to what is against our better nature and the will of God;* and if we are to subdue the will and turn it to what is good we must do violence to ourselves" (p. 27; emphasis added).

The question of who or what is in control is crucial for each person, and only that person can supply that answer. There comes a moment in the life of every Christian when he must honestly, without subterfuge, face the problem of the extent to which he is *dependent* on drink, food, tobacco, sweets, TV, or any other physical pleasure that has within it the possibility of taking command over one's life.

To repeat: anything that is good can be used badly. Rightly used, food, drink, sex, etc. can be the material of holiness; wrongly used, they become the material of sin. Vann tells us that there are degrees of indulgence and renunciation which will differ according to the particularities of circumstances, personality, and way of life. "But they should all, from the strictest asceticism to the most generous good-living, be motivated not least by an appreciation of what is either renounced or enjoyed: the very renunciation and enjoyment being referred to God in love of whom they find their motive" (p. 34). As a good Thomist, Vann insists strongly that it is just as wrong to despise and scorn God's gifts as it is to misuse them or allow them to enslave a person. Such a negative attitude, however, would seem to be fighting a negative battle in the face of modern advertising.

The Example of Christ

The life and example of Jesus himself tell us a great deal about the proper use of God's good things. His very first miracle took place at a wedding feast, and each of those words is important—"very first," "wedding" and "feast." There is something very significant in that Jesus chose to inaugurate his public ministry and saving act of redemption at a wedding feast and that he does it by miraculously supplying the guests with an over-abundance of the best of wine. No one could reasonably conclude from this fact that Jesus looked down either on marriage or on wine or on feasting. On the contrary, the miracle at Cana might well be the foundation for the opinion of Father Vann that:

> Marriage is one of the divinely appointed paths to holiness; real and deep human love, integrated in the inclusive love of God, not only perfects the human personality, mind, heart and will, and gives it, in the most potent way, that training in selflessness and self-giving which is the essential of holiness, but at the same time raises man and wife to a dignity for which there is nowhere else an exact parallel, making them, in the words of Pope Pius XI, "ministers of the divine omnipotence" (p. 33).

The Gospels go on to tell about Christ's enjoyment of meals at Levi's house in the midst of sinners and, above all, of the friendship he enjoyed at the home of Lazarus and his sisters Martha and Mary. We can only conclude from Christ's own example that friendship is one of God's most precious gifts. Much has been written about the blessings of friendship, and no praise can be exaggerated. To have a person or persons to whom one can confide one's most secret ideas, feelings, ambitions, and hopes is to have a treasure of inexhaustible value. On the other hand, there is so much truth in the old saying, "A friend is one in whose presence you can be silent." Not to have or to want to have friends is one of life's tragedies, and it need not be. There is no more pitiable person in all the world than the crusty, self-sufficient, yes, selfish man or woman who insists on "going it alone" through life, who refuses to want friends or to make himself available to someone in need of friendship. That is not the path to holiness!

Nor need one worry that human friendship is detrimental to one's love-relationship with the Lord. St. Thérèse of Lisieux wrote: "A heart given to God loses nothing of its natural affection . . . on the contrary the affection grows stronger." However, here again a certain degree of caution may be in place. If friendship with one person becomes *exclusive,* that is, if it is allowed to become so consuming of one's time and thought that it cuts one off from the needs of other persons in the family, in society, or above all in a religious community, it can be self-defeating and injurious.

Jesus had his special friends in Martha, Mary, Lazarus, and especially John, the "beloved disciple," but his heart was great enough to be shared with all the apostles, with the crowds (to say nothing of the billions of his friends who have lived since his day).

From this chapter I hope that the reader will conclude that *moderation* is the key idea that best guides Christians in coming to terms with all the elements that constitute their life in the world.

Social Aspects of Christian Living

Christ, in his lifetime, demonstrated his concern for the whole human person, not just his spiritual side. He healed people as people. We may conclude from his example and from the writings of the popes from Leo XIII to our time that the Church's concern likewise extends to *all* areas of life, social as well as spiritual. Indeed, the one (social) flows directly from the other (spiritual). Christ continues his saving work and his concern for every element of human life in and through his Church, which is called by St. Paul "the body of Christ" (1 Cor. 12:27). It is impossible to think of a Christian apart from his membership in the Body of Christ. It is Christ who acts in and through his members who in turn become his hands, his feet, his mouth, his heart.

Fr. Michel Quoist draws valuable conclusions from this Pauline doctrine:

> The Church, then, is the People of God. But the Church is also that terrestrial institution, founded by Jesus Christ, to which new members are joined throughout the course of history. The Church is therefore both visible and invisible, in time and beyond time. In Christ, the Church is fully realized and sanctified; in her members on earth, the Church is incomplete and *in via [on the way]*. The Church, therefore, is the Body of Christ; but she is, at the same time, the one who generates that Body in history.
> *Christ Is Alive*, (Garden City, N.Y.: Doubleday and Company, 1971), pp. 10-11.

It is significant that Quoist maintains that in her members the Church is incomplete and on the way. To live as a member of Christ in this world is, then, a redemptive kind of life that aims at extending the redemption in the world, in society, in all of society's institutions, in people. It is time for all Christians to realize and appreciate their dignity and potential as members of the Church. And not only their dignity but also their obligations. Oft-repeated though it is, the French saying is applicable here: *Noblesse oblige*, "Noble birth imposes the obligation of living in a noble manner." Having been born into the nobility of Christ's Body through baptism, we necessarily share all the obligations and tasks as well as the privilege of membership.

I do not believe it is mere Christian romanticism to maintain that the Christianizing of the world by helping people to live in accordance with their Christian dignity extends to the developing of our own country, to the progress of science, especially medicine, the proliferation of inventions, the creation of opportunities for work, the overcoming of racism, and the struggle towards nationhood by underdeveloped countries. Too many people in our world find it impossible to live Christian lives because it is not possible for them to live human lives. It may not be practical or even possible for all Christians to be actively involved in the task of helping people to make progress, but all can and must care about that progress and contribute to it in every way possible.

What to do in a practical way presents a problem for many social-minded Catholics, especially those living in small cities, towns, and in the country. City parishes usually have social action programs whose purpose is the perfecting of the institutions that condition modern areas of life. The goals of the so-called "specialized Catholic Action" movements—Young Christian Workers, Young Christian Farmers, Young Christian Students—may have been more or less successfully achieved (although there is always a place for improvement in each of those fields), but no parish will ever run out of the need for organizations like the Christian Family Movement and Marriage Encounter groups which help promote Christian family life and encourage couples and parents to live up to their vocations as husbands, wives, and parents.

In the chapter on the parish, I already mentioned the very special "problem" of the aged, the sick, the shut-ins. Caring for them and for their needs—especially their feeling of being unwanted, useless, and left-out, their loneliness—is an aspect of parish living and Christian social action that never ends. And who ever thinks of visiting the prisons?

In a word, there is no limit to the possibilities for Christian social action (which, may we not forget, is carrying on the redemptive work of Christ) for the Christian endowed with a minimum of curiosity and social concern. The harvest is as ready now as it was in the time of Christ.

Leisure and Recreation

Leisure and recreation are not the same, although they are probably related. Leisure is not escapism, it is not just "having a good time." For too many people their work is a drudgery and so mechanized that it requires nothing creative from them. The result is that they seek relief in activities and pastimes that do not re-create or refresh them. The very idea and meaning of the word "recreation" has vanished from the minds and values of many Americans. They spend the whole week living for and looking forward to the weekend, and after they have lived through the weekend, they are hardly more renewed, that is "re-created," created anew, than they were before.

Someone has said that leisure is a time for love, which indicates how essential leisure is for everyone. It is for building love in the family, for uniting family members who have necessarily been scattered by various occupations during the week. This does not mean that individual family members do not need personal leisure. Everyone has to discover the possible talent(s) he has and develop them. There are very few men or women who are incapable of achieving something creative and perfecting some skill.

In reflecting on leisure and recreation, it seems necessary to say a word about television. It was surely a praiseworthy invention; it can provide genuine recreation if used wisely, but there are few families that would dismiss the possibility that TV can disrupt family harmony. It can readily distract parents from their obligations as parents and turn both parents and children from their genuine duties. It can in many cases cause people to live in a dream world and can destroy personality. I am thinking, for example, of the complaints of so many wives during the football season (which now extends over half the year). Husbands who spend all of Saturday afternoon, all of Sunday afternoon, and all of Monday evening watching football games hardly seem to have the best possible conception of leisure. And in their case leisure is hardly a time for love.

We may not even think of leisure without some consideration of the importance of reading. And I do mean more than a dedicated devouring of the weekly news magazines and the daily papers, important as these may be for keeping one informed about the nation and the world. That kind of reading is the bare minimum. Only slightly less sad and diminished than the priest who does not read (and it is all too obvious in his sermons) is the laymen or laywoman who scorns good novels, poetry, plays, and, above all, books on the spiritual life. Unfortunately, too many Catholic men and women graduate from schools and colleges where they were never challenged to respond to the wealth of knowledge of human nature and human experience that is the stuff of literature. Unfortunately again, it seems that it would take a special effort to begin serious reading if one has neglected to form the habit when young. But with some guidance it need never be too late for one who is at all concerned about becoming a well-rounded human person.

Recent Catholic authors delight in quoting the ancient phrase of one of the earliest of the Church Fathers, St. Irenaeus: "The glory of God is man fully alive." Irenaeus surely does not intend the phrase "fully alive" to mean that a person exuberantly bubbles over with enthusiasm and good cheer. The man or woman who is fully alive is one who has grown to the utmost of his human potential—grown not only physically and intellectually, but also aesthetically, spiritually, and socially. As John Garvey puts it so beautifully, "Man fully realized is more than a man, he is in some way divine" *(Saints for Confused Times* [Chicago: Thomas More Press, 1976], p. 9). A person who is fully alive is surely one in whose presence people will say, 'It is good for me to be here!"

And that could be the last word. Living in the world (and living in a convent or monastery as well), family life, social life, education, apostolic activity, recreation, and leisure—everything we have considered in this chapter and anything that we have missed—all must coalesce into the forming of a Christian man or woman who is not only good to everyone whom he meets, but he is also good *for* those people. And being good for others is harder than being good to them. There is no higher ideal in all the world, for it was the ideal that Christ himself lived out in his lifetime. And the best thing about it is that it is within reach of any one of us.

11

A Spirituality for Christians

In the winter of 1978 the film "Beyond and Back" attracted considerable attention throughout the United States. In relating the stories of men and women who had apparently been killed and then brought back to life, it attempted to give some idea of what death and the beginning of the afterlife was like. I do not know how successful the movie was in achieving its purpose.

However, there once lived a man called Lazarus who knew about the reality of death and the afterlife and who came back to the reality of this world. He lived and died during the lifetime of Jesus Christ; he spent four days in the tomb and then Jesus recalled him to live again in this world. That Lazarus did not leave any written record of his extraordinary experience has not prevented at least one spiritual writer, Fr. Gerald Vann, O.P., from speculating on how Lazarus might have reacted. Vann surmised that on returning to this world Lazarus must have been more recollected than he was before, that he was quiet, distracted, and even uninterested in the life he had once lived.

I wonder if it would not be just as reasonable to suppose that upon his return Lazarus enjoyed an insight into this life that he had never had before, that the real value of living in this world came home to him through his personal experience of dying. And what is the real value of living in this world? It is that it is possible to find God *in* this life, *in* this world.

Finding God in This Life

During our everyday life in this world we work, suffer, seek truth, we grow physically, emotionally, intellectually, and socially. We live as members of families and communities, we learn to love and to keep our ears and eyes open to the message of goodness, beauty, truth, and wonder that God tries to communicate to us through his word and the world around us. The most elementary task of Christians is to be attuned to life and to the Author of life anywhere and everywhere we find ourselves. There is no experience in life that God cannot use as a conveyor of the message of his loving concern for us.

Too many serious-minded Catholics seem to want to live in an exclusively spiritual universe that has little or no relationship with life in this world. It is time for them to return to their "mother country," to become human beings again and stop trying to live like angels. What I am getting at is that if eternity is life with God, it can and must begin now, and that, I believe, is what Lazarus discovered. The Christian does not look on death as the end of everything, as the pagan does. For the believer death means the beginning of a new life, or more exactly, the un-folding of a life that is already his, once he has been reborn in baptism and has Christ living within.

The possibility of meeting God in our daily life may seem strange and unreal to many Catholics, especially those of us who grew up in the earlier part of the century. We had the impression that to find God one had to go off to a monastery or a retreat house where one could stock up on or renew one's "spiritual life" and then return to the humdrum, wicked, godless old world. And it would be unheard of and presump-tuous for the "ordinary" layperson to entertain any aspirations to holi-ness without a radical break with lay life.

With but slightly veiled sarcasm, the French priest Michel Quoist lists several classes of Christians. The first comprises the privileged class of "super-Christians" who live in solitude apart from the world. The second class is a kind of spiritual bourgeoisie of men or women who have the time and the money to make retreats, to spend days or weeks in monasteries, and who have plenty of time for spiritual reading and other spiritual exercises. They generally appear to be quite unconcerned about becoming involved in trying to make this a better, more humane, more socially acceptable world. Finally, and in last place, is the great mass of ordinary people who struggle to make a living to raise their families, victims all of the demands of daily living, housework, worry, distraction, pain, and concern with the wherewithal to care for the family, with hardly enough time for any kind of spiritual reading or mental prayer, to say nothing of finding a couple of days for a weekend retreat.

Quoist claims that if God is present only "in the desert" and in silence, then he is inaccessible to most Christians today. "And in that case, if the purpose of the Incarnation was to join Christ to the whole of life, we may say that the Incarnation has been a fiasco" *(Christ Is Alive, p. 37)*. He insists that Christ is present in life, waiting for people in the heart of this world, eager to be discovered. In a word, the success of the Christian's life lies in finding God in his ordinary, day-by-day living.

Helps for Finding God in Daily Life

I agree with Father Quoist. I am convinced that it is possible to find God (and to find fulfillment for all the deep longings in the human heart) in everyday living. But the question is *how?* A living awareness of that divine Presence might well require as great an act of faith as believing in Christ's presence in the Eucharist. Finding God in one's daily life is closely linked to growth in awareness of who and what one is as a member of the Body of Christ, awareness of the full implications of St. Paul's conviction that "it is no longer I who live, but Christ who lives in me; and the life I now live in the flesh I live by faith in the Son of God, who loved me and gave himself for me" (Gal. 2:20). This kind of aware-ness should be possible for even the busiest person.

But whether or not one is aware of it, no one will ever exhaust the depth of meaning in the fact of living the life of Christ, of being a member of his Body, and the inestimable worth that fact gives to the daily existence of the Christian.

While insisting on the possibility of finding God in our daily life, it hardly seems necessary to insist on the oft-repeated conviction that this possibility does not eliminate the need for whatever specific moments and periods of prayer and spiritual reading that one's daily life permits. Fr. Henri Nouwen writes: "We have fallen into the temptation of separating ministry from spirituality, service from prayer. Our demon says: 'We are too busy to pray; we have too many needs to attend to, too many people to respond to, too many wounds to heal. Prayer is a luxury, something to do during a free hour, a day away from work or on a retreat.' But to think this way is harmful. . . . Service and prayer can never be separated" *(The Living Reminder* [New York: Seabury Press, 1977], p. 12).

Earlier I insisted that if one's religion and prayer life do not nourish daily living and vice versa, there is something faulty with the way one lives or with one's understanding of religion. Surely there is something deficient in an understanding of religion that does not make a person more and more aware, not only of the value of life, but of his personal union with other members of the Body of Christ. Fr. Quoist is again to the point: "To be a Christian is to bind oneself to Christ, but to the total Christ, head and body, in order to live consciously, every day, that mystery of love which is the historical realization of the eternal plan of the Father" *(Christ Is Alive,* p. 10). It is no secret that this vital awareness of one's union with others is not easy to come by for most people, preoccupied as they naturally must be with their own personhood.

Importance of Self-acceptance

What I have been saying thus far in this chapter is closely related to the idea of self-acceptance. I am who I am and no one else, and I've got to understand that the person who I am is God's own creation, his idea alone. I may well be dissatisfied with the way I live my life, with the kind of Christian I am, with what I have allowed my life to become, or even with the way life has treated me. Surely, I may want to become a better human being, a better person, but not a different person. God created me, I am unique, and I must accept my uniqueness, this person who I am, and not try or want to be anyone else.

Accepting myself for who and what I am includes accepting the gifts and talents God has given me and working at developing them. With most people it is necessary to discover talents, and everyone can use help in that area of life. There is no person alive who does not need another person or persons who trust and believe in him. There seems to be no limits to the personal growth of a human being who has parents, teachers, friends, spouses who create self-confidence and self-acceptance by showing that person real trust. Sad and wounded, on the other hand, is the human being who grows up without such providential helpers.

The fact of God's having chosen me, given me my being and personhood is beautifully illustrated in this verse from the prophet Isaiah: "The Lord called me from the womb, from the body of my mother he named my name" (49:1). When I am ready to accept having been loved and chosen and known by God—chosen by him to be, to be *me,* then I am on my way to arriving at a healthy spirituality, to a genuine loving communion with my God.

But arriving at a firm conviction of God's personal love and choice of each of us to be is not always easy to come by in a world and a society that so frequently diminishes and levels human beings to a status of nonpersonhood. There may also come times in all our lives when we are tempted to complain with Israel, "The Lord has forsaken me, my Lord has forgotten me" (Is. 49:14). But the Lord will never permit such defeatist thinking. He comes right back with what has been called the most consoling verse in the Old Testament: "Can a woman forget her suckling child, that she should have no compassion on the son of her womb? Even these may forget, yet I will not forget you" (Is. 49:15).

Enemies of Self-acceptance

The worst enemy of healthy self-acceptance is a sense of guilt arising from an awareness of one's actual or presumed sinfulness. Many older Christians grew up and were instructed in an idea of a "watchman God," ever ready to catch us in wrongdoing and to condemn us for the deed. A sense of sin, together with a consciousness of one's frailty, is good for one, but when personal sinfulness assumes a greater importance and reality in our minds than the image of a loving, compassionate, forgiving God revealed to us in both the Testaments of the Bible, then we have never understood his word and deeds. We have to be convinced that there is *nothing*, absolutely nothing that we can do, no sin that we can commit, that can destroy God's everlasting, ongoing love for us. Accepting and living with that idea of God is crucial in building a Christian spirituality.

Life-changes, for example, seeing children grow up and leave home, losing a job, or forced retirement, can do untold damage to one's self-image. Allowing oneself to become the prey of any kind of depression arising from such misfortunes can become deadly. The human heart is very vulnerable and fragile, indeed. As long as we live we need to be reminded again and again that the love of God, his esteem for us, is everlasting, that he never takes it back, that each of us is of infinite worth in his sight.

The near infinite value of each human person is brought home to us most of all by the incarnation and redemption of Christ. When I become convinced that everything that Christ was and did, he did for me, then I am on my way to growth into a healthy mentality. Christ's personal care for each of us, begun with his many miraculous healing words and actions during his lifetime, continues now in and through the sacraments, the extensions of his humanity (we will come to that in a moment). We can permit St. Paul to have the last and best word in the matter of God's personal concern and love for us: "God shows his love for us in that while we were yet sinners Christ died for us" (Rom. 5:8).

Self-acceptance Invites Self-improvement

Self-acceptance, together with a grateful acceptance of Christ's redeeming grace, should not, of course, discourage anyone from wanting and trying to improve oneself in every area of life. There is no one who could not become a better person on all levels through personal cooperation with the grace of God and the directives of a spiritual director or confessor. The whole idea and purpose of this book is to facilitate conversion which always begins with a certain dissatisfaction with oneself and one's limitations.

On the human level there is always room for growth into a more Christ-like personality through the developing and perfecting of one's talents. It is neither Christian or human to allow one's gifts and talents to go undiscovered or undeveloped. Developing one's talents and natural gifts has almost unlimited possibilities and potential. It can actually lead a person to surpass himself. Such an ideal cannot but glorify God, for it reflects his own perfection. And it all begins with self-acceptance.

Christian Morality

If the notion of treating Christian morality seems out of place in a chapter on spirituality for the layperson, it may be that one's concept of morality can stand some improvement or implementation. In the past it has been common to think of morality primarily in terms of ethical behavior, with behavior seen mainly as the kind of conduct that will not get us into trouble either with God or with the laws of human society. We conceived of holiness in much the same way, as John Garvey indicates in his *Saints for Confused Times.* "Our idea of a good life is one which involves behavior more than the heart. We see saints as people whose standards of behavior were much better than our own, whose actions reflected their dedication perfectly" (p. 9).

Garvey claims that the true center of every saint's life is the firm belief that God is real. The belief, even more, the knowledge, of the reality of God in the lives of the saints does involve moral behavior to some extent, but, says Garvey, it involves much more. It involves a *wholeheartedness* that is central to being Christian. "Saints are not people whose ambition is to be saints or to fit into any other human definition. They simply want to be what God wants them to be" (p. 12).

I believe that there is a close relationship between this wholeheartedness that is so central to the very idea of being a Christian and the ideal of Christian morality as it is conceived by Fr. William Shannon in his article "The Uniqueness of Christian Morality" in the February 1978 *Sisters Today.* Shannon speaks of morality in the biblical sense as response or responsiveness to the goodness of God and to his great deeds on behalf of his people, and this kind of morality is true of both the Old and the New Testaments. The responsiveness is naturally tinged with thanksgiving.

New Testament morality more particularly is responsiveness in gratitude for what Christ Jesus has done for us. The chief difference is in the nature or "specificity" of our response. In the Old Testament the nature of human response to God's goodness was spelled out in a written code which was handed down mostly in the Books of Exodus and

Deuteronomy. Accordingly, Old Testament morality has been called a "code morality." There is a considerable difference between obeying a set of rules and relating to a person with love.

New Testament morality, claims Father Shannon, is much less specified. "It makes no attempt to spell out what Christian man must do in particular situations. It is, as Paul says in Romans, *a new way* of serving God—not the way of the written code, but the way "of the Spirit" (p. 382). New Testament morality tells us not so much *what* we are to do but *that* we are to live and act from a motive of deepest love for God. As members of Christ, sharers in his very life and Spirit, the Christian is a new creation, possessing and possessed by the Holy Spirit, the source of their lives (Gal. 5:25). It is the Spirit who is to direct the lives of Christians (Rom. 8:4).

St. Paul insists strongly on this truth. Much of his apostolic life was spent opposing those converts from Judaism who insisted on retaining their Old Testament conception of morality as primarily obedience to a code (with obedience to the Law seen as saving) and worse than that, imposing it on their fellow Christian converts from paganism. The sense of security that results from carefully following an external code of laws is tempting, and many modern Christians seem to prefer it to the less specifically defined observance of the Law of the Spirit. They want to know what they are to do and the details of how to do it.

No one would claim that written law is alien to New Testament morality. It definitely has its place, but the place is not number one. Father Shannon quotes approvingly from St. Thomas:

> That which is preponderant in the law of the New Testament and whereon all its efficacy is based is the grace of the Holy Spirit which is given through faith in Christ. . . . Consequently, we must say that the New Law is in the first place a law that is inscribed in our hearts, but that secondarily it is written law.
>
> *Summa Theologica*, I-II, q. 106, a. 1

Christians do have codes, and they need them, since it is not always easy to know in which direction the Spirit of Love is to lead them. But they must constantly be on their guard lest they see the code as an *end* which is equivalent to the law of Christ and of the Spirit. Being a Christian means more than literal observing of a set of rules. Jesus Christ and St. Paul had enough trouble with that kind of morality and religion in their time. We do not have to add to it by an inadequate understanding of morality today.

From what has been said here about morality, it seems obvious that morality has a great deal to do with spirituality—that it is impossible to conceive of spirituality apart from morality. In his article "Contemplation and the Sacraments" in the June-July 1978 *Sisters Today*, Father

Shannon goes more deeply into the relationship between morality and spirituality. He insists that:

> Jesus did not come simply to make us better persons (though he certainly did that); primarily he came to make us new persons. The sequence is not that we improve our conduct and thereby become better persons; rather the sequence is that we become new persons in Christ, and because we have become new persons, our conduct is different. Jesus came not just to change what we do but to change who we are (p. 686).

What is "spirituality"? It is the dynamic motivating force of our life. It colors and characterizes our ideas, our judgments, our opinions, our actions and reactions. For the Christian there can be no other motivating force than his vivid awareness that the deepest reality of his being is Christ living in him.

The Nature of Sin

No treatment of morality is possible or complete without some consideration of its opposite, namely, immorality. We all belong to a fallen, sin-inclined race, and sad experience reveals our vulnerability again and again. We all have to come to terms with sin and the possibility of sinning. This consideration is an essential element in our growth to maturity in our faith, our love-relationship with Christ. The Christian life is definitely not characterized by security of any kind, least of all, security or exemption from the possibility of injuring that relationship by sinning.

Once we understand that we are frail, vulnerable, and readily inclined to sin and join that understanding to the deeper, more consoling fact of God's eagerness to forgive sin, we are less likely to become crushed by guilt and victims of despair or depression if or when we sin. I do not by any means wish to give the impression that, because of its universality and "popularity," sin is to be taken lightly. On the contrary. But this observation does seem necessary in the light of the self-image in so many Christians resulting from their sinful weaknesses, their selfish failure to remember the right relationship to God that they know they ought to have.

This brings us to a consideration of the nature of sin. The familiar definition of sin as "a violation of the law of God or of the Church" hardly seems adequate in the light of the above reflections on morality. Sin is best seen as a refusal to love, a non-response to him who is Love, Goodness, and Beauty in Person. This is obviously the way in which Mary Magdalene saw her sins. Once aware of the holiness and lovableness of Jesus, her past failures to respond to that love forced her to her knees in tears.

Most Catholics were trained to distinguish between "mortal" and "venial" sins, the former seen as serious offenses against God and his law, committed with full freedom and sufficient reflection on what is being considered, while the latter was thought of as a lesser offense or an offense committed without much deliberation or choice. This distinction between kinds of sin seems reasonable to Catholics (civil law and practice also makes such a distinction), although it is good for them to realize that it is unacceptable to most Protestants for whom all sin is evil and hateful.

In a booklet explaining the new ritual for the sacrament of reconciliation *(The Savior's Healing,* The Liturgical Press, 1974), I have enlarged on the old idea of sin by drawing on an article by Fr. Ladislas Orsy, S.J., in *America.* Orsy believes that it would be useful to broaden our thinking to three types of sin: *venial, serious, mortal.*

His description of venial sin as "basically on the refusal to grow" is most interesting. He means, of course, refusal to grow responsibly into a deeper love-relationship with Christ. The next category is *serious sin* which may include many acts that "betray evil trends in the heart of man but do not necessarily bring about a radical break with God. They are like failings in a loving family." For example, Peter's denial of Jesus in a moment of weakness, fear, and distress was serious, but because of the circumstances of fear and distress, it did not destroy his love-relationship with Jesus. Judas, on the other hand, betrayed Christ after a long period of deliberation and of deliberate alienation from Jesus. His was a *mortal sin,* which Fr. Orsy describes as a "free and permanent option by man to remain alone and to exclude God from his life. Its consequence is damnation; God ratifies what man chose freely. . . . It is all a fatal, mortal choice."

It is quite evident from this opinion that—while serious sins brought on by momentary weakness and emotional excitement may be fairly common in our lives—a genuine mortal sin is probably quite rare or nonexistent, which may or may not be good news. Mortal sin is possible, and that is tragic. But the fact of God's forgiving love for us *is* good news. That love can never be wiped out or destroyed, no matter how seriously or mortally we offend him. God's love is unconditional, and because of his love there is no sin, however serious, however mortal, that he is unwilling to forgive. What seems difficult for us is to absorb and welcome his forgiveness. We are much too hesitant to accept what St. John wrote: "In this is love, not that we loved God but that he loved us and sent his Son to be the expiation for our sins" (1 Jn. 4:10).

In this connection it is good to recall Christ's treatment of Peter. When they were all together again after the resurrection, Jesus did not accuse

Peter. He did not say, "Peter, you denied me three times." All he did was to ask Peter three times, "Simon, do you love me?" This is a perfect description of how God feels about the weak, sin-inclined people that most of us are. Jesus was simply being true to his own principles as laid down in the parable of the prodigal son. There the father set no conditions for the prodigal's reconciliation. He did not even give him a chance to blurt out his prepared confession: "Father, I have sinned against heaven and before you; I am no longer worthy to be called your son" (Lk. 15:18-19). The father simply opened his arms and clasped his repentant son to his heart. Then he had a big party to celebrate the occasion. The prodigal son was no longer prodigal; he was a new creation.

There can be no better transition to an insight into the nature of the sacrament of reconciliation (penance) than to recall the cast of characters, the nature of the thought processes of each character, and the perhaps surprising ending of the parable of the prodigal son. The son's decision to return to the father (prompted undoubtedly by God's grace . . . with a bit of help from the son's degrading life-situation) and, above, all, the father's anxious eagerness to forgive and receive him back into the family tells us more about the sacrament of reconciliation than a long book of theological speculation.

12

The Sacraments and

Christian Spirituality

What Jesus did for Peter he wanted to do for sinners in every age. It was this desire to provide all sinners who were tired of their alienation and eager to return to loving union with the Father the very same opportunity to have their desires fulfilled.

During his lifetime the reality of sin was undoubtedly more present to the consciousness of Jesus than any other human problem. To be sure, he saw physical illness and bodily deficiencies such as blindness, disease, and crippled limbs wherever he went. Such human wounds were offensive to him, and the Gospels tell us again and again of his eagerness to heal all manner of suffering. But it is significant that he usually related internal healing, that is, the forgiveness of sins, with the healing of bodies. Typical was his treatment of the paralytic as related in Luke: "Man, your sins are forgiven you" (5:20), and then he restored the man to perfect physical health.

The sacrament of reconciliation (a name more descriptive of its overall purpose than "sacrament of penance") is a logical follow-up to Christ's very existence as Savior, to say nothing of his subjective, personal, day-by-day attitude towards the people to whom he preached. He saw the need for inner healing, not only for his contemporaries, but in every age, and that is why he decided to extend his personal power to forgive sins and heal souls by instituting the sacrament of reconciliation. On the very first day of his new existence as the risen Lord, he appeared to his apostles and said to them: "Peace be with you. . . . As the Father has sent me, even so I send you." Then he breathed on them and said to them: "Receive the Holy Spirit. If you forgive the sins of any, they are forgiven; if you retain the sins of any, they are retained" (Jn. 20:19-23).

The deep truth that gives meaning and genuine importance to this sacrament is that *it is Christ himself who, in the person of the priest, greets the penitent, hears about his sinful problems, counsels him and then restores to that person inner health and innocence.* If anyone is a sinner in any degree of seriousness and has allowed his basic inclination to evil to rise to the surface in a sinful act, word, or thought, that person *needs* this sacrament.

It is true, there are many ways whereby we can have our sins forgiven, the most prominent being the Mass itself; also the fervent recitation of the Lord's Prayer and "perfect acts of contrition." But, as Fr. Peter van Breemen, S.J., tells us, after pointing out the difficulty most of us have in forgiving ourselves and accepting God's forgiveness, "If we do not verbalize our sins in a conversation with a fellowman and hear his absolution spoken in the name of God, the forgiveness may not reach the heart. We have to express our guilt, and we cannot do that alone" *(As Bread That is Broken* [Denville, N.J.: Dimension Books, 1974], p. 74).

Everyone is aware that in "the old days" confessions were much more frequent than they are now. Religious sisters, priests, and brothers made it a practice to confess once a week, whether they "needed it or not." That may have been an extreme of sorts, and in many cases it "mechanized" confessions to the extent that penitents quite regularly recited off a list of sins that never varied, giving confessors the impression that the "firm purpose of amendment" required for a "good" confession was not taken too seriously. The other extreme is what we are witnessing in the Church today—the almost complete neglect of the sacrament of reconciliation.

Making Confession More Fruitful

I think it is important to remind conscientious Christians that the sacrament of reconciliation not only heals internally, but also it is or can be a very worthy aid in one's growth towards that total conversion and that maturity in religion and discipleship we have been considering in this book. It provides the kind of personal encounter with Christ, of worship and celebration (and I mean those two words to be understood literally) without which religious growth would appear to be very difficult. We too readily think of the word "confession" as simply the telling of our sins, forgetting the most ancient meaning of the word as the expression of praise and gratitude. *The Confessions of St. Augustine,* for example, is much more a hymn of praise, worship, and thanksgiving to

God than a relating of his youthful sins.

There are probably few Christians who are really satisfied with their confessions. Confession does not seem to help them to improve and become better persons, which is surely one of the purposes of this sacrament. It is good for them to be reminded that few of us become saints in a hurry and that for most Christians conversion and maturity in the faith is a life-long work.

There may, however, be something we can do about our failure to make the spiritual progress we hope for. It is important to remember that this sacrament is not only for the forgiveness of particular sins; it is also for the *inner healing,* for the correcting and re-directing of the deep-down attitudes that shape our lives. Sin has to do more with what we *are* than with what we do or say—what we are to one another, to our community, to our God, to the world around us. It is the whole person who sins, who loves, who believes, who betrays, who injures. And it is the whole person that needs healing and rejuvenation.

So, in preparing for confession, we would do well to examine the basic attitudes that govern and sometimes poison our lives, our relationships with others, above all, with God. Do we seriously face up to the conscious, freely chosen attitudes that are simply evil: selfishness, prejudice, vindictiveness, neglect, stubbornness, pettiness, impatience, envy, and callousness about the feelings and needs of others? These are tendencies in our hearts. It is the heart that is sick and in need of Christ's healing. Like an infection in the body, these tendencies and attitudes can poison the whole system of our relationships with God, with others, and with our inmost being. It is these attitudes that provide us with the causes of the deeds, words, and thoughts that make us feel guilty and in need of forgiveness and reconciliation. It may be useful to take advantage of the opportunity provided in the new ritual's provision for a face-to-face encounter with the confessor in order to ask his help in digging into the causes of sins, along with the attitudes that make sin possible.*

---

*The New Rite of Penance decreed by Vatican Council II (1975) seeks to make use of the deeper understanding of the theology of the sacraments as "extensions" of the humanity of Christ" (St. Leo, fourth century) and as manifestations of the compassion and mercy of Christ for the special need Christians have to be reconciled to their God and their community. As sin is being understood more and more not only as an offense against God but also against the Body of Christ, so in the new rite a special effort is made to emphasize that the sinner is reconciled not only to God but also to the community.

The new rite is much the same as the old one, but also different. The possibility for anonymous confession for those who desire it is still available in the new

To sum up, every confession should be prepared by a searching look into our hearts. This in turn will make us dissatisfied with what we are; it will make us want to be changed by Christ and by this sacrament into that better person formed after the heart and mind of Christ that we are capable of becoming. What confession aims at is the enlargement of our capacity for loving. It all adds up to seeing the sacrament of reconciliation as a hunger for change, a thirst for newness of life, for growth, for wholeness, for holiness.

While confession must make us aware of our sins and desirous of overcoming them, it is necessary to insist that too much preoccupation with sin, with the negative in all its varieties, either in oneself or in others, is spiritually unhealthy. Too many Christians, Catholic and Protestant, conceive of their religion mainly in terms of combatting evil. However, the spiritual life is much more demanding than avoiding sin or even living up to an ethical code of laws and rules. Many pagan humanists do better at being ethical than do many Christians.

The essence of the spiritual life consists in believing with all our being the teaching of Christ and St. Paul that as members of Christ's Body he dwells in us and wishes to dwell in us more and more. This relationship has to be our chief preoccupation, and in the light of that truth we can and should look into ourselves to discover the obstacles in our hearts and lives which prevent Christ from living more fully in us. This is a far

"penance rooms" in most parish churches, but the room is now lighted, and the dark and forbidding atmosphere of gloom that used to discourage children (and many converts) is now gone. The room is arranged so that the penitent can, if he desires, sit in a chair facing the confessor and confess to him face to face.

A surprising number of Catholics of all ages now use this option of a face-to-face confession. I believe that confessing in this way helps them to avoid the "mechanical" recitation of a list of sins that made them dissatisfied with the old way of confessing.

The rite itself is the same for both the anonymous and the face-to-face confession. It begins with a greeting by the priest, and the Sign of the Cross made by both penitent and priest. The priest then invites the penitent to trust in God's mercy with a phrase that draws heavily on the mercy of Christ as the Gospels depict him. There follows next a short reading from Scripture which emphasizes the mercy of God and his eagerness to forgive the sinner. The penitent then confesses his sins and is counselled by the confessor, after which he makes an "act of contrition" in his own words or with a verse from Scripture. Follows next the words of forgiveness by the priest as he extends his hand or hands over the head of the penitent and invokes the Holy Spirit. The penitent gives his consent to being forgiven with an Amen, and the confession ends with a brief dismissal by the priest, "Give thanks to the Lord, for he is good," to which the penitent responds, "His mercy endures forever." Then, "The Lord has freed you from your sins. Go in peace."

cry from the self-hatred that sin and confession too often create in some Catholics. That is not what God wants, and it is certainly not the reason why Jesus gave us this sacrament.

Doris Donnelly wrote a few years ago in the *National Catholic Reporter* that penance is the

> sacrament of discovery . . . the place where we sense the truth about ourselves and discover that even then we are loved beyond our imagining. That discovery has the power to change us mightily and radically. . . . At the root of the sacrament of penance is a self-acceptance in harmony with the way our Father accepts us. What I am accepting is the self that God loves. We are loved lavishly, prodigally, unrelentingly. And all this *before* the sacrament, irrespective of our sin.

Baptism, Penance, Eucharist

It should be obvious from all that has been said in this chapter that confession, inspired by a genuine desire and determination to repent and be converted, is a crucial step on our way to fulfillment as human persons, to say nothing of the fulfillment of our being as baptized Catholics. The call of John the Baptist to conversion and repentance (which is as timely now as when it was first issued) is a summons to become the fully developed and responsible persons that is our destiny as Christians. Conversion builds and takes off from the lack of unity in our lives. It responds to a universal human need, the need for wholeness, the need to put together the scattered pieces of our lives.

Seen in this perspective, the sacrament of reconciliation brings us face to face with Jesus Christ in whom we see the breadth and depth of what it means to be a whole person. In him we see what our own lives are meant to be. Above all, in him we see what mature Christian thinking about God, about religion and daily living, including all human relationships, is meant to be. I do not see how it is possible for Catholics to be sincere and earnest about their commitment to Christ without this sacrament as an essential element and experience in their Christian lives.

This is above all true when penance is seen as a renewal of one's baptismal dying and rising with Christ. I hope I am not being too imaginative in claiming for penance what St. Paul claims for baptism when he writes in Romans:

> Do you not know that all of us who have been baptized into Christ Jesus were baptized into his death? We were buried therefore with him by baptism into death, so that as Christ was raised from the dead by the glory of the Father, we too might walk in newness of life. . . . We know that Christ being raised from the dead will never die again; death no longer has dominion over him. . . . So you also must consider yourselves *dead to sin and alive to God in Christ Jesus* (6:3-11; emphasis added).

Baptism introduces a person into a redeemed community by joining the person to the death and resurrection of Christ. Penance reconciles him to that redeemed community if serious sin has severed him from vital membership. As in all the sacraments—especially baptism and the Eucharist—penance receives its full meaning only in the context of the community of the redeemed, the Body of Christ.

Historically and theologically baptism and the Eucharist go together. Through baptism one enters into and makes his own the death and resurrection of Jesus; the Eucharist *celebrates* that death and resurrection. The Eucharist completes and perfects what is begun in baptism. Accordingly, there can be no consideration of the spirituality of the Christian apart from the tandem of baptism (penance)—Eucharist. This tandem initiates spirituality, it shapes it, nourishes it, brings it to its highest development.

Before considering the Eucharist, I want to correct an inadequate impression of the sacrament of reconciliation I may have given earlier in this chapter. Once I heard a person say in the confessional, "Father, I'm just not a very good person." When I heard that, my reaction was: here is a Christian who really knows what the sacrament of penance is all about. Now I am not so sure.

It seems to me now that the person's self-appraisal might very well reveal the faulty understanding of morality and spirituality that I have criticized earlier, namely, that of confusing spirituality or union with God with ethical conduct. To be sure, ethical conduct is an important element of spirituality, but it is not the whole of it. The attitude betrayed in the remark, "I'm just not a very good person" seems to overemphasize *human effort* to the extent of down-playing God's personal action and influence in our lives.

There are undoubtedly several ways of interpreting the parable Jesus tells about the rich man who had such good crops that he planned to tear down his barns and build bigger ones so as to have room for the surplus. The foolish plan hardly met with Jesus' approval. He puts these words in God's mouth: "Fool, this night your soul is required of you; . . ." And Jesus concludes: "So is he who lays up treasure for himself, and is not rich toward God" (Lk. 12:20-21).

I believe that the best way to make oneself rich in the eyes of God is to empty oneself of everything but one's hunger and desire for God. Such an attitude is the best possible preparation for the Son of God's own ideas for satisfying our hunger and making us rich—the sacraments of reconciliation and the Eucharist.

The Eucharist

It may or may not seem strange that what has been most a part of me throughout my lifetime, the area of religion I have studied most, namely, the Mass, is apparently most difficult for me to write about. In all probability, my trouble has been that I want to write something striking, original, and fresh, and I find myself overwhelmed by a multiplicity of ideas and bits of information arising from my study of some fifty years. Actually, all I want to do is to write about the Mass in such a way that it will enter into the consciousness and become the foundation of my readers' spirituality.

How does the average Catholic look upon Sunday Mass? Does he say or think on a Sunday morning (or a Saturday night): "It's Sunday. I've got to get Mass in"? Or does he simply go off to the parish church out of force of habit, without even thinking about a reason? Most people adjust themselves to a routine, and there is nothing very wrong about that. But there is nothing very profitable about it either.

If someone were to ask what I think ought to be in the minds of Catholics on a Sunday morning, I would simply suggest this idea: "It's Sunday. I want to come together with my family and with my parish family *to remember Jesus Christ.*" After all, isn't that the reason why we have the Mass—the reason given to us by Jesus himself? The fact is simple: if we really want to understand the Mass and to understand why we want to be present at it, the best thing for us to do is to go back to the New Testament accounts of the first Mass, the Last Supper, to recall what Jesus said and did on that occasion, and to follow his command: "Do this in remembrance of me." Thousands of books have been written about the Mass, but if any one of them misses that simple fact, its author has simply not grasped its meaning.

Why did Jesus want his followers to remember what he had done? There are several reasons, the main one, I believe, being that he wanted to increase love in the world, our love in particular, and he knew that the best way to enkindle and nourish love would be by bringing to our minds all that he has been and all that he has done for us. I believe he also wanted us to come together to remember so that the members of every parish community would be more and more united in mutual love for one another and for him. Just coming together would be important. The Last Supper was a family meal—it was the Passover meal which Jesus celebrated with and for his beloved disciples. It was a very special occasion for them and for him. He wants it to be very special for us: "I have earnestly desired to eat this passover with you before I suffer," he told his apostles (Lk. 22:15). Jesus intended the Last Supper to be a love feast, and such is his intention for every making-present-again of the

Last Supper at the Mass.

What did Jesus do at the Last Supper that he was so insistent on their remembering? Surely he wanted them to remember *him* and all that he has done and will do at the last Passover meal. We have pretty detailed accounts of what he did that night. He spoke a lot, he taught, he prophesied the coming of the Holy Spirit, and he was very active. The high point of the action was, of course, his taking bread, breaking it, giving thanks, and saying: " 'This is my body which is [given] for you. Do this in remembrance of me.' In the same way also the cup, after supper, saying, 'This cup is the new covenant in my blood. Do this, as often as you drink it, in remembrance of me' " (1 Cor. 11:24-25).

This act and these words constitute the heart of that first Mass, even as they constitute the heart of every Mass since that time. Our Lord's command, "Do *this*. . . ." is very likely limited in the thinking of most Catholics to Jesus' changing bread into his body and wine into his blood. Few of us would be likely to extend his command to all that he said and did at the Last Supper. But why not?

At that Last Supper, Christ also washed the feet of his disciples the most menial and servile act of service any person could do for another. This gesture was ordinarily performed by slaves for their masters. But Jesus did it for them; and when he was finished he said to them: "Do you know what I have done to you? You call me Teacher and Lord; and you are right, for so I am. If I then, your Lord and Teacher, have washed your feet, you also ought to wash one another's feet" (Jn. 13:12-14). It is plain that Jesus wanted the memory of his personal act of loving service to remain with them forever and to inspire them to perform the same kind of service when they in turn would be shepherds and pastors.

But why stop there? Why not make all future gatherings of Jesus' followers "to break bread" the occasion for calling to the mind of the Christian communities all that Jesus was, all that he had said, all that he had done and all that he had meant to that original group of disciples? And this is what I think ought to be uppermost in our minds when Sunday comes around and we prepare to join our parish community for the celebration of the Eucharist: "I, we, want to remember Jesus."

A New Kind of Remembering

But we must be careful here. Our remembering of Jesus and all that he said and did throughout his life and especially at the Last Supper is not a mere exercise of instant recall on our part; it is not an imaginary memory trip into the distant Palestinian past. In commanding the apostles to do what he had done, Christ obviously gave them the power to do what he had done. Catholic theology maintains that when Jesus commanded,

"Do this. . . ." he ordained them priests and so endowed them with the power to change bread and wine into his body and blood as he had done. Catholic theology also maintains that at the Mass not only the Last Supper, but Calvary, in fact, the entire redeeming life and work of Jesus Christ *is made present here and now*. The community of the redeemed in a parish gathers together not only to remember but also to *celebrate* and to be present at the redeeming act of Christ, their Lord and brother. But more than to be present at and to celebrate, it means giving personal consent to that redeeming act, both as a community and as individual members, saying YES to it.

There can be no doubt that the first Christians were obedient to Jesus' command. St. Luke in Acts does not go into great detail, but the main ideas are there: "They devoted themselves to the apostles' teaching and fellowship, to the breaking of bread and the prayers. . . . And all who believed were together and had all things in common; . . . And day by day, attending the temple together and breaking bread in their homes, they partook of food with glad and generous hearts, praising God and having favor with all the people" (Acts 2:42-47).

It is possible to follow the "evolution" of the Mass in the epistles of St. Paul, particularly in 1 Corinthians 11, where Paul becomes very angry at one of the customs his Corinthian community had settled on. It seems that the "agape," the love-feast with which earlier Eucharists had been associated, had degenerated among the Corinthians into an occasion for unholy partying and argumentation. When Paul heard about this, he sat down and wrote some of the toughest words in the New Testament: "When you meet together, it is not the Lord's supper that you eat. For in eating, each one goes ahead with his own meal, and one is hungry and another is drunk. What! Do you not have houses to eat and drink in? Or do you despise the church of God and humiliate those who have nothing? What shall I say to you? Shall I commend you in this? No, I will not" (20-22).

After that "blast," Paul provides us with what is considered the most detailed description of the Last Supper that we have. And he wasn't even there! But his source was good:

> For I received from the Lord what I also delivered to you, that the Lord Jesus on the night when he was betrayed took bread, and when he had given thanks, he broke it, and said. "This is my body which is for you. Do this in remembrance of me." In the same way also the cup, after supper, saying, "This cup is the new covenant in my blood. Do this, as often as you drink it, in remembrance of me." For as often as you eat this bread and drink the cup, you proclaim the Lord's death until he comes (23-26).

Paul's description of the first Eucharist is then followed by a description of the Church as the Body of Christ (chapter 12) and by his renowned essay on love (chapter 13). I do not believe we are reading too much into the mind of St. Paul when we see the Eucharist, the Church, and charity as belonging together in his mind, the one being incomplete and inadequate without the other two. The Eucharist, the Breaking of Bread, is the act of the Church: it makes and creates; it fosters love, and without love no Christian belongs at the Eucharistic celebration.

Here it would be impractical and impossible to follow the development of the Mass from those primitive times to our own. One thing we can be certain of: in the midst of diversity, there is always a core of "sameness," namely, the description of what Jesus said and did at the Last Supper, along with this command, "Do this. . . ." This diversity and sameness, together with a very important response on the part of the community to the president's prayer of thanksgiving (the consecratory prayer) is clearly and simply indicated in the following description of a Mass around the year 150 by St. Justin Martyr:

> . . . And on that day which is called after the sun, all who are in the towns and in the country gather together for a communal celebration. And then the memoirs of the apostles or the writings of the prophets are read, as long as time permits. After the reader has finished his task, the one presiding gives an address, urgently admonishing his hearers to practice these beautiful teachings in their lives. Then all stand up together and recite prayers. After the end of the prayers . . . the bread and wine mixed with water are brought, and the president offers us prayers and thanksgivings, as much as in him lies. The people chime in with an Amen. Then takes place the distribution, to all attending, of the things over which the thanksgiving has spoken, and the deacons bring a portion to the absent. [He had previously remarked, "This food itself is known amongst us as the eucharist. No one may partake of it unless he is convinced of the truth of our teachings and is cleansed in the bath of baptism."] Besides, those who are well-to-do give whatever they will. What is gathered is deposited with the one presiding, who therewith helps orphans and widows.
>
> *First Apology*

It is obvious that all the elements of the Mass as we know it today are there—the readings from the writings of the apostles and prophets, the collection, the preparation and bearing of the gifts to the altar, the Eucharistic prayer or canon which Justin calls "prayers and thanksgivings, as much as in him lies" (indicating that the Eucharistic prayer at that time depended entirely on the spontaneity of the president, the one requirement being the consecratory words used by Jesus at the Last Supper: "This is my body . . . this is my blood . . . Do this in remembrance of me"). In Justin's Mass there is also the response of the people to the sacrifice, their Amen! And finally there is a distribution of the gifts, Holy Communion, which is also brought to members of the community who are not at the service.

There has been but one "canon" or Eucharistic prayer in the Roman Church for the past thousand years. It was in Latin and was invariable, except for small insertions on very special feasts. The new revised rite of the Roman Mass (1969) now provides us with four canons, one of them being the old Roman canon just mentioned. These Eucharistic prayers are similar in essentials, differing only in some wording and in historical background and emphasis. The newer canons also give greater emphasis on the Holy Spirit as the divine Person especially invoked for changing the bread and wine into the Lord's body and blood. We can learn a great deal about the nature and meaning of the Mass from these Eucharistic prayers, especially the fourth, which contains a brief history of sacred salvation, of the life of Jesus, reaching its culmination in the Last Supper and the aftermath of the passion, death, and resurrection.

With all its holy details, the fourth Eucharistic prayer helps us fulfill Christ's command to do what he had done in remembrance of him. Unfortunately, because of its length, it is seldom used on Sundays in most parishes, and so most Catholics are deprived of the opportunity to review with love and gratitude all that Christ has done for them. As missalettes are available in almost every parish church, I strongly recommend that my readers leisurely examine the text of this fourth Eucharistic prayer. Their appreciation of the Mass will then be greatly enhanced.

Hearts Burning Within

Earlier I commented on the incident in St. Luke's Gospel in which Jesus appeared to two disciples as they were making their way to Emmaus from Jerusalem on the first Easter afternoon. They did not recognize Jesus when he asked why they were so sad. When they told him of the collapse of their dreams about Jesus as a possible political rescuer from Roman domination, he accused them of being "Foolish men, and slow of heart to believe all that the prophets have spoken" (Lk. 24:25). As they walked along, "he interpreted to them in all the scriptures the things concerning himself" (24:27). They experienced a peculiar sensation within themselves, and they asked each other, "Did not our hearts burn within us while he talked to us on the road, while he opened to us the scriptures?" (24:32).

Actually, what Jesus accused them of when he said they were slow of heart to believe was the failure to know him as he was in reality—as the God-man, the Messiah, the Lord, whose kingdom was not of this world. Their knowledge of him was purely "notional," it was primarily a bundle of facts and impressions about him and his accomplishments (mingled with their own fanciful dreams of what they thought the Messiah ought to be).

The true meaning of Jesus dawned upon them in a flash, the moment when he performed the familiar gesture of taking bread, breaking it, and blessing it. Then they recognized him, as they later claimed, "in the breaking of the bread." The Jesus who had died a few days earlier and had now risen from the dead, who had risen into a new kind of existence that morning is now known to them at long last. Or more exactly, they have made a giant step in coming to know him. The full understanding of the Christ will be brought home to them (as to the other disciples) only when they receive the gift of the Holy Spirit on Pentecost. It is, above all, the Holy Spirit whose function is to bring about that "heart-knowledge" without which Christianity is only a superficial veneer of thought and practice.

Likewise, it is the Holy Spirit who—with his special gifts of wisdom and understanding—can conduct us into the inner heart and mind of Jesus, his life and his work, above all his greatest gift, the Holy Eucharist. And the best way to open ourselves to those divine gifts is by meditating on the word of God, as Jesus helped his two disciples to meditate on the word on that first Easter afternoon.

The Mass is never celebrated without readings from the Old Testament and/or the New Testament, from one of the letters of the apostles, and from the Gospels. The importance of these readings cannot be over-emphasized. They can be found, of course, in every one of the variety of Mass books that are published by our religious presses. The readings are as essential to us as Jesus' unfolding of the Scriptures to the two Emmaus-bound disciples. But the scriptural readings have to be "unfolded" if we are to expect those burning hearts that best condition us for the full participation in the Eucharist.

This "unfolding" is primarily the work of the celebrant who preaches the homily, the chief purpose of which is to bring the congregation to a deeper knowledge of and love for Jesus Christ. But the zealous Christian can help the process of the "unfolding" a great deal by reading and thinking over the readings beforehand and, if possible, looking at the explanatory notes for the text in such editions as the New American Bible, the Jerusalem Bible, or the Reading Guides of both Old and New Testaments published by The Liturgical Press.

At the beginning of this treatment of the Eucharist, I proposed that our main purpose in celebrating Mass is to remember Jesus. By now it should be evident to all that our remembering—in addition to mental recall of what Jesus said and did and was—involves a never-ending process of understanding that is love and love that is understanding more and more and more. We cannot live without the Eucharist. We believe Christ's word to us, "I am the living bread which came down from heaven; if any one eats of this bread, he will live for ever" (Jn. 6:51).

The Deepest Reality of Life

As this chapter concludes, it is imperative again to insist strongly on the reality that has been the foundation and background of all that I have written about spirituality and the place of the sacraments in spirituality. It is the fact of our having become new beings in Christ. "If any one is in Christ, he is a new creation; the old has passed away, behold, the new has come" (2 Cor. 5:17).

Christian spirituality has been defined as "the deepest reality of life in persons when it is lived in and through the spirit of Christ. It is there that we find the heart of Christianity" (Institute of Spirituality, Collegeville, Minnesota, February 1978). As we have seen, this "deepest reality" is our new being in Christ. It is not a question of acquiring a new kind of spirituality. We have it already, surely, at least, in its beginning. It is Christ in us, our "hope of glory" (Col. 1:27). And it is our being in him. For us it is a question of growing in awareness and appreciation of the new being that we are and allowing that awareness to control and direct our lives. Perhaps the first moment of our conversion is the first startling awakening to this new reality that Jesus has given to us.

Awareness of our new being in Christ has to be the motivation of all of life, especially our moral life. But this awareness does not take away the need we all have to die daily to the flesh, that is, to our selfish, self-centered ego, so that God may be the center of our being. It has to become "a lived experience," as Fr. William Shannon tells us in the June-July 1978 *Sisters Today* (p. 690). And it takes a lifetime.

And this is where the sacraments come in. Father Shannon sees the sacraments primarily as "celebrations" of realities already present in the Christian and the Christian community. He sees them as "peak moments" in the ongoing, never-ending experience of the extending of the new creation into the reality of our lives. "The sacraments are key moments in our lives when we ritualize and celebrate our new birth into God's life and the conversion process whereby we live out in daily life the implications of that new birth" (pp. 690-91). The idea is that the more we celebrate the more we grow in the spirit of Christ.

I like this idea very much, but with some reservations which I shall come to presently. I especially like the idea that at Mass we celebrate our being as a community of people, all born again, all united to Christ and to one another. Celebrating this reality cannot but intensify it. And along with doing what Jesus did in remembrance of him, this adds a new and beautiful dimension to our Sunday Mass.

I take back nothing of what I have already said about finding Christ in our daily life, work, and suffering. But it seems to me that being able to celebrate (and to look forward to) the "peak experience" of the Mass more than any other exercise can help us keep that divine Presence in our consciousness. The statement of the American Bishops' Committee on the Liturgy published in *The Place of Music in Eucharistic Celebrations, 1968* could not be more appropriate:

> We assemble together at Mass in order to speak our faith over again in community and, by speaking it, to renew and deepen it. We do not come together to meet Christ as if he were absent from the rest of our lives. We come together to deepen our awareness of, and commitment to, the action of His Spirit in the whole of our lives at every moment. We come together to acknowledge the work of the Sprit in us, to offer thanks, to celebrate.

See *Sisters Today* (June-July 1978), pp. 692-93.

Father Shannon follows through with the same idea of the sacraments as celebrations of present realities in his treatment of the sacrament of reconciliation. For him this sacrament is also a celebration of a reality that is already there, namely, our repentance and God's universal love and forgiveness. Here is where my reservation comes in: if we are already assured of God's forgiveness, experiencing the ever-present reality of that forgiveness in our lives (p. 694), what is the point of Christ telling the apostles, "If you forgive the sins of any, they are forgiven" (Jn. 20:23)? And what is the point of the priest's absolution?

Father Shannon's idea is a welcome corrective to the negative conception of confession many of us older Catholics grew up with—the idea that confession is a kind of spiritual shower bath. It is more than that, however. People sin. They feel the need for relief from guilt. The best (and cheapest) way to acquire relief is to unburden one's soul to a confessor. The mere unburdening is already a psychological relief, as psychiatrists assure us. But when that relief is backed up by the firm belief that our sins are actually forgiven by the priest's absolution, it is a great deal more satisfying than seeing a psychiatrist.

I would like to add to Father Shannon's theory of the sacraments as celebrations of realities already present the personal theory that sacraments are also living encounters with Christ—with Christ the Savior—for particular needs of our life. The Christ we encounter in the Eucharist is also the Christ who says to us as he said about the woman who washed his feet with her tears of repentance, "Her sins, which are many, are forgiven, for she loved much" (Lk. 7:47).

Linking with Everyday Life

Throughout this book I have been obsessed with the danger of writing in a spiritual vacuum and proposing ideas and theories that do not correspond to or in any way affect the daily life of Christians, particularly the laity. I know that it would be difficult to find an adult Christian (or an adolescent or child, for that matter) who does not wrestle with varying degrees of anxiety. It does not require a great leap of faith to believe that for most people life is conflict, struggle, pain, worry—most of which results from concern about loved ones.

It may not have been too evident, but the reality and universality of human pain has never been far from my consciousness all through this book. Now as I come to the end of these two chapters on spirituality—especially this one on the sacraments of reconciliation and the Eucharist —I have to ask myself if the ideas here proposed are in any way related to daily life as it is lived by most Catholics. What help can the Christian find in these chapters that will provide more meaning for his life?

Hopefully, some meaning might be found in the word and idea of "reconciliation." I emphasized earlier that the main purpose of the sacrament of reconciliation is reconciliation of the alienated penitent with God, with one's community, family and friends, and finally with oneself. May I now extend this idea of reconciliation to life itself and express the hope that through this sacrament the Christian may *become more reconciled to his human condition,* with all its content of joy, sorrow, worry, hope, failure, disappointment—without, however, the willingness to settle (in a defeatist kind of way) for evil conditions that could be changed by some human effort?

But it is the Eucharist par excellence that not only invites but effects reconciliation to the human condition, not only to one's personal human condition but also to the human condition of Jesus in its essence. More than at any other sacrament, at the Eucharist we literally stand at the Redeeming Act of Christ, we say our personal YES to it, we become one with the divine Victim. In the Eucharist all of life is reconciled to the Father. In the Eucharist we make our own the sentiment of Christ who, when he came into this world, said:

> "Sacrifices and offerings thou hast not desired,
> but a body hast thou prepared for me;
> in burnt offerings and sin offerings thou has taken no pleasure.
> Then I said, 'Lo, I have come to do thy will, O God,'
> as it is written of me in the roll of the book" (Heb. 10:5-7).

He has also fashioned a body for each of us and called us to a particular vocation in this life. But the only sentiment that can give any meaning to our life (as it did to Christ's life) is, "Lo, I have come to do thy will, O God." There is no more effective way of expressing that sentiment than the Eucharist.

Father Shannon insists that conversion, *metanoia,* is a life-long process. We need to die daily to our selfishness. For me life is not all celebration. It is a combination of triumph, success, personal and material failure, sorrow, joy, defeat, victory. The sacraments, especially the Eucharist and reconciliation, are there for every one of life's needs. They shape life, give it form, direction, and meaning. I cannot conceive of life without them.

13

The Virgin Mary and Christian Spirituality

A book which aims at deepening a Christian's conception of spiritual realities and of conversion to Christ must consider the Virgin Mary, who has been called the Perfect Christian. What we human persons need much more than verbal and written directives is the living example of flesh and blood people like ourselves who came to know and experience Christ in an intimate and personal way. No one has ever known and experienced him in the same way that Mary did, and yet her way is the way most available and open to all Christians.

Mary, Model of the Christian Life

Spirituality—Christian spirituality above all—is a relationship between persons, a relationship that becomes the dynamic motivating force of one's life. It colors and characterizes one's ideas, judgments, opinions, actions, and reactions. It is the deepest reality of life. Spirituality is the relationship between the Person who is Christ and the person who is each of us. Our task and never-ending goal is to try to understand that relationship with a view to perfecting and deepening it. The best way to do this is to examine with loving care the most perfect example of Christian spirituality that Christianity has ever known, namely, Mary, the Mother of Jesus.

As limited human beings, we all need guidance, enlightenment, and encouragement; we need the feeling of not being alone on our quest. No one, no saint, ancient or modern, can provide us with that guidance and enlightenment and encouragement in a more practical and available way than Mary.

The first truth to be established and emphasized about Mary is that she was a human being. This may seem like a strange statement until one realizes the perverse efforts of "pious" artists, sculptors, and some writers to picture her as a pretty doll-like figure who spent all her time praying with eyes rolled heavenward, confident no doubt that the angels would do her housework for her. But Mary was a real human being, a real woman in every way, except sin. She was a Jewish mother who worked with her hands, doing in her home all that needed to be done. She was a wife and a mother who took care of all the personal human wants of her husband and son; she cooked, sewed, cleaned, and did the washing. She taught Jesus by word and example, and it was with and through her and her husband Joseph that Jesus "increased in wisdom and in stature, and in favor with God and man" (Lk. 2:52).

In a word, Mary *experienced* life, she knew from firsthand experience what it was to live in this world as a wife and a mother, above all as a woman. She was aware of the mystery of life—its sorrow, pain, joy, and happiness—and came to terms with it all without, however, understanding it any better than we. Through her experience of growing and living in Nazareth as the wife of Joseph and the mother of Jesus, she perfected herself more and more as a human being, a daughter to the Lord.

Mary loved Joseph her husband; she saw herself as his equal, and knew she was not a sex object, as were many of the women of that time and area of the world. Unlike those women, she experienced no self-hatred. She realized her personal dignity, not only as the Mother of God, but as a human person, as a woman. Even before she became aware of God's special choice of her to become the Mother of his Son, she was aware of God's special choice of her to be a Jewish woman, a human person, a member of the Chosen People.

It is Catholic belief that Mary was a virgin all her life, that she and Joseph never had physical intercourse, but I do not believe that her sinlessness (also part of Catholic belief) and her perpetual virginity in any way diminished or "spoiled" her life as a wife and mother. It was this marvelous sense of her own dignity as a human person that was at the foundation of her whole attitude towards God and therefore of her spirituality, her religious convictions, which she expressed so wonderfully in the Magnificat:

> "My soul magnifies the Lord,
> and my spirit rejoices in God my Savior,
> for he has regarded the low estate of his handmaiden.

For behold, henceforth all generations will call me blessed;
for he who is mighty has done great things for me,
and holy is his name.
And his mercy is on those who fear him
from generation to generation.
He has shown strength with his arm,
he has scattered the proud in the imagination of their hearts,
he has put down the mighty from their thrones,
and exalted those of low degree;
he has filled the hungry with good things,
and the rich he has sent empty away.
He has helped his servant Israel,
in remembrance of his mercy,
as he spoke to our fathers,
to Abraham and to his posterity for ever" (Lk. 1:46-55).

Basis of Her Spirituality

Mary sets forth her whole spirituality in this Magnificat. The heart of that spirituality is the old biblical truth to be found in the lives of the great leaders of her people like Abraham, Isaac, Joseph, Judith, Esther, and all the psalmists and prophets—the truth which her Son will preach day in, day out, the truth that St. Paul will fight for all his apostolic life, namely, that all good, all favor, all grace, privilege, and salvation come from God and God alone, that it is all undeserved and unmerited: "He who is mighty *has done great things for me,* and holy is his name." Those made proud and rich by their asceticism and perfect obedience to the Law the Lord sends empty away. Those mighty in words and worship performed for self-gratification he puts down from their thrones, but on the other hand he exalts those who acknowledge their creatureliness, their absolute need for God:

> "He has filled the hungry with good things,
> and the rich he has sent empty away.
> He has helped his servant Israel,
> in remembrance of his mercy,
> as he spoke to our fathers,
> to Abraham and to his posterity for ever."

Unlike the first Eve who wished to be like unto God, Mary recognized and acknowledged the Lordship of Jahweh and so became the second Eve, the true Mother of all the Living. As it was with the Mother of God, so must it be with us. The Lord has to be the Lord of our lives, too.

A Model for Every Christian

I have referred to the danger of failing to see Mary as a human being and overemphasizing her great privileges as the only human being (other than her Son) who remained sinless all her life, who was a virgin before, during, and after her giving birth to Jesus, and whose body was assumed into heaven when she died. The Catholic Church asks us to celebrate these personal prerogatives of hers and along with her to praise and thank the Father for them all, but neither she, nor her Son, nor the Church would be happy if in celebrating these divine favors we forgot that Mary was human and placed her on a pedestal where she would have nothing in common with us. "If we admired her to the point of making her unapproachable, we'd nullify her message. Mary's more than a jewel of God's: she's a mother, our mother, and what she wants is children who are like her, who are willing to be servants, just as she was" (Louis Evely: *That Man is You*, [Westminster, Md., Newman Press, 1965], p. 246).

But it was the young Englishwoman Caryll Houselander, who died prematurely shortly after World War II, who to my knowledge first insisted on the humanness of Mary and drew the inevitable conclusion from that fact, namely, that of all the saints Mary was the one whom we can most readily imitate. Each of the canonized saints had his own vocation. They all distinguished themselves in extraordinary ways, for example, by martyrdom, by high degrees of contemplation, crippling self-mortification, etc., but Mary's whole way of life was ordinary (apart from her privileges as Mother of God). Miss Houselander puts it so well:

> Our Lady had to include in her vocation, in her life's work, the essential thing that was to be hidden in every other vocation, in every life. She is not only human, she is humanity.
>
> The one thing that she did and does is the one thing that we all have to do, namely, *to bear Christ into the world.*
>
> Christ *must be born from every soul,* formed in every life. . . . If we had a picture of Our Lady's personality, we might be dazzled into thinking that only one sort of person could form Christ in himself, and we should miss the meaning of our own being.
>
> Nothing but things essential *for us* are revealed to us about the mother of God: the fact that she was wed to the Holy Spirit and bore Christ into the world.
>
> Our crowning joy is that she did this as a lay person and through the ordinary daily life that we all live; through natural love made supernatural, as the water at Cana was, at her request, turned into wine.
>
> *The Reed of God* (New York: Sheed and Ward, 1951),
> p. xii; emphasis added.

I am quite convinced that even before Mary was found to be with child by the Holy Spirit (Mt. 1:18), she found God in her daily life through her duties as a Jewish girl and later as a wife and mother. It is in this "ordinariness" and then in her faith and trust that Mary becomes a perfect model for the Christian in any age who is deeply concerned about achieving intimacy with Christ.

Earlier I said that God wishes to enter the world through us human persons. The process he began with and in Mary he wishes to carry on through us. The best way for us to carry out our God-given vocation of being God-bearers is to be and do as Mary did, i.e. form Christ from our lives as she formed him from hers.

Forming Christ from Our Lives

Again I am indebted to Caryll Houselander for many of the ideas of this section. One of Jesus' favorite images was that of seed. Remember, "the seed is the word of God." Actually, he himself was a seed, a divine Seed, containing in it the life of the world; this divine Seed was planted in Mary's womb where it grew in her and from her. *She formed him from herself,* from her physical self and from the simplicity of her daily life. Working, eating, sleeping, visiting neighbors, she was forming his body from hers. From her humanity she gave him his humanity.

Every beat of her heart gave him his heart to love with, his heart to be broken by love that was to be rejected and repudiated. All her experience of the world about her was gathered to Christ growing within her. Looking upon the flowers, she gave him human vision and sight. Breaking and eating the bread, drinking the wine of the country, she gave him flesh and blood—she prepared the host and the wine for Mass.

What Mary did for Christ then, we can and must try to do for him now in our world, our environment. He wants to be formed from our lives now. He wants our eyes to see with, our ears to hear with, our mouths to speak with, our hands to serve with, our hearts to love with. During the advent of Mary's pregnancy, Christ was totally dependent on her for everything. He was absolutely helpless. He could not speak. His breathing had to be her breathing, his heart beat with the beating of her heart. Today he is likewise dependent on us. We must carry him everywhere—wherever he wishes to go. And there may be many places where he may never go unless we take him.

When Mary, with Jesus in her womb, went off to visit her cousin Elizabeth, John the Baptist quickened in Elizabeth's womb—he leapt for joy. Later, in his own adulthood, Jesus will say, "I came that they may have life. . . ." (Jn. 10:10). Even before he was physically born, his presence gave life. So must it always be. If we carry Christ wherever he wishes to go, people will become aware of his presence in us, not by our outward appearance, but in the way the flower buds become aware of the presence of the sun, by a growing and unfolding in themselves. This is Christ's favorite way of being recognized in any age.

Giving our being and our life to Christ so that he can be formed from our being and our life has meaning, too, for our work. No one should make or do anything except in the spirit in which a mother bears a child, in the spirit in which Mary formed Christ in her womb, in the love with which the Creator made the world.

Before you make anything, you must have it in your heart. "And his mother kept all these things in her heart," says St. Luke (2:51). If we work and create in the spirit of Mary forming Christ in her womb, then when the work is finished, we can say in our own way, "The word was made flesh." This applies to anything we make or do—cooking a meal, writing a poem, painting a picture, creating a piece of music, sweeping a floor, working in an office or a classroom, running a truck or tractor— anything and everything. Above all it includes suffering. As Christ received everything of his humanity from Mary then, so now does he wish to receive everything of his new presence from us.

The Nature of Mary's Faith

All the above requires faith on our part, but no more, indeed, not as much—as Mary's vocation demanded of her. Elizabeth's tribute to Mary when Mary came to help her in her pregnancy can be said to have characterized her entire life, not just her acceptance of the request of the angel: "Blessed is she who believed that there would be a fulfillment of what was spoken to her from the Lord" (Lk. 1:45). Mary lived on faith from day to day, all through her life. Faith for her was accepting God, receiving his requests, trusting in his will, and making that divine will the dynamism of her life. "Behold, I am the handmaid of the Lord; let it be to me according to your word" (Lk. 1:38), she answered when God through the angel asked her to become the Mother of the Son of God.

What was faith for Mary? She is the best example I know of for the claim that faith is not so much acceptance of doctrine or a system of truths as it is accepting God as the guiding force in her life and trusting her whole life to him. "Be it done to me according to your word" meant for Mary "I trust myself and my life entirely to you, Father, my life is entirely in your hands, no matter what comes." When Mary gave her consent to God's request, she accepted the future, with all its unknown elements, she said YES to whatever the Lord would continue to ask of her. Here again she becomes the perfect model for all dedicated Christians. Indeed, it is her faith more than any other of her gifts that makes her the "perfect Christian," the ideal that enfolds every other ideal. The words of the *Dogmatic Constitution on the Church,* no. 45, of Vatican II are to the point:

> In the most holy Virgin the Church has already reached that perfection whereby she exists without spot or wrinkle (cf. Eph. 5:27). Yet the follow-

ers of Christ still strive to increase in holiness by conquering sin. And so they raise their eyes to Mary who shines forth to the whole community of the elect as a model of the virtues. Devotedly meditating on her and contemplating her in the light of the Word made man, the Church with reverence enters more intimately into the supreme mystery of the Incarnation and becomes ever increasingly like her Spouse.

The Documents of Vatican II, Walter M. Abbott, S.J., ed. (New York: America Press, 1966), p. 93.

The Passion of Mary

Mary's faith could never have been easy for her. How she must have wondered about having to give birth to the Son of God in a stranger's stable in Bethlehem! Then the prophecy of Simeon at the circumcision of Jesus had to puzzle her:

"Behold, this child is set for the fall and rising of many in Israel,
and for a sign that is spoken against
(and a sword will pierce through your own soul also),
that thoughts out of many hearts may be revealed" (Lk. 2:34-35).

She knew instinctively that the threat of that sword had to involve the being she loved most in the world, her Son. In this connection we must not forget how proud and concerned all Jewish mothers feel about their sons. What Mary could not have realized in the beginning was how her Son would himself give her cause to experience the sword. In his book *The Lord,* the great German theologian Romano Guardini makes the point that Mary gradually had to watch Jesus grow away from her, even before he left home to begin his public life.

Her Son's words can be toned down and even somewhat explained away now as we read or hear them in retrospect, but they must have sounded harsh to Mary when she first heard them. For example, at Cana when she simply remarked to him, "They have no wine," he responded, "O woman, what have you to do with me? My hour has not yet come" (Jn. 2:3-4). (The translation of the New American Bible is only slightly less severe: "Woman, how does this concern of yours involve me?").

Again, when someone said to him, "Your mother and your brethren are outside, asking for you," his response must surely have seemed harsh to his mother, "Who are my mother and my brethren? . . . whoever does the will of God is my brother, and sister, and mother (Mk. 3:32-34). In Luke Jesus is even more explicit: "My mother and my brethren are those who hear the word of God and do it" (Lk. 8:21). Hearing God's word, being open to his will, is surely a grace that is available to every earnest follower of Christ, and it is most consoling for us who hear it now. But no one could find any fault with Mary if her first reaction was one of pain, for she was surely not aware at the time of the future St.

Augustine's opinion that receptive faith, willingness to do the Father's will, is a greater dignity even than being Christ's Mother in the physical order, nor could she realize then that of all people who would ever live she was the only one who would ever achieve perfection according to both ideals.

The point here, of course, is that Mary knew human pain, sorrow, and anxiety even as each of us does. Indeed, because of her extreme sensibility, she probably felt it more keenly. I do not believe that any of Mary's great endowments or achievements were momentary events. Her faith, for example, her "let it be done to me according to your word," had to be constantly renewed, and she had to live on faith all through her life. She had to struggle with faith, even as we do. So, too, the sword that Simeon had foreseen. As her Son grew more and more remote from her, when he left her home and gave himself completely to his work with the people and the apostles, the sword entered more and more deeply into her soul, the final thrust being, of course, when she stood beneath the cross, looking up at him, seeing him in his pain, *suffering with* him. This is compassion in its truest sense.

We do not forget that she was a *Jewish mother*. She could and would continue to make her act of faith, but not without the most heart-rendering struggle the world has ever seen. Some insight into God's plan must surely have come to her after her Son's resurrection, but complete understanding had to wait until the Holy Spirit came upon her and the apostles at Pentecost and made them into the Church, the New Christ, of whom she was still the Mother.

What Imitation of Mary Really Means

In writing about Mary, I have necessarily used the past tense as she did live some two thousand years ago. But Mary, like her Son himself, belongs to our age and every age. She lives now. This is the real meaning of her assumption. No book presents this truth more realistically (and beautifully) than *A New Catechism:*

> Mary has already been raised from the dead, body and soul. Of the other dead we may also say that they will be made alive, that they are about to arise, but we acknowledge that Mary is already glorified. It is true that her glory—like that of Christ—will only be perfect when the whole of mankind is gathered together. Just as Christ's resurrection is effective among us through his forceful, vivid presence in the life of the world, so, too, we may say, the glory of the "Assumption" of Mary. This means that she *is more in the world than any other woman*. Cleopatra is remembered. *Mary is addressed*. She is the *most closely present of all women*. The risen Christ and Mary assumed into heaven—the true Adam and Eve of mankind—are not to be sought far away from us, as though heaven were an immense theatre full of purely spiritual souls where only two places were bodily

occupied, those of Christ and Mary. Once again, it must be remembered that imagination in terms of space and time is powerless here. *We can experience the presence of Christ and Mary by living on earth in the Spirit of Christ* and by speaking to them in prayer. The same may be said of the other dead. Some great saints and good men are more powerfully present than others.

(New York: Herder and Herder, 1967), p. 475; emphasis added.

There are libraries full of books on the Virgin Mary. This is not the place to recite all her privileges and endowments. What I have wanted to do was to show how her life is truly the example of the life of the Christian, to show how the life of the Christian not only parallels hers, it can draw its inspiration, its dynamism, its guidance from her and her life. It was especially in that gradual, day-by-day growth in the likeness of Christ that she truly becomes our model, our example. As her whole life was a high road pointing to Pentecost, so too ours. Then and only then shall we understand.

From this it should become clear that our imitation of Mary is not a mere superficial imitation. We do not try to copy her life and spirit as an artist might copy the style of a great master or as a young athlete might try to make his own the mannerisms of a great player. This is not the way we imitate either Christ or his Mother. The person that I am is not the same as the person Mary is. Imitating her means entering into a personal relationship with Jesus as she did, but it is *my* personal relationship— one that *I* live here and now in this vocation that is mine, this body and personality that is unlike that of any other person who has ever lived. It may help to see my imitation of Mary as my doing and living now as she would do and live if she were in my place.

But more than anything else it means forming Christ (as she did) from the routine and substance of my daily life. When the Child was born, he surely looked like her. It is also that way with us. Christ grows in us, we grow in him, as Mary did. We form him from our daily life, as she did. The Christ each of us brings forth is our very own. I hope it is not too imaginative to express the hope that he will also look like us!

I can't think of a better way to finish this chapter than by quoting from Caryll Houselander's *The Reed of God:*

In giving her humanity to God, Mary gave all humanity to Him, to be used for His own will.

In wedding her littleness to the Spirit of Love, she wed all lowness to the Spirit of Love.

In surrendering to the Spirit and becoming the Bride of Life, she wed God to the human race and made the whole world pregnant with the life of Christ.

"I am come," Christ said, "that they may have life, and may have it more abundantly."

Mary knew in what the joy of the world was to consist, what it would be that would make everyone call her blessed, for it would simply be her own joy.

Everyone who wished it could be wed to the Spirit, not only solitaries living in lonely cells but everyone in the world; not only young girls and boys or children who had been somehow spared from sin, but sinners, too; not only the young but also the old: because the Spirit makes everything new. The life filling her own being, the life leaping in little John the Baptist, the life breaking out in her jubilant song . . . all that would be given to everyone who asked for it.

She had given mankind the key. *Indeed, she had unlocked and opened the door of every heart. Now men had only to leave it open.*

p. 67; emphasis added.

My prayer is that this book and especially the example and inspiration of Mary will aid us all always to make our own the sentiment of the psalmist:

> My heart is steadfast, O God,
> my heart is steadfast! . . .
> Be exalted, O God, above the
>   heavens!
> Let thy glory be over all the earth!

Ps. 57:7, 11

14

Love: the Heart of Spirituality

Let us again consider the scene in Scripture where Jesus asks Peter three times, "Simon, son of John, do you love me?" After the third query, Simon Peter bursts out, "Lord, you know everything; you know that I love you" (Jn. 12:15, 17).

Peter had heard Jesus speak about love many times before that day. He had been present when his master had proclaimed the great commandment of love of God and love of neighbor: "You shall love the Lord your God with all your heart, and with all your soul, and with all your mind. . . . You shall love your neighbor as yourself" (Mt. 22:37-39). And at the Last Supper Peter had heard Jesus say: "A new commandment I give to you, that you love one another; even as I have loved you, that you also love one another. By this all men will know that you are my disciples, if you have love for one another" (Jn. 13:34-35).

But for Peter—as for countless numbers of Christians since his day—there is apparently a great difference between hearing about love, being told to love, even telling God that you love him, and actually and truly carrying out that love in practice.

Freedom Necessary for Love

In Peter's case the realness of his love undoubtedly resulted both from the vivid, bitter memory of his having denied knowing Jesus after the latter's arrest and the now overwhelming realization that Jesus had not only forgiven him but that he still trusted him and loved him in spite of everything.

In this book we have been seriously concerned with conversion to Christ and with the "spirituality" that necessarily must result from such an intimate experience. With admittedly limited success, I have tried to put into words that special relationship to Jesus that I believe spirituality to be. I've used phrases like "life in persons lived in and through the spirit of Christ," "the dynamic motivating force of our life," the Christian's vivid awareness that the "deepest reality of his being is Christ living in him."

All of those phrases add up to a total picture of the nature of spirituality, but now as I come to the end of the book it seems to me that this deep reality can only be fully described in terms of *love*—love based on the realization of how very much Christ has loved us. This realization can come about in any number of ways, with the way of repentant Peter open to most of us. To repeat: there can be no genuine love for God (and ultimately for neighbor) without a realization of our first having been loved. What makes God's love for us so great is that it is a forgiving love, and true love for God on our part understands this.

The Pharisee asked Jesus: "Which is the greatest commandment in the law?" Was it a good question? Can love be commanded, forced, prescribed, purchased? I have never heard of true love resulting from any such transaction. Love has to result from a *free choice*. God is he who is supremely free. That is why he can love so magnanimously and so universally. We humans are made in his likeness—which means not only that we can think and reason and choose, but, above all, that we can love. That is why God has such admiration, such reverence, for our human freedom.

The French poet Charles Péguy puts these sentiments in God's mouth:

> A beatitude of slaves, a salvation of slaves, a
> slavish beatitude, how do you expect me to be
> interested in that kind of thing? Does one care
> to be loved by slaves?
> My might is manifest enough in all matter and
> in all events. . . .
> But in my creation which is endued with life, says God,
> I wanted something better, I wanted something more.
> Infinitely better. Infinitely more. For I wanted
> that freedom.
> I created that very freedom. . . .
> When once you have known what it is to be loved freely,
> submission no longer has any taste.
> All the prostrations in the world
> Are not worth the beautiful upright attitude of a

free man as he kneels. All the submission, all
the dejection in the world
are not equal in value to the soaring up point,
the beautiful straight soaring up of one single
invocation.

> "From a love that is free," *God Speaks* (New York:
> Pantheon, 1945), p. 40; emphasis added.

The Difficulty of Loving

The conclusion is inevitable: it is in loving that we humans attain the highest degree of our humanity; it is in loving that we become, to a certain degree, divine. But unless we exercise our freedom by constantly, deliberately recommitting ourselves to the love of God and of neighbor, we run the risk of losing the freedom and becoming mere mechanical men and women. That is why we need constant reminders of how much Jesus has loved us. It does not take too much imagination to attach to a crucifix the question Jesus asked Peter: "Do you love me?" Unless we are free and aware of our freedom, there will never be any substance to our response, "Lord, you know everything; you know that I love you."

But loving God, loving one's neighbor, one's enemies—even loving one's wife or sweetheart or friend—is *hard*. To love anyone genuinely is the most difficult task in the world. There is a great difference between telling someone (including God) that you love him and actually carrying out that claim. The familiar phrase of Dostoevski comes to mind: "Love in action is a harsh and dreadful thing compared to love in dreams." The example of history's saints and closer to us moderns, the example of Dorothy Day and Mother Teresa of Calcutta, demonstrates the truth of that statement.

The booklet by Fr. John Powell, S.J., entitled "Why Am I Afraid to Love?" continues to retain its popularity among young people. The question may sound strange to American ears, accustomed as they are to TV and film dramatization of the ease of "falling in love." But the question demands an answer from every Christian. My answer is that we are afraid to love because we instinctively realize that loving makes such terrifying demands upon us, the chief one being that it requires the decentralization of self. It requires that we learn how to live for others, above all, for the beloved, rather than for self, as we had been accustomed to doing. Fr. Adrian van Kaam tells of another reason why we are afraid to love: to open oneself to love means to open oneself to being hurt, and most people are hesitant about that.

Again, we are afraid to love because to tell someone that we love him or her (above all, God) means that we have to admit our own poverty and emptiness; we have to admit our total dependence on the beloved, our absolute need to be enriched by the beloved. This is especially the case when we tell God that we love him. This admission of poverty and dependence was the heart of Peter's confession to Jesus: "Lord, you know everything; you know that I love you." His brashness, his over-confidence, his pride at having been made the chief of the apostolic band is gone. He stands naked and empty in the presence of Jesus. At long last he is now capable of genuine love.

Allowing Oneself to Be Loved

I think that there is another element in Peter's experience on this particular occasion that often escapes us. It is that Peter finally under-stood the necessity of *allowing himself to be loved*. Quite understand-ably loving someone—a wife, husband, a fiancé(e), a child, a friend—can present a challenge to a person's desire to do something for the beloved. There are many lovers who can simply spend themselves in the service of others; there is no limit to the things they want to do.

This can be a very laudable attitude, but only on condition that it be balanced by the willingness to accept the same demonstration of love from the beloved. Allowing oneself to be served with love requires humility; again it admits dependence and is therefore the more difficult aspect of the experience of loving.

It may be dangerous to generalize, but I personally believe that if a person is successful in a profession or in human relations of any kind, if anyone is admired and respected and has many friends, the chief credit has to go to those who have trusted, believed in, and loved that person.

When you know that someone really believes in you, the possibilities for personal growth are unlimited. Love gratefully and graciously accepted is creative. That surely was the way with Peter. When he finally realized how much Christ had loved and done for him (despite Peter's weaknesses and denials), he became a new creation. There was more to Peter than there was before.

Love of Self: Basis of Love of Neighbor

This truth leads to another even more basic one. In repeating the ancient Mosaic commandment (and in fact giving it a new meaning) Jesus tells us: "You shall love your neighbor as yourself" (Mt. 22:39). Not a single word of that divine imperative may be omitted, especially not "as yourself." What Jesus is saying is that love of self, that is, esteem, respect for oneself as God's special creation—known by him from all eternity and chosen to exist at this particular moment in mankind's history—and the self-acceptance that goes with knowing one is so loved, is the basis of the loving attitude and the service one gives to his neighbor.

To repeat: there can be no genuine love of neighbor that does not have its roots in genuine love of oneself. But what about this love of neighbor, what does it entail? When Jesus was asked, "Who is my neighbor?" he told the story of the Good Samaritan. The Samaritan saw a human being who had been victimized by robbers. He went out of his way not only to give the victim first aid but also to provide for his future care. In the lives of Christians the variety of victims is limitless and so also the degree of help needed.

The first demand on our loving service must necessarily go to those nearest us in our own families and communities. Anyone who is in need, anyone who is unloved, anyone stricken in any way—physically, morally, or psychologically, of any age—is a proper recipient of our merciful service.

Jesus himself is our exemplar here: Peter described Jesus' life beautifully: "He went about doing good and healing all that were oppressed by the devil" (Acts 10:38). At the Last Supper, Jesus performed a very symbolic act: he washed the feet of the disciples and wiped them with a towel. When he had finished this work of service (actually, it was the work of a slave), he said to them: "Do you know what I have done to you? You call me Teacher and Lord; and you are right, for so I am. If I then, your Lord and Teacher, have washed your feet, you also ought to wash one another's feet. For I have given you an example, that you also should do as I have done to you" (Jn 13:12-15). Our Lord was not here describing the nature and extent of Christian service; he was simply laying down a way of life for his disciples and for his followers in any and every age.

The Works of Mercy

In his description of the Last Judgment (Mt. 25), Jesus gives a criterion whereby men will be judged, i.e. they are to feed the hungry, give drink to the thirsty, welcome strangers, clothe the naked, visit the sick and those imprisoned. Those who perform these works of mercy are blessed and they will inherit the kingdom prepared for them from the foundation of the world (Mt. 25:32-37). Those who refuse or neglect these works of mercy are to be sent to eternal fire (25:41).

In providing his followers, including us, with these principles, Jesus did not, I am convinced, wish to give desire of heavenly reward or fear of hell as essential motives for doing the works of mercy. The real motivation for doing works of mercy is rather that he, God's own Son, identifies himself with all the victims he here mentions. He says to the blessed ones: "Truly, I say to you, as you did it to one of the least of these my brethren, you *did it to me"* (Mt. 25:40; emphasis added). And in judging the self-centered people who refused or neglected to do the works, he says: "Truly, I say to you, as you did it not to one of the least of these, *you did it not to me"* (25:45; emphasis added).

It would seem then that there can be no love for Christ unless it finds its way into the lives of those who are in need of any kind. "Love in practice is a harsh and dreadful thing compared to love in dreams."

It is equally true that it is in the Christian's belief that Christ is identified with all victims that the Christian's love differs from that of the good pagan, the humanist, which is not to downgrade the love of a good pagan who simply sees a human person (not Christ) in those he is kind to. Reverence for the human person of anyone is basic for the Christian as for the pagan. But over and above, or beneath and below, the human person, the Christian also sees an even greater dignity, Christ Jesus himself.

Our Lord's listing of the works of mercy in Mt. 25 is undoubtedly the source of the list of "Corporal Works of Mercy" to be found in the old catechisms: to feed the hungry, give drink to the thirsty, clothe the naked, shelter the homeless, visit the sick, ransom the captives, and bury the dead. It is not an exclusive list. Surely, Jesus would not want to exclude some of the favorite recipients of modern charity—alcoholics, displaced persons, fallen women, citizens of skid row, and inhabitants of underdeveloped countries.

The so-called "Spiritual Works of Mercy" are probably not as well-known: to instruct the ignorant, counsel the doubtful, admonish sinners, bear wrongs patiently, forgive offenses, comfort the afflicted, and pray for the living and the dead.

Conversion to Love

One hardly needs to insist that the works of charity that Jesus demands of his followers and which this chapter has sought to propose as an ideal have to be *personal,* as far as that is possible, in whatever vocation the Christian follows. Writing a check for the Community Chest every year is laudable, and it may be all that many busy business and professional men and women can do. But it is also too impersonal, and it is doubtful that it releases the Christian from his Christ-given obligations as a Christian. It is hardly an adequate substitute for the personal attention, the human touch, the heartfelt smile and word of encouragement, that Christ cries out for with the mouths of so many sick, lonely, discouraged, and unloved persons with whom we daily rub elbows. Even more than financial aid, these unfortunate persons need to be recognized and received in all their human dignity. They need the same reverence and respect that we might give to Christ himself.

The aim of this book has been to encourage genuine and lasting conversion to Christ by Catholics. I am by no means satisfied with what I have written. Now at the conclusion, I have finally come to recognize that conversion to Christ is nothing other than conversion to love. It is accepting from the heart of him who is love incarnate our personal vocation to become the presence—and the channels—of his love into whatever places and situations we find ourselves. It is quite evident that "God, who is rich in mercy, out of the great love with which he loved us" (Eph. 2:4) wants us to be worthy of that love by sharing it and passing it on.

Come, Holy Spirit

The fear of loving, the difficulty, the harsh demands it makes on a person, together with the need to love that most of us instinctively feel can result in only one conclusion: true love for anyone is impossible without divine help. This fact Jesus himself recognized at the Last Supper where he associated the power to love with the coming of the Holy Spirit: "If you love me," he told the apostles, "you will keep my commandments. And I will pray the Father, and he will give you another Counselor, to be with you for ever, even the Spirit of truth . . . you know him, for he dwells with you, and will be in you" (Jn. 14:15-17).

We know how the coming of the Holy Spirit on Pentecost more than fulfilled Jesus' promises. The Holy Spirit completed Jesus' work; he gave understanding of Christ and the courage and enthusiasm to the apostles to carry out Christ's mission. It was the Holy Spirit, too, who initiated, carried through, and finished off God's plan for Mary. It was he who gave her full understanding of her Son and his work.

So, too, Catholics living now. Love fulfills and completes a person. If ordinary, human love can do that, think of the possibilities of completion and fulfillment when divine Love personified, the Holy Spirit, takes possession of a being. That possibility is available to any person who holds out his love-starved heart and begs in the words of what might be the most necessary of all prayers,

> Come, Holy Spirit, fill the hearts of the faithful,
> and kindle in them the fire of your divine love. Amen.

15

Personal Testimonies to Faith

This final chapter is not an afterthought. It has been in my mind from the beginning that a book of this nature could best be completed by the personal testimony of serious-minded representatives of the various vocations in the Body of Christ.

But it was not easy to find people who would be willing to examine their hearts and reveal in writing what their Catholic faith really meant to them. A few consented right off, but later when they perceived the risk and the possible pain of such an intimate self-manifestation, they begged off, and I don't blame them in the least. The reader who asks, "What does faith mean to me?", will immediately understand that what I had requested amounted to a painful invasion of privacy, and granting my request required more than a bit of heroism. So I hope that my readers will join me in a deep expression of gratitude to the brave contributors of the following pages.

What I actually requested was that the writers try to put down what mature Christianity really meant to them, and I wanted them to do this out of the context of the particular vocation of each. This will make for considerable variety in the chapter—variety in more ways than that of the differing vocations. Each writer obliged in his own way, and I am sure that the readers will find worthwhile ideas for their own spiritual growth in all of the testimonies. I personally believe it is the most stimulating and interesting of all the chapters.

The arrangement of the testimonies follows no certain order as none is essential. The testimonies, whether they be from a college student, a young married woman, a single man, a single woman, a priest, a mother of ten, or a sister, speak from the heart about Christianity as lived by that particular Roman Catholic.

Janet Smith

When Janet Smith wrote this testimony, she was a sophomore at the College of St. Scholastica, Duluth, Minnesota, where she majored in history and was a star on the basketball team. Janet is from Crosby, Minnesota.

* * *

I see maturing in Christianity as a gradual realization of my own personal relationship with God, with my fellowmen, and with the community offering itself as one to God in the Church. I feel that in any kind of relationship one gets involved in, there should be a firm foundation of faith; otherwise there can be no hope of furthering the maturing and development of this fellowship.

To me this is the most difficult aspect of Christianity to follow. At times it appears that God and my religion is so distant and apart from my life. I may believe that God exists, but I find myself failing to trust what I believe in, most of all myself.

When I am weighed down by the pressures of everyday life, my faith loses sight of Christ's promise that, when one door closes, another will open for me. I have begun to realize that in the times when I am struggling with my own life, my relationship with God, with the Church, and with the community around me actually grows stronger. I realize finally that I am not alone and that the love and help of Christ is always there at hand if I will only reach out for it.

I see that when I refuse to accept Christ's outpouring of love, I not only cripple my relationship with him, but with other people. Christ's love is given to all and is meant to be shared with each other as he shared it with us. This is the greatest hindrance to becoming an adult Christian. Faith and love must exist in myself first before I can attempt to reach out to others.

Christ's commandments for us are to love God with our whole heart and soul and to love our neighbor as ourselves. How is it possible to give totally of myself if I am lacking these ingredients of faith and love to begin with? Without them I would become susceptible to an increasing self-love within myself. I look for love from the outside first, then from within. Thus I would not be satisfied with the type of person I am. I would not be honest with myself or with others as God wants me to be. This would be the greatest sin against myself that I could commit. I would be hurting my relationship with God and with those around me because it is not an honest relationship to begin with. It would be very easy for me to fall prey to all other kinds of sins that would only be more damaging to myself and others.

My favorite example of the meaning of faith is in Lk. 8:22-26 when Christ was in the boat with his disciples crossing over the lake. A storm came up while Jesus was asleep and his followers became frightened. Afraid of being lost, the disciples awakened Jesus. He quieted the storm and then questioned their lack of faith.

I think that throughout our lives we too are in that same boat; it is Christ's Church, crossing over a sea of turmoil and temptation which threatens to destroy our faith. But Christ is present to us, with us. I have learned that maturation as a Catholic is not a smooth and rapid development. Rather it emerges very grudgingly and at different levels throughout my lifetime. One thing I know is that I must believe that Jesus is there for me and that his love for me will never perish.

Joan Bresnahan Lasslo

Since her graduation from the College of St. Benedict, St. Joseph, Minnesota, in 1975, Joan Lasslo has worked in a parish in Price, Utah, has been a construction laborer, and has recently married. She and her husband Steve live in Price where they are active in parish affairs.

* * *

"What does it mean to me to be an adult Catholic?" Before answering this question, I want to give some of my background. I was raised in a Catholic home, attended public grade school and high school, attended a Catholic college, worked as a volunteer in a Catholic parish, and am presently twenty-five years old, newly married and unemployed.

First, my faith is in Jesus Christ. To me knowing Jesus personally is the most important thing in my life. Everything else grows and comes from this. My participation in Catholicism would be meaningless without this relationship to him. Jesus is all-powerful. He has complete control over all evil. He guides me in my life and gently frees me from my many fears. He forgives my sins and encourages me onward. He shows me which things are important and which are not. He protects me from all that is not true by gradually revealing himself and his wishes to me. He gently and lovingly, through joys and sorrows, asks me to trust him in everything. He is the focus and support of my life. I could do nothing without him.

This faith I have in Jesus finds its expression primarily in the community of our Catholic parish. This community offers me people with whom to live, grow, love, serve, pray, and share the Eucharist. Sharing the Eucharist in a community is important—I am nourished by the prayers, music, sermons, the sacrament. I can also affirm that, "Yes, these people know and love the same God that I know and love." This enriches my life very much.

I have also been deeply enriched by larger Catholic communities. The first is the Catholic college I attended. The witness and faith of the dedicated nuns who run the college have greatly influenced my faith. Their most powerful influence has come through their theology classes, especially those in biblical studies. The latter have changed my entire outlook on Jesus and on life in general. I am so thankful to the Catholic Church for its biblical scholars who give us a clearer understanding of the Bible through the study of cultures, languages, and literary forms.

There are three further reasons for my feeling particularly indebted to the larger Catholic community. The first is the tradition of the mystics with their deep love for God and the manner in which they expressed their experience of him. The second reason for appreciating the Catholic Church is because it has stood up for the ideal of natural family planning. Third, I deeply appreciate the Catholic community's involvement (although hesitant) in charismatic renewal. This movement has deeply affected my life. It has helped me to understand so much more deeply what our Christian life is all about.

I am strongly committed to my Catholic faith. I cannot conceive of a life apart from this Church, except for two situations, the first being a world catastrophe in which the organizational structure of the Church would be destroyed and there would be no access to priests. In such a situation, I would try to follow Jesus either alone or with those who would share my faith.

The second situation would be a community in which the priest-pastor would not allow his parishioners to grow towards Jesus and freedom, away from the rigidity of rules. I would either continue my lay leadership, realizing that my own service was worthwhile, or perhaps I would withdraw for a while. It would be very difficult for me to affirm by my presence something I did not believe in. In such a situation I would rely totally on the will of God as he revealed it to me.

In my daily life I try to spend some time in prayer and in Bible reading. I listen to God and try to spend each day trusting in him and allowing myself to be guided by his Spirit. My "active" life consists in taking care of my husband's needs and being of service to my friends, also those with whom I come into contact every day. I think that at this moment in my life my call is to listen to God and calmly and peacefully to share Jesus' love with no shame or pretense. I do this by visiting people and taking their problems and joys upon myself.

I love Jesus very much, and I love the community of the Catholic Church. My roots, however, are in Jesus. I could follow him without the Church, but I could not be part of the Church without him.

Patricia Gits Opatz

Patricia Opatz, who has been married twenty-seven years, is the mother of ten children and a graduate of the College of St. Benedict, St. Joseph, Minnesota. While bringing up her family, she earned a master of arts degree in English from St. Cloud State College and has also taught at that institution. She and her husband Ralph, a businessman, live in St. Cloud, Minnesota.

* * *

It's a good exercise for any wife and mother, I suppose, to spend the eve of her fiftieth birthday looking back to see what influence Jesus Christ and the Church have had on her vocation. One thing is certain: when I try to imagine what I might have been had I grown up outside the Catholic Church, I turn out to be someone else, not me. There isn't any part of my life that has not been shaped by my being a Catholic Christian.

Because I was a Catholic youngster in a militantly Protestant community, I grew up praying a lot and reading every religious book I could find—often for argumentative and defensive purposes, I'm afraid.

Also because I was a Catholic, I went to a Catholic college that was noted for its religious atmosphere and its values of prayer and work, its motto of doing everything for the glory of God. Oddly enough, the theology and Scripture classes are forgotten; I am not aware of their having had any influence on my life at all. It was in philosophy and literature classes (especially Dante) that I learned my most important lesson in college: the absolute necessity of setting a time aside daily for prayer and spiritual reading. There was ample opportunity to practice that lesson as I moved from college to marriage.

Anyone who married and started a family around 1950 knows what it meant to be a Catholic then. Large families were *de rigueur;* noise, clutter, embarrassment, fatigue, sickness, austerity, the feeling it would never end—was all "offered up." For many of us, there was a kind of love-hate relationship with the Church in those days. It was because we took our Catholic faith seriously that we had so many children in the first place, and frequently the Church was the only source of encouragement we had. Who else was speaking of children as a blessing, of the beauty of family life? Those were hard years. For me, one means of surviving and even enjoying them was that daily "quiet hour" I had learned in college. (That and a very good husband—and I probably would not be married to him either had I not been a Catholic!)

Now, like any adult, I am what I have been in the process of becoming all my life. Today I see the difference between my early years as a Catholic wife and my present life as something like the difference between the Old and the New Testaments. All the things I learned about God, about Christ's life in us, about prayer, I firmly believed—but mostly in my head. Now these truths are firmly rooted in my heart. I experience them. I know them to be true, personally. The motivation for many good things in those days was frequently guilt; now it is more likely to be joy—or at least conviction. During those years I thanked God for the good things and "offered up" the hard ones. Now I am learning to thank him for the good and bad alike. In those days I said, "All for the greater honor and glory of God," and professed that praise was the highest form of prayer. Now I am discovering how powerful the prayer of praise really is in one's life, and I do it in my own words all the time. Jesus is very real to me, and I find myself discussing everything with him. Learning to listen is harder. Lest this sound overly pious, and lest my family fail to recognize me in this description, I must add that I still have my life-long problems with ego and a sharp tongue and failures in love, but I am more forgiving now than I used to be, both of myself and others. I like to think it is Christian maturity; it may be only old age.

Like many another Catholic wife, I have learned that there is no marriage manual so successful, no housekeeping or child-rearing skill so essential, as prayer—done as faithfully as making the beds and sweeping the kitchen floor. And because prayer has to be nourished by reading, I am grateful to the Church, to the Benedictines, and to those childhood adversaries who headed me toward that practice.

Today I am thankful that the Church, on the one hand, stood firm on marriage, and on the other, took the risk of opening up to renewal and all that followed, especially ecumenism and the charismatic renewal. It is the charismatic renewal which is largely responsible for having moved me from the Old to the New Testaments. I never could have done it outside Catholicism, however, so I am thankful that this new life is possible in the familiar, comfortable arms of old Mother Church.

Sr. Marie Fujan, O.S.B.

Sister Marie is a member of St. Paul's Priory, St. Paul, Minnesota. She has taught in parochial schools of the archdiocese of St. Paul and is presently a counsellor at St. John Vianney Seminary, St. Paul.

*   *   *

The encounter of Jesus with the woman at the well in the fourth chapter of St. John's Gospel offers me an insight into the way Jesus has come into my life and what it means to be an adult Christian woman and a religious.

The Samaritan woman was astounded that Jesus would talk to her. She became more and more aware of her human frailty just by being in his presence, but it was also the presence of Jesus that called forth the beauty that was within her. Because of his love and acceptance of her, she was able to experience, perhaps for the first time, that she was lovable. What a liberation she must have experienced to be able to leave the well (to which she had come at noon because no one else would be there) and to return to the village to share with everyone her "Good News!" "Come, see a man who told me all that I ever did. Can this be the Christ" (Jn. 4:29). She sensed that he was the Anointed One, the one who would free the nations from bondage as he had freed her—and he loved her just as she was.

The struggle entailed in learning how to love and to accept love that most of us experienced as adolescents ceases to seem impossible when we come to believe in the unconditional love of God. As we mature, our faith grows in the God who loves not only the world, but me, unconditionally. It is confidence in that kind of love which bids us leave our adolescent expression of the Christian life and which gives us the strength and courage to try to follow the Lord. Having become an adult Christian does not mean that the struggle is over but that we have the "armor of God" ready to protect us. St. Paul, writing to the Ephesians, spells out each part of that armor: "Stand therefore, having girded your loins with truth, and having put on the breastplate of righteousness, and having shod your feet with the equipment of the gospel of peace; above all taking the shield of faith, with which you can quench all the flaming darts of the evil one. And take the helmet of salvation, and the sword of the Spirit, which is the word of God" (6:14-17).

Having experienced that unconditional love of Jesus, I feel compelled, as did the woman at the well, to tell the world about it. Recently, I have come to understand my life as a sister from that same perspective.

Briefly, it goes like this: If the fact that God loves us is one of the most important facts in the world, then people need to be told and reminded over and over. That means that it is necessary that people who are convinced and willing do the telling. If it is such important news, in fact, the "Good News," then it is important enough for some people to give their whole lives to proclaiming it. That's what it means to me to be a sister. I believe that God has called me to give my life to proclaiming the Good News of God's unconditional love. I know that I fail to follow through many times, but it is that conviction and that love of Jesus that sustains me.

God has gifted me with a joyful, optimistic view of life, and I am grateful. There are many contributing factors to this view. Among them is, first my awareness of, and second, my experience of the power of the Spirit that Jesus desires to release to all. The release has brought me a greater awareness of God's presence in and around me. It has placed within me a hunger for the Word of God and for the Eucharist. Perhaps the most powerful and sustaining element is my confidence in the loving forgiveness that my Lord constantly offers me. I am often amazed how the Lord chooses to work through me, bringing people to himself, ministering to their brokenness in spite of and sometimes through my own.

Added to these gifts are the people, especially the friends, who are sometimes with me "at the well," listening to Jesus; at other times proclaiming the Good News to the "townspeople," but always with me on the journey. They give me the support and encouragement, and they need me to reciprocate. It is that journeying that the Christian life is all about, and I delight to be traveling with sisters and brothers, grateful for the gift of each new day. For I know that each day I have the opportunity to grow in my awareness of the Father's love for me as manifested in the Lord Jesus and in the power of his Holy Spirit.

Let all that lives and breathes give glory to God!

Jerry Rudolph

Jerry Rudolph was a junior at St. John's University, Collegeville, Minnesota, when he wrote the following testimony.

* * *

When I was young I thought I had a pretty good idea of what Catholicism was all about. It seemed to be a set of rules set forth in the Baltimore catechism that were to be followed without fail. If you broke one of the rules, you either went to confession or to hell. I was also taught that Christ resided in the church and that to see or receive Christ we had to go to church. Things were pretty cut and dried.

When I reached the age of infinite wisdom and maturity, the teens, I also thought I had things figured out. The Catholic Church was totally wrong. Its main objective was to keep teenagers from having fun. I was determined not to let anyone tell me what to do. I was smarter than any old priest.

I don't know how smart or mature I am today, but at least I know that nothing is ever cut and dried. Not all things can be seen or touched. Some truths require faith to be grasped. That, to me, is the first criterion for being a mature Catholic. One has to have faith. We have to realize that Christ is not just living in a church building. He is living in all of us. He is manifest in everything we see. We receive him and give him out in everything we do.

Another criterion is that we realize that we are not being forced to run our lives in a certain fashion. Rather, through the Scripture we hear during Mass, Christ tells us how we can be better people *if we want to be.* These are not rules. They are guidelines for our conscience. We still have the final decision on what is right and wrong.

So for me being a mature Catholic does not mean that I have to follow a strict set of rules and spend all my time in church. Likewise it does not mean deciding for myself what is right and wrong with no regard for anyone else. Rather, it means being able to integrate the ideals Christ set forth in Scripture into our everyday, college-student lives. When we do this, we strengthen our faith in Christ and live in harmony with that part of him that is manifest in everything around us.

Fr. Terence Carroll, O.S.B.

Father Terence is a monk of St. John's Abbey, Collegeville, Minnesota. He is seventy-seven years old, has been ordained for forty-three years, and has spent all of his priestly life in parochial work. At present he is chaplain at the Garrison Memorial Hospital, Garrison, North Dakota, where he spends his "leisure" time doing missionary work among the Indians of the area.

* * *

Living eighteen miles from the parish church before the time of automobiles, with only prairie roads to travel on, our family did not have much opportunity for church-related religious influence or instruction. Added to the hardship caused by distance and transportation difficulties was the poverty of our large family of eleven children, of whom I was the sixth.

I was about ten years old before I attended church services. Up to that time our home was the only source of the knowledge of God. Family life centered around prayer, especially the Rosary. Lessons in catechism came from a large Deharbe's text and a Bible history with pictures. Nature was another source of divine knowledge for me. The harsh winters in western Minnesota, the three-day blizzards, taught us dependence on God. The coming of spring gave hope of better things, spiritual and material. It meant that we might get to church. Lowering storm clouds sent down flashes of lightning from heaven to earth, revealing dust-laden twisters rising skyward. The fear of approaching hail clouds urged us to serious prayer. Then there was Haley's comet! We rejoiced in the beauty of the flowers, especially the ladyslips. We matched the migration of waterfowl. The death of my sister Mary, four years my junior, when I was nine brought family and neighbors together in prayer and united us in a deep sense of the power of God.

Finally I was able to go to church. The tall bell tower and the high church roof spoke of men who had a lofty opinion of the importance of God. I loved the high altar, the stained glass windows, the statues, and paintings. All this proclaimed that this village thought that God deserved good things. The priest at the high altar, the solemn strains of organ music, the awful silence as the bell rang at the consecration, a procession around the church with the Blessed Sacrament all made deep impressions on me. The fragrance of incense gave a new dimension to the importance of God at these processions. I also remember vividly the four men carrying the canopy, the long white cope on the priest, and older boys holding back the edges, and, of course, there was the monstrance with its sacred Host!

To these religious influences was now added catechism instruction by the pastor after the 10:30 high Mass. I do not recall any of this instruction. After one of the instructions, I remember my mother remarking to our neighbor lady, "I had them all to confession." Later our group of three families received Holy Communion in the McGurke's farm house. As the roads and transportation improved, we were able to attend Mass and receive Communion more frequently. We had a parish mission which wasn't very strong on instruction, during which we were glad to learn that we belonged to God's people, not the "Rollers," the "Jumpers," the "Bumpers," and the Lord only knows them all!

Thanks to the generosity of my godmother-aunt, I enrolled in a private school where there was ample time for prayer and the opportunity for daily Mass and Communion. The example of the Benedictine monks showed me that grown men could dedicate their lives entirely to God. Their daily choir chant across the quadrangle was a lesson in how those same men could join in praising God. A sermon by Father Method urging the students to develop a personal love for Jesus Christ was challenging. It still is.

True, it is impossible to know the external evidence which brings one to increased dependence on Christ the Savior. And there is always the working of grace. I became a member of the Order myself and was deeply influenced by two early years I spent in a Benedictine foundation in Peking, China, where the "way, the truth and the life" of Christ was in sharp contrast with anything Confucius could say or do. The sudden death of a favorite brother and three weeks before my ordination the death of my mother helped to lessen worldly concerns and enable the figure of Christ to surface more and more in my life.

After my ordination in 1935, I was immediately assigned to parish work. I spent almost thirty years in a New York parish, once a middle-income neighborhood which gradually became a slum. My convictions about the importance of Christ in my life continued to grow. I was deeply impressed by the faithful followers of Christ who kept themselves unspotted from the world. Valiant volunteer co-workers helped others to overcome the problems of their surroundings and to find the love of Christ in unlovely "ruins." I noticed them growing in the knowledge of the Lord and reception of the sacraments helped many to lead holy lives.

I read a lot and in later leisure years I had time to read Pelikan's books on the Christian tradition and McDonnell's *Calvin*. In these books I became acquainted with many of the troubles endured by the Church throughout her history, up to and including the present.

It has been a good life. It has been, is now, and ever shall be—Christ yesterday, today, and the same forever!

Fr. Renè McGraw, O.S.B.

Father Renè is a member of St. John's Abbey, Collegeville, Minnesota, where he teaches philosophy at St. John's University. He has been a monk for twenty-two years and a priest for sixteen.

*   *   *

What is difficult to separate out is my experience as a Christian from my experience as a teacher, a monk, as middle-aged, male, priest, and coming from a particular family background. Let me then begin this testimony by saying that I write this as this person, describing what is important to me, what I would find difficult to give up or change.

The first experience: I find myself very much in tune with Paul's "I do not do what I want, but I do the very thing I hate" (Rom. 7:15). Natasha's experience in Tolstoy's *War and Peace*, "Can't you understand, I have no will," rings true for me. To a degree this remains frightening, but also what is of great value in this experience is that little surprises me about myself—I come to feel more accepting of my own weakness and sin.

The second experience: Prayer in community, the psalms, become, surprisingly to me, more central in my life. I find the time of prayer creating for me a zone of peace where I can let go of my day-to-day concerns.

Third: The support of this monastic community and specifically of a close group of friends within this community remains central in my life. People who know me, yet accept me; people who struggle to live what I find, at least theoretically, important, but don't do very often. These people become emotionally and religiously central in my life. The other side of the coin is more disturbing; as I grow older, I become less tolerant of people's sins and weaknesses or even differences, though I expect them to be patient with mine. That ought to be just the opposite as I grow older, I think. But I discover a readiness to judge others and an impatience with masks, a desire to rip off their masks and expose what they are doing to themselves and to everyone else.

Fourth: Within the specifically Christian domain, the word of Jesus to Philip, "Have I been with you so long, and yet you do not know me, Philip? He who has seen me has seen the Father" (Jn. 14:9, makes more and more sense. I have little understanding or appreciation of the mystical experience of God as God or of the so-called "oceanic feeling." The God I know is the God who appears in Christ Jesus.

Fifth: More and more I believe that the "City of God—City of Man" is a dichotomy. I believe that Christians ought ever to be a thorn in the side of states. The citizen-Christian is almost a contradiction, but not quite, since like Jeremiah in the Old Testament, we live and love in a particular country and come to love that place and those people. But more often than not, the role of the Christian vis-à-vis the State—any State, Communist, capitalist, papal—is that of the outside critic calling the State away from what it is doing, without giving a clear message of what it ought to be.

Sixth: I find myself uncomfortable with the kind of instant intimacy that a number of Christians feel happy with. To hug someone I do not know or love seems false to me. To bare my religious sentiments before a group who are not personally close appears embarrassing to me.

Seventh: Somewhere along the line I have happily lost the feeling that I am extraordinary, that the world is waiting for something very special from me. Neither my virtues nor my sins seem especially remarkable. Neither my talents nor my weaknesses are likely to gain me notoriety. I do not fantasize the world weeping at my funeral.

Finally, my hopes: As I move on in my middle-aged Christianity, I would hope to concentrate more and more on the Lord, who comes to save, rather than on this person who needs salvation. I would hope to be more loving and generous to those in need of help. And I hope to continue to find the joy and peace that monastic life has so far brought me.

Fr. James Scheuer

Father Scheuer is engaged in pastoral ministry in Duluth, Minnesota. Ordained in 1959, he has been involved in the Office of Priestly Life and Ministry and has been Bishop Paul Anderson's liaison with the charismatic movement in the Duluth Diocese. What his faith means to him will be evident from the following interview.

* * *

Fr. Emeric A. Lawrence: How do you think our Catholic people ought to look upon Christianity?

Fr. James W. Scheuer: I would hope that their perception would be basically experiential. I believe that the Christian is first and foremost one who has in some way come to experience Jesus Christ—to experience in him the unconditional love of God for them and for others.

EAL: How do you expect the ordinary lay person to acquire that kind of experience?

JWS: I would begin by admitting that such an experience, such a heart-felt awareness of the risen Lord is surely a special grace from God. It cannot be programmed as such. It does happen, however, in surprising ways and surprising situations. I have observed that people seem to be led to such an experience where there has been a real community experience, mainly through small groups meeting, praying, discussing together. I mean groups like the Cursillo, Marriage Encounter, etc. The charismatic renewal and the "Life in the Spirit" seminars bring together adults who are searching for something more in their lives. Those present at these meetings see in the lives and faces of others a joy and a strength that they come to desire for themselves as they are exposed to some very basic Christian and biblical teachings in a community context.

EAL: Such experiences of Christ can surely happen apart from the presence and influence of a priest, but a priest could surely be very instrumental in guiding the people towards this experience of Christ. How do you perceive your vocation as a parish priest in this regard?

JWS: I see my vocation as a diocesan priest in the pastoral ministry as very much involved in evangelism. I once discussed this with a lay leader who was known for his pastoral role with other lay people. He convinced me that the fundamental thrust of my preaching ought to be evangelical rather than catechetical. By that he meant simply inviting people in every sermon to get back to the basic meaning and teaching of God who has revealed himself in Jesus Christ, inviting them to a personal encounter with the living God, as he has revealed himself to us. Basic evangelism of this sort is the basic thrust of all my preaching.

EAL: Do you mean that in this way you are able to lead the people to an encounter with and an experience of Christ?

JWS: That is right.

EAL: Let's try that theory on one of the Sunday Gospels—the one about love of neighbor and specifically about forgiving one's neighbor if he has offended or hurt you. Peter asked the Lord, "How often shall my brother sin against me, and I forgive him?" (Mt. 18:21). Now, how would you make a sermon on this topic into an occasion for an encounter with Christ?

JWS: O.K. In the past I would have stressed the moralizing element very much; I would have insisted that they have to forgive one another over and over, again and again, seventy times seven times. I would have "laid it on them." "If you will not forgive again and again, you cannot be Christ's follower." Now I would approach it in a more doctrinal way, trying to show that the seventy times seven times illustrates the unconditional love of the Father for us. It is only in stressing that divine initiative of forgiving (rather than my response to it)—putting the emphasis on grace; it is only when I realize God's unconditional love for me in forgiving me over and over again that I am enabled to hear the word of Jesus and keep it. Simple willpower in relation to the Gospel mandate can get me nowhere.

EAL: That's very good. I like that very much. It reminds me of an article in *Sisters Today* in which the author, Monsignor Shannon, bases the whole idea of Christian morality on our response to what God has done for us.

JWS: I am convinced that unless one has some sort of experience of what God has done for one, the response will not be forthcoming. A lover whose life has been changed by love will be concerned about the one responsible for that love. In the process of falling in love, two people gradually see their reaction to one another changing. Their whole outlook on life changes, too.

EAL: That's fine. That's what I wanted. In other words, you see your vocation as a priest in the pastoral ministry in terms of bringing your people to a vivid experience of Christ—Christ living now in them?

JWS: That is right. I strive for basic scriptural evangelizing; and then I would also try to promote an ongoing experience of Church, of small community experience which alone can sustain the experience of God's unconditional acceptance of and love for the people. Thus I would see my role in the pastoral ministry as being very much involved in the formation of smaller communities within the larger parish community.

EAL: Small communities within the larger community? But how?

JWS: I think we have to have lay people "pastoring" lay people in this matter, lay people helping others realize that they are all gifted in some way. The priests could do the coordinating and the overseeing; they could facilitate this experience of Church.

EAL: But we are a long way from such an idea and ideal in most of our parishes.

JWS: I would agree, although I think I see things happening. As I never have before, I see lay people unafraid of speaking about love. I see them able to speak about Jesus, sharing their experiences of Jesus.

EAL: And you have more and more priests involved in the charismatic renewal who are leading their people along that way. When you think of the large number of priests who go to Stuebenville every summer for the charismatic renewal meetings, they are bound to become a leaven on the others.

JWS: Well, I don't think there is a sizable number of priests involved in the charismatic renewal in our diocese, but somehow I believe that our priests in general—this is a presumption now—are finding themselves becoming more and more evangelistic in their preaching. They are speaking about their personal relationship with Jesus, and they are able to perceive a noticeable reaction from their people.

EAL: Thank you very much, Jim.

Charles House

Charles House represents the "singles" vocation. He is a graduate of the University of Minnesota in Duluth and went on to graduate school at the University of Minnesota in Minneapolis where he graduated in business. He works as a C.P.A. in Duluth.

*   *   *

Twenty, even ten years ago, I had acknowledged the existence of Christ. It was a part of my family's belief and foundation laid through the rigid catechetical discipline of the 1950's, the "Baltimore" catechism and all. My knowledge of Christ was one fraught with respect bordering on fear rather than love.

What has happened to get me to where I am today? My own involvement with the Christian Church began to progress when I became affiliated with a national association of parish clergy of all faiths, known as the Academy of Parish Clergy. It was not through the influence of this organization itself, but through the friendships and relationships of fellow board members of the APC that Christ first put a hand on my shoulder and walked with me. These relationships continue today and are a source of growth, love, and caring in my life.

The walk with Christ continued to include a growing, caring Christian community in a neighborhood parish. This community became another continuing source of growth—a family—caring, loving, and surprisingly concerned. I say concern, because often such a community exists only on Sunday mornings.

About this time, I think Christ moved his hand from my shoulder to take hold of my hand and lead me very strongly. I can't exactly tell when this happened, but I can clearly identify a Sunday in December 1974 as somewhat of a turning point. My friend Fr. Gerald J. O'Bee was sharing a homily on faith at St. Christine's parish in Detroit. Looking back, he was talking about and to me. By no coincidence Jerry served on the board of the APC with me.

My walk continues toward my involvement with the Welch Center in Duluth, which was established in 1962 by the Duluth Diocese to serve as a center for diocesanwide Youth Ministry Services, local United Way community services, and renewal activities.

Here is where Christ has turned around and embraced me. I now clearly see him as father, friend, teacher, companion, and lover. His love is so overpowering that it is most difficult to write about that love.

Accepting Christ's love has made such a significant change that a friend in Washington, D.C., recently wrote about a meeting where we had shared a meal, love, and a lot of ourselves. He said that he could physically see the peace and love radiating from me. Maybe so, I don't know if it shows that much, but I do feel Christ's presence within me.

This is not to say that our relationship is perfect. Every so often he puts me to another test. I trust he has a reason for such tests—maybe it is his way of giving me some benchmarks for my own growth.

Whatever, I feel my faith, God's love through his son Christ, and it feels O.K.

Carolyn Schmidt

Carolyn Schmidt represents three vocations—that of a convert, of a single person, and that of a victim of serious illness. Her biography emerges from the following three pieces. I cannot think of a better way to conclude this chapter.

* * *

On November 28, 1978, I celebrated the thirtieth anniversary of my conversion to the Roman Catholic Church. This call to Church membership and the events which led to my first reception of the Church's sacraments in 1948 I refer to as my first adult CALL TO LOVE: LOVE OF GOD THE FATHER, OF THE SON INCARNATE, AND OF THE HOLY SPIRIT.

Invariably converts to the Church are asked, "How did it happen?"

I can cite long-standing intellectual struggles with and probable misunderstandings of childhood Protestant beliefs, spiritual crises exacerbated by a pagan atmosphere in university humanities and philosophy classes, and a germ of faith which my God-loving mother implanted so firmly in me in childhood that somehow it survived my walks through agnosticism, secular humanism, and deism to lead me back to institutional Christianity years later.

Why that turn to institutional Christianity led me to the Roman Catholic Church was influenced by equally complex factors. I knew no Catholics at the time and had never attended Catholic worship services. But Anglican friends had fed me richly on the writings of Thomas à Kempis, St. Thomas Aquinas, St. Augustine, St. Paul's letters, C. S. Lewis, and that marvelous seventeenth-century writer John Donne, who spoke so eloquently on the ideas of the Mystical Body of Christ, which had impressed me so profoundly in St. Paul's writings. Long and repeated readings of St. John's Gospel and Epistles deepened my understanding of the depths of love which God was teaching man through his redemptive incarnation and the concept of the Mystical Body, the vine and the branches, which remained pivotal in my understanding of the social organization of Christianity. The time came when I knew I could no longer deny Christ as my Redeemer, nor could I accept the rationale for the dividing of Christendom. Thus, on November 28, 1948, called by Christ, I responded by joining the Church which I believed Scripture, history, and tradition supported as the Church established by Jesus.

Yet, to suggest that this brief resumé of personal history is the full explanation of my first vocation, the call to love in conversion, is grossly misleading. I know in my heart that the instigating hand throughout the years of struggle prior to receiving this full gift of faith was divine, not human. In the years in which I had left God, he had never left me. The call was from him. Why this call was made so insistently and why I responded as I did remain mysteries. Perhaps closest to the truth is a comment made by a wise priest friend: "Carolyn, ultimately every convert is a walking miracle of God's grace." Thank you, Lord, each day, for letting me experience this miracle in my life.

* * *

My second vocation, that to the single state, is shared by many persons in our society, but my own living of this state is not typical. With me it evolved as a deliberately chosen form of total dedication to God. In this state Christ is my spouse forever and my life is not open to the possibility of marriage as so many singles' lives are.

From the earliest years as a convert, my relationship to our triune God and his role for me in the Body of Christ were propelling issues in decision-making regarding professional and lifestyle options. Because converts might have special insights to offer to "cradle Catholics," I chose a Catholic girls' school as the focus of my professional services in college teaching. All this time the words of our Lord to his apostles kept coming to mind:

> You did not choose me, but I chose you and appointed you that you should go and bear fruit and that your fruit should abide; so that whatever you ask the Father in my name, he may give it to you. This I command you, to love one another (Jn. 15:16-17).

Did these words have special meaning for me? By 1953 their meaning was clear in a challenge to respond to the second CALL TO LOVE: THE CALL TO THE DEDICATED SINGLE STATE. The first five years as a convert had been a rich and wholesome preparation for this state of life, giving daily opportunities to grow in Christ in the liturgical atmosphere of the Benedictine college in which I taught and lived. These days were filled with fun, romances, and community-living experiences which were later to be strong stabilizing elements in helping me to make a free and healthy choice of vowed celibacy. In the early years marriage remained a tempting option, but ever more strongly I felt God's call for me to give myself totally to him and his work; to become steeped in the study of theology, to share with others as a lifetime commitment my personal and academic knowledge of the Lord, and to share at a level of intensity and involvement which I believed could best be accomplished in my case in the single state. Because of complex family responsibilities, I could not join a religious community, the customary mode of living a life of total dedication in those days. I had been warned that the single state as a state of dedication was rare and exceedingly difficult. But with prayer and spiritual guidance, this state has evolved as a permanent lifestyle and commitment, sealed by a perpetual vow of chastity and dedication to the Lord's service.

It is not easy to be a single and celibate person in American society, geared as it is today to pairs, families, and active sex for singles. Loneliness, isolation from many activities open to others, and a sense of being different are constant temptations. My own living of this state is enriched by and, for me, simplified by my vowed status. But single Christians without vows, single on a temporary basis or single for life, abound and they too want to live fully the life which our Lord describes in Sacred Scripture. In a society in which sexual activity has become synonymous with normalcy, this is indeed difficult.

I believe the Church has far to go in developing a theology of and an apostolate for singles. It has far to go in being the sound support for and inspiration that it could be to them. Too little has been done in exploring options of Christian community living and community social involvement and service for singles. The single state is often a genuine call from God to serve the Body of Christ in a unique way. I thank God for the special freedom, the special energy, and the special accessibility to serving people which this state has given to me. Daily I hear the words of the psalmist, "As a hart longs for flowing streams, so longs my soul for thee, O God" (Ps. 42:1). Daily I long to help others to experience this thirst for God and to be able to be an instrument used by the Lord in sharing his love with my fellow humans.

It is my hope that eventually the Church will devote more considered and energized efforts to the single state and that some day every parish will help its single members to realize the fullness of their potential as special co-workers with Christ. Only when the single state is recognized by the Church as a special and authentic way of serving the Lord can the single person experience fully the joy and dignity of knowing that by living this state response is being made to God's call.

* * *

The year 1975 heard the full voice of my third CALL TO LOVE: THE VOCATION OF ILLNESS. For years I had been fighting a progressively disabling complex of collagen diseases (systemic lupus erythematosus, scleroderma, polymyositis) with inoperable vascular complications which were eventually to force me to spend major portions of time in bed as I must do now. By 1963 I was in a wheelchair most of the time, but I continued to teach and work heavily. A successful battle with breast cancer in 1971-1972 gave a temporary sense of physical invulnerability and my teaching efforts became more enthusiastic than ever. This was not to last long. The collagen disease advanced, energies ebbed, more and more time had to be spent in bed, and by March 1975 I became medically categorized as "totally disabled." Today my shut-in status is augmented by the fact that drugs which control further advancement of the disease are agents which depress immunity, and I must avoid all personal contacts which might involve infection risk, especially during months of colds and influenza.

Illness has brought many new dimensions to my life. On a human level, it showered me with an intense outpouring of love and caring from family and friends, and I have seen Christ's love witnessed through many beautiful persons I never knew before. It has freed me to give time to help persons I neglected to find time for when I was well. It has made me sensitive to suffering on many planes I had never thought of before. It has given a new value to time, making me ask more frequently than I did before, "Do I use it well?" On a spiritual plane, in becoming more isolated from people, as I have been forced to be by my infection-proneness, I have been able to be drawn closer to God in the sense of spending more time in prayer and contemplation. My days of active parish involvement have been changed by circumstance to days of offering for the parish. I miss Mass attendance intensely, but our Lord has proved himself to be generous in being close in other ways. Most beautifully, through illness, I am developing a new understanding of Christ's suffering which deepens daily. He has never been as real to me in the fullness of his humanity and his divinity as he has been since my withdrawal from active life.

I am often asked if my illness has embittered my life. No, but there have been times of disillusionment and frustration.

Disillusionment has come chiefly in the realm of friendships. Some persons who were once identified as "close friends" are no longer part of my life since I can no longer be part of their group. Others care, but avoid contacts because they don't know how to express their caring.

Frustration has come mainly from societal attitudes toward the ill. So often because the ill are shut-in, they are shut out. The Church is not guiltless in this regard. An ill member remains a member, affecting the Body and as surely being affected by the Body as when he was well and present. But too often there is so little development of ministry to the sick outside of institutional settings that the shut-in at home feels more like a severed twig than a living branch. I plead with all the love which Christ has shared with me that the Church may become more sensitive in this area—not only recognizing its need to minister *to* the shut-ins but also recognizing the potential of a ministry *by* the shut-ins to the Church in terms of the contributions of prayer, works, and sacrifices which the ill can make.

By nature I am not a masochist. I dislike pain and I naturally fear a future of progressive disability. Thus when persons ask if I have prayed for the gift of healing, my spontaneous response is, "Yes, often and with great faith—and so have many of my friends in my behalf." But even more I have prayed, and have asked them to pray, that God's will may be done and that I may accept it, whatever it is. I believe that there is a gift as miraculous as the gift of healing and that is the gift of being able to accept with faith and hope that which is not healed. So far, God has given me this great gift and I have been able to live rejoicing in each new day. If our Lord is calling me to a prolonged life of illness, to use it redemptively for the people of God as he has so often used sickness for a higher purpose throughout history, then I shall pray to be able to be his willing and loving handmaid. I have learned the truth of the words: "God writes straight with crooked lines." In eternity, if not in time, we shall see the patterns of our lives fall fully into place.

The Author

Fr. Emeric Lawrence, O.S.B., currently is the chaplain at St. Scholastica's Priory, Duluth, Minnesota. From 1938-1967 he taught French and theology classes at St. John's University, Collegeville, Minnesota. From 1967-1969 and from 1971-1975 he was a visiting professor at Luther College, Decorah, Iowa, and from 1969-1971 at Concordia College, Moorhead, Minnesota. His previous publications include *The Week With Christ* (1950), *Meditating the Gospels* (1957), *Homilies for the Year* (1965), *Understanding Our Neighbor's Faith* (1972), *A New Meditating the Gospels* (1977), all published by The Liturgical Press, and *Each Week With Christ* (1961), published by Helicon Press.

Cover by Sr. Mary Charles McGough, O.S.B.